Study Guide

to accompany

Psychology
Science & Understanding

Barry D. Smith
University of Maryland

Prepared by
Dr. Valerie Levine

McGraw Hill

Boston   Burr Ridge, IL   Dubuque, IA   Madison, WI   New York   San Francisco   St. Louis
Bangkok   Bogotá   Caracas   Lisbon   London   Madrid
Mexico City   Milan   New Delhi   Seoul   Singapore   Sydney   Taipei   Toronto

McGraw-Hill

A Division of The McGraw·Hill Companies

Study Guide to accompany
PSYCHOLOGY: SCIENCE & UNDERSTANDING

4 5 6 7 8 9 0 QPD/QPD 9 0 9

ISBN 0-07-289144-0

www.mhhe.com

Table of Contents

Preface

How to Use This Study Guide

The field of psychology is broad in scope and complex in nature. You may find that the introductory course covers more material in greater depth than you had anticipated when you first considered taking the course. You may also discover topics in the textbook that you had no idea were included in the field of psychology. But there is no reason to panic. If you approach the material with a good attitude, an open mind, and the desire to meet a challenge well worth your time and effort, you can master the material in Barry Smith's *Psychology: Science & Understanding.* Your willingness to do so will enhance your knowledge and your life.

The purpose of this *Study Guide* is to facilitate your mastery of the material in the textbook. It is a supplement to, and *not* a substitute for, the textbook. If you use the *Study Guide* appropriately, it is likely that you will perform better in the introductory course.

There is a one-to-one correspondence between *Study Guide* and textbook chapters. The chapters of the *Study Guide* have been designed with a consistent, easy-to-follow format, described below.

Chapter Outline

To tie the *Study Guide* and textbook together, the chapter outline that opens each *Study Guide* chapter is the same as the chapter outline presented at the beginning of the corresponding chapter of the textbook. Seeing the chapter outline in both the text and the *Study Guide* will provide you with repetition of the structure of each chapter. Repetition and structure are both important learning tools. You can use the chapter outline as a guide by following along with it as you read the chapter in the text to keep track of the flow of the material. Read through the chapter outline before reading the material in the text, as a way of orienting yourself.

Chapter Overview

The chapter overview is a narrative summary of the chapter and touches upon all the main topics and concepts covered in the chapter. Each chapter overview is organized to correspond with the associated chapter, section by section. Read the chapter overview after reading the chapter outline. It would also be useful for you to read the summary of each main section of the chapter in the overview after reading that section of the text. Read the entire overview again after completing the chapter in the text. Remember—the overview is not a substitute for the chapter. It is simply a helpful tool.

How to Master Chapter

This section is the heart of the *Study Guide,* because it is the goal of the *Study Guide* to help you master the material in each chapter. The remainder of the chapter is subsumed under this main heading.

Refer to These Learning Objectives

The learning objectives are designed as a guide to what you need to be able to do or need to know after mastering the material in each chapter. To help you keep track of how the learning objectives correspond to text material, the learning objectives are organized by the main chapter headings. Notice that each learning objective starts with an action verb, like *Discuss, Explain, Distinguish between, Give examples of, Define,* or *Describe.* Because learning and the demonstration of learning are active processes, your learning objectives or goals must be active as well. As you read and study chapter material, you can use the learning objectives to focus your attention on what you should be able to do to prove mastery. Along with the chapter outline, you can keep the learning objectives available as a guide to keep track of the chapter material. You can check off the objectives as you master them to give yourself both reinforcement for your efforts and information as to what you know and what you still need to work on.

Debate These Myths

This section provides you with a structured format for debating myths that take the form of overgeneralizations, simplifications, extreme viewpoints, and misstatements. The myths were derived from misconceptions that many students have expressed over the years in the introductory psychology course. Even if you do not believe these myths or harbor these misconceptions, debating them can help you learn the course material in a meaningful way. This section of the *Study Guide* gives you the opportunity to challenge your thought processes and achieve a deeper level of learning and understanding. The structure of each myth exercise will lead you through a logical sequence toward turning each myth into a true statement. Although you will need to refer to the text in order to fill in some of the information, the thinking, wording, and logical conclusions will have to come from you. Do not neglect the part of each myth exercise that asks for *other statements and examples for debating MYTH ___*. This is the part of the exercise that gives you the opportunity to express your own ideas.

Test Yourself: Multiple-Choice Questions

Under this heading, you will find fifty multiple-choice questions for each chapter. Some of the questions test factual information in a direct way, whereas other questions will challenge you to show a deeper understanding of the material and an ability to apply it to new situations. Be willing to take a risk when you are unsure of an answer. Remember, you are testing yourself and need to know what you know and what you don't know in order to review the material properly. Correct answers are provided in the **Answer Key.**

Test Yourself: Fill in the Blanks

Under this heading, you will find twenty fill-in-the-blank questions for each chapter. This type of question tests your recall of new terminology and names. As with the multiple-choice questions, be willing to take a risk if you are unsure. Don't worry about the spelling of technical terms or names of people the first time around. The important thing is to know the correct content to fill in each blank. Correct answers are provided in the **Answer Key** section.

Test Yourself: Matching Questions

Under this heading, you will find fifteen matching questions for each chapter. There is only one correct match for each item in column I. Correct answers are provided in the **Answer Key** section.

Test Yourself: Answer Key

Under this heading, you will find answers to all the multiple-choice, fill-in-the blank, and matching questions. Page numbers of the correct answers to the multiple-choice questions are included.

Do These Mini Projects

These are simple, not elaborate, projects that are designed to hold your interest and enhance your mastery of the concepts presented in the text. Because you will be busy mastering the material in this course, and perhaps in other courses, the projects are designed not to require a great deal of your time. The projects vary. They include such activities as writing down observations, interviewing people, gathering information, and brainstorming. Doing as many projects as you can will help make the material come alive and will help you gain a deeper understanding of the field of psychology.

Pull It All Together

The purpose of this last section of the *Study Guide* is to help you integrate the material you are mastering. It will help you (1) relate the material in each chapter to material you mastered in previous chapters; (2) relate the material in one part of a chapter to material in another part of the chapter; and (3) relate the information in the chapter to your own life experience. Integration helps solidify your mastery and is a logical last step for each chapter before proceeding to the next chapter.

Preparing this *Study Guide* has been a challenging and rewarding experience for me. I hope you find it to be a useful supplement to Barry Smith's textbook, *Psychology: Science & Understanding.* Using the *Study Guide* faithfully will enhance your mastery of the textbook.

Valerie J. Levine, Ph.D.

CHAPTER 1
INTRODUCTION: THE FIELD OF PSYCHOLOGY

Chapter Outline

Chapter Overview

Chapter 1 introduces the field of psychology. The chapter begins by defining the field of psychology as the scientific study of behavior and underlying mental processes. The author points out that although not all psychologists would include underlying mental processes as part of the definition of psychology, the acknowledgment and study of mental activities such as thought or cognition has increased in recent years. The existence and workings of mental activities are inferred from observable behavior and measures. In spite of disagreements concerning mental processes, psychologists agree that psychology is empirical, where empiricism is the assumption that knowledge is acquired through careful and precise observation. It is empiricism that makes psychology a science. The science of psychology will be the topic covered in chapter 2.

Chapter 1 contains four major sections: (1) "The Big Picture: Evolution, Heredity, and Environment," (2) "Psychology Begins," (3) "Models and Perspectives in Psychology," and (4) "The Field of Psychology:Areas and Careers."

The first section ("The Big Picture: Evolution, Heredity, and Environment") begins with a discussion of the nature-nurture issue, or the influence of heredity (nature) and environment (nurture) on human behavior. Rather than forcing you to decide which is more powerful, the author explains that the current view is that nature, nurture, and the interaction between them are all involved in the determination of behavior. Charles Darwin's theory of evolution and more modern evolutionary theories are briefly examined for the purpose of shedding light on the interaction between heredity and environmental factors in the development of the species. Asking whether behavior is based on biology or is a product of experience is the wrong question. The better question is: How do biological and environmental factors work separately and together to influence behavior and mental processes, and to what extent is a given behavior influenced by each? The author points out that, historically, views on the weight of these two factors have gone through changes. Currently, the pendulum swings near the center of the continuum, perhaps a bit toward the biological side.

The second section ("Psychology Begins") provides a brief history of psychology, starting with the field's early roots in philosophy and physiology. In terms of philosophy, the work of Aristotle and Plato (and, later, Descartes) dominated thinking about human functioning for almost two thousand years. Nineteenth-century physiologists began to demonstrate that psychological processes and behavior could be studied objectively. The most credit for establishing psychology as an independent discipline is given to Wilhelm Wundt, who opened a laboratory for the study of psychological processes in Leipzig, Germany, in 1879 using the method of introspection. The first major American psychologist was Wundt's contemporary William James, who developed the school of functionalism. Other schools of psychology include structuralism, developed by Edward Titchener; behaviorism, developed by John Watson; and humanism, developed by Carl Rogers.

At the same time as these schools of psychology were being researched in America, there were early psychologists working and developing theories and research abroad. Ivan Pavlov, a Russian physiologist, began the formal study of learning processes based on stimuli and responses. Sigmund Freud developed psychoanalysis. Gestalt psychology, which proposed that perceptions and mental operations can be best understood as wholes, was developed in Germany by Max Wertheimer, Wolfgang Kohler, Kurt Kofka, and Kurt Lewin. Back in America, G. Stanley Hall organized the American Psychological Association (APA) and became its first president. The APA, which had only 31 members at its first meeting in 1887, had grown to over 75,000 members in 1993. From the beginning of the twentieth century through the present time, many applied areas of psychology have sprung up, women's contributions to the field have been increasingly acknowledged, and the field has become more diverse.

The third section ("Models and Perspectives in Psychology") describes five schools of thought that are prevalent today. The first is the neuroscience or biological model, which holds that understanding behavior requires knowledge of underlying physiological processes. The second is the psychodynamic model, which proposes that there are powerful biological and psychological forces within all of us that motivate us at an unconscious level. The third is the behavioral model, which accepts only observable behavior as appropriate subject matter of psychology. The fourth is the humanistic model, which proposes that humans are innately good and strive to achieve goals and fulfill their potentials. The fifth is the cognitive model, which suggests that we use mental processes such as thought, attention, and expectation to search for and process information. All these models have been influential in the field. Remember that there is no one correct way to view and understand human functioning.

The final section ("The Field of Psychology:Areas and Careers") describes briefly some of the subdisciplines in the diverse field of psychology, including experimental psychology, neuroscience, cognitive science, health psychology, developmental psychology, social psychology, personality psychology, clinical psychology, counseling psychology, industrial/organizational psychology, environmental psychology, school psychology, and educational psychology. The author distinguishes among various careers and degrees in the field and points out the difference between psychology and psychiatry.

How to Master Chapter 1

Refer to These Learning Objectives

You should be able to achieve the following learning objectives after mastering the material in chapter 1:

The Big Picture: Evolution, Heredity, and Environment

1. Define psychology and list the major goals of the field.

2. Define empiricism, and explain how this concept is central to the definition of psychology.

3. Discuss the nature-nurture question and explain why this question is an important one in psychology.

4. Describe how views on the nature-nurture question in the field of psychology have changed over the past thirty years.

5. Discuss what is meant by the "right" and "wrong" ways of asking the nature-nurture question, and explain the best way to answer the question.

Psychology Begins

6. Name the earlier disciplines from which psychology has arisen, and explain how those disciplines have influenced the current field of psychology.

7. List the names of the early pioneers in the field of psychology, and describe what each of these individuals contributed to the development of the field.

8. Discuss the historical and current roles of women in psychology.

Models and Perspectives in Psychology

9. Describe and give examples of the major characteristics of the following models in psychology: neuroscience or biological; psychodynamic; behavioral; humanistic; cognitive.

10. Explain how the model you adopt affects the research you do and the theories you develop.

The Field of Psychology: Areas and Careers

11. List the specialty areas in the field of psychology, and describe their major characteristics.

12. Name the type of degree required to be called a psychologist, and explain the difference between a psychologist and a psychiatrist.

Debate These Myths

MYTH 1: *We must decide whether all human behavior is based on biological factors or on experience.*

Strategy:

Discuss what is meant by the nature-nurture question:

3

Discuss how views about the influence of biology and environment have shifted over the years:

Give examples of human behaviors and characteristics that are influenced by both heredity and environmental factors:

Other statements or examples for debating MYTH 1:

Change MYTH 1 into a true statement:

MYTH 2: *There were no major contributions made by women in the development of psychology as a field.*

Strategy:

List the names of six women who contributed significantly to the development of the field of psychology and describe the contributions of each:

Explain why historians have not typically included women among the major figures in the field:

Explain why women have not achieved the same status as men such as Wundt, James, or Freud:

Other statements or examples for debating MYTH 2:

Change MYTH 2 into a true statement:

MYTH 3: *All the models in the field of psychology consider human beings as basically good.*

Strategy:

Name five major models in the field of psychology:

Indicate which of these models consider human beings as basically good, which consider human beings basically evil, and which models do not consider this dimension at all:

Other statements and examples for debating MYTH 3:

Change MYTH 3 into a true statement:

MYTH 4: *The field of psychology focuses primarily on the theory and practice of psychotherapy.*

Strategy:

Name the number of divisions contained in the American Psychological Association (APA), each of which represents an area of psychology:

Examining table 1-4, compute the approximate percentage of divisions that focus on psychotherapy:

Discuss the role and position of the American Psychological Society (APS) in the field of psychology:

Name at least a dozen areas in the field of psychology that have nothing to do with psychotherapy:

Other statements and examples to debate MYTH 4:

Change MYTH 4 into a true statement:

Test Yourself: Multiple-Choice Questions

Directions: Circle the best response for each of the following questions.

1. There is general consensus that psychology is:
    a. humanistic
    b. therapeutic
    c. empirical
    d. cognitive

2. Mental operations can be studied by making them:
    a. objectively observable
    b. carefully limited
    c. more generally accepted
    d. behaviorally determinative

3. Mary is a sociable, outgoing individual who enjoys parties and good conversation, whereas Laura prefers to spend time by herself at home reading novels. The differences in the personalities between Mary and Laura are most likely due to:
    a. inherited traits
    b. different experiences
    c. the interaction of heredity and environment
    d. neither biological nor environmental factors

4. Charles Darwin developed the theory of:
    a. empiricism
    b. evolution
    c. humanism
    d. cognition

5. The types of attributes that are generally passed onto the next generation are:
    a. nurturing
    b. adaptive
    c. teleological
    d. modern

6. All of the following scientists engaged in the study of evolution, except:
    a. Darwin
    b. Buss
    c. Scarr
    d. Fechner

7. Which of the following is the best example of an evolutionary mechanism?
    a. dislike of vegetables
    b. underachieving in school
    c. fear of bugs
    d. obesity

8.   Modern synthesis refers to the combination of Darwin's theory of evolution with:
      a.   genetics   c.   empiricism
      b.   cartography   d.   ornithology

9.   Gregor Mendel's groundbreaking work in the field of genetics first became known in:
      a.   1800   c.   1900
      b.   1850   d.   1950

10.   It would be considered adaptive for women to:
      a.   have children   c.   fight in wars
      b.   live alone   d.   drive sportscars

11.   Which of the following statements regarding alcoholism is the most accurate?
      a.   You can become an alcoholic even if you don't consume alcohol.
      b.   Alcoholism is strongly influenced by genetic factors.
      c.   Peer pressure is the primary underlying cause of alcoholism.
      d.   Most alcoholics are also extroverts.

12.   At the end of the nineteenth century, most scholars believed that behavior was determined primarily by:
      a.   experiences   c.   religious forces
      b.   random factors   d.   biology

13.   The field of psychology has its early roots in:
      a.   philosophy   c.   both philosophy and physiology
      b.   physiology   d.   neither philosophy nor physiology

14.   The philosophers Socrates, Aristotle, and Plato lived:
      a.   in the 1800s   c.   in the fifteenth century
      b.   at the end of the nineteenth century d.   over 2,000 years ago

15.   The first psychology laboratory was opened in 1879 by:
      a.   Wilhelm Wundt   c.   Edward Titchener
      b.   William James   d.   Carl Rogers

16.   Which one of the following descriptions of the method of introspection is the most accurate?
      a.   The researcher would draw conclusions based on the observable behaviors of the participant.
      b.   The participant was required to report sensations and thoughts as accurately as possible.
      c.   The researcher had to draw together the elements of the participant's mind.
      d.   The participant had to demonstrate adaptive behavior during data collection.

17.   Functionalism, the study of the adaptive significance of consciousness, was a nineteenth-century school of thought developed by:
      a.   William James   c.   Wilhelm Wundt
      b.   Edward Titchener   d.   Sigmund Freud

18.   Structuralism is to functionalism as:
      a.   humanism is to behaviorism   c.   element is to process
      b.   maladaptive is to adaptive   d.   nature is to nurture

19.   Edward Titchener and G. Stanley Hall were students of:
      a.   B. F. Skinner   c.   Max Wertheimer
      b.   Ivan Pavlov   d.   Wilhelm Wundt

20. John Watson was best known for basing his theories of human functioning on:
    a. observable animal behavior
    c. underlying mental processes
    b. psychoanalytic concepts
    d. introspective techniques

21. The field of clinical psychology became solidly established:
    a. at the end of the nineteenth century
    c. when Freud proposed his theories
    b. after World War II
    d. only in the past ten years

22. Historians have not typically included women as major figures in the field of psychology because:
    a. gender roles have been rigid until recently
    b. no woman has ever been president of the American Psychological Association
    c. hardly any women have made significant contributions to the field
    d. no woman founded a psychology laboratory until the 1960s

23. Leta Hollingsworth is best known for:
    a. serving as president of the APA
    c. coining the term *gifted*
    b. working with John Watson
    d. her studies on memory

24. Knowing how white male college students socialize can provide information that would be valid to generalize the social behavior of:
    a. white male blue-collar workers
    c. white female college students
    b. white male high school students
    d. other white male college students

25. The field of psychology is moving increasingly in the direction of studying:
    a. individual differences
    c. child development
    b. the unconscious
    d. the middle class

26. There is a growing recognition in the field of psychology of the importance of considering:
    a. the contributions of female psychologists
    b. the impact of cultural differences in theory and research
    c. how biological and environmental factors interact to influence behavior
    d. all of the above

27. The issues of hedonism, teleology, holism, and human nature are:
    a. old-fashioned concepts that are not relevant to modern perspectives in psychology
    b. philosophical issues that are considered in hypothesis formulation and testing
    c. valued only by psychologists who believe in the psychodynamic model
    d. applicable only when underlying mental processes are studied empirically

28. The behavioral view that a boy in second grade will do his homework because in the past his completion of homework resulted in parental praise and his homework avoidance was met with disapproval is based on the concept of:
    a. holism
    c. hedonism
    b. human nature as good
    d. human nature as greedy

29. Of the following models, the one based most on the concept of genetic predisposition is:
    a. behavioral
    c. neuroscience
    b. psychodynamic
    d. humanistic

30. The idea that heredity combines with early life experience to determine the personality and behavior patterns of the adult is most closely associated with which of the following models?
    a. psychodynamic
    c. behavioral
    b. neuroscience
    d. cognitive

31. Sarah stays in her relationship with her boyfriend even though he cheats on her and ridicules her in public. According to the psychodymanic model, Sarah stays because she:

   a. has a biological disposition for being abused

   b. is driven by unconscious forces

   c. finds the boyfriend's behavior rewarding

   d. has biased perceptions regarding the relationship

32. Referring back to Sarah, according to Carl Rogers and Abraham Maslow, Sarah stays in this unhealthy relationship because of:

   a. powerful biological forces that drive her

   b. her hedonism

   c. her subjective perceptions

   d. an unconscious panic about being alone

33. Referring back to Sarah, according to John B. Watson and B. F. Skinner, Sarah stays in this relationship because of:

   a. environmental reinforcers

   b. primitive physiological and psychological drives

   c. her predisposition to sensation-seeking activities

   d. her unrealistic expectations that he will change

34. Psychologists who follow the humanistic model are concerned with the issue of:

   a. reinforcement   c. internal conflict

   b. neurological processes d. self-concept

35. Cycles of thoughts and actions are studied by:

   a. psychodynamic psychologists   c. behaviorists

   b. cognitive psychologists   d. structuralists

36. A psychodynamic researcher would study alcoholics in order to discover the:

   a. environmental factors that maintain their drinking patterns

   b. subjective perceptions that help them justify their alcoholism

   c. unconscious motivations and conflicts underlying their behavior

   d. genetic history of this disease in the family tree

37. A behavioral psychologist would study children with learning disabilities to discover:

   a. how this problem affects children's self-esteem

   b. the history of learning disabilities on both sides of the children's families

   c. environmental factors that help and hinder the children's school performance

   d. to what extent these children's primary drives were thwarted in infancy

38. Generalizing findings from animal studies to the functioning of human beings is most closely associated with:

   a. the behavioral model   c. the humanistic model

   b. the cognitive model   d. the psychodynamic model

39. Regarding the models of psychology, an accurate statement would be that:

   a. even though they disagree in philosophy, they all consider human nature in their theories and research

   b. they are all based on the principle that humans move toward pleasure and away from pain

   c. they all consider the impact of early life experience as irreversible

   d. there is no one correct approach to view or study human functioning

40.   The number of divisions contained in the American Psychological Association is:
a.   18   c.   38
b.   28   d.   48

41.   How people influence each other's attitudes, actions, emotions, and thoughts is a typical question asked by:
a.   industrial psychologists   c.   social psychologists
b.   developmental psychologists   d.   experimental psychologists

42.   The prevention and treatment of mental disorders is the province of:
a.   clinical psychologists   c.   personality psychologists
b.   health psychologists   d.   educational psychologists

43.   The relationship between stress and cancer would be studied by:
a.   neuroscientists   c.   experimental psychologists
b.   health psychologists   d.   counseling psychologists

44.   At a major corporation, employee absenteeism began increasing and productivity decreasing. Motivation was at an all-time low. What type of psychologist should be called in to help with these problems?
a.   clinical   c.   educational
b.   industrial   d.   social

45.   Psychoanalytic theory, humanistic theory, and trait theories are most closely associated with:
a.   counseling psychologists   c.   developmental psychologists
b.   cognitive psychologists   d.   personality psychologists

46.   How we think, solve problems, and make decisions are processes studied primarily by:
a.   cognitive psychologists   c.   experimental psychologists
b.   health psychologists   d.   personality theorists

47.   The American Psychological Association is divided into:
a.   models   c.   divisions
b.   schools   d.   careers

48.   To be called a psychologist, you must obtain what type of degree?
a.   master's   c.   bachelor's
b.   doctorate   d.   M.D.

49.   Before a psychologist is allowed to administer psychological tests or treat clients, most states require that he or she:
a.   be licensed   c.   do research
b.   teach on the college level   d.   graduate from an APA-approved program

50.   Unlike a psychiatrist, a psychologist cannot:
a.   administer standardized tests   c.   engage in the practice of neuropsychology
b.   work in a research laboratory   d.   prescribe medication

Test Yourself: Fill in the Blanks

Directions: Fill in the blanks with the correct term or name.

1. _____ is the scientific study of behavior and underlying mental processes.

2. In Charles Darwin's book *The Expression of the Emotions in Man and Animals* (1872), he wrote about his theory of _____.

3. The influence of genetic and environmental factors on human behavior is explored in the _____ question.

4. The greatest credit for establishing psychology as an independent discipline is usually given to _____ (1832–1920).

5. _____ was a nineteenth-century method of self-observation in which the subject focused on his own physical sensations, analyzed his consciousness, and verbally reported the results of the analysis.

6. The first major American psychologist, _____ (1842–1910), wrote the first major textbook in the field, *The Principles of Psychology,* in 1890.

7. Studying the adaptive significance of behavior, rather than the structure of consciousness, was the guiding principle of the school of thought called _____.

8. Edward Titchener (1867–1927) founded the school of psychology known as _____.

9. John B. Watson (1878–1958), a student of William James, developed the school of thought known as _____.

10. Humanism emerged as a psychological school in the 1940s primarily as a result of the work of _____ (1902–1987).

11. Psychoanalytic theory, one of the most influential theories in psychology, was developed by _____ (1856–1939).

12. _____ psychology proposes that our perceptions and mental operations can be best understood as organized wholes, not elementary parts.

13. _____ (1844–1924) founded the American Psychological Association and became its first president.

14. _____ is a philosophical assumption that behavior is driven by the desire to maximize pleasure and avoid pain.

15. _____ is the philosophical question asking whether behavior is random or purposeful.

16. The philosophy of _____ assumes that the organism cannot be studied by being broken down into elements.

17. The philosophical question of _____ asks whether human beings are basically good or evil.

18. A _____ is a way of organizing thinking about the various components of behavior and the ways in which they relate to each other.

19. A _____ attends medical school and receives an M.D. degree and then completes four additional years of training specifically in the field of psychiatry.

20. A _____ is an individual with a doctoral degree in psychology rather than medicine.

Test Yourself: Matching Questions

Directions: For each item in column 1, *select the item in column II that is most closely associated with it.*

I	II
_____1. nature-nurture	a. environmental determinism
_____2. empiricism	b. processes of thought and attention
_____3. structuralism	c. heredity and environment
_____4. hedonism	d. unconscious conflicts
_____5. behaviorism	e. elements of experience
_____6. cognition	f. stress and disease
_____7. humanism	g. assessment and treatment
_____8. psychodynamic	h. careful, precise observation
_____9. neuroscience	i. trait theories
____10. health psychology	j. practical problems
____11. clinical psychology	k. adaptive significance
____12. personality psychology	l. self-concept
____13. industrial psychology	m. genetic predisposition
____14. applied psychology	n. pain and pleasure
____15. functionalism	o. employee productivity

Test Yourself: Answer Key

Multiple Choice

1. c	(4)	11. b	(9)	21. b	(17)	31. b	(21)	41. c	(25)
2. a	(4)	12. d	(10)	22. a	(18)	32. c	(22)	42. a	(25)
3. c	(4)	13. c	(12)	23. c	(17–18)	33. a	(21–22)	43.b	(24)
4. b	(5)	14. d	(12)	24. d	(19)	34. d	(22)	44. b	(25)
5. b	(5)	15. a	(12)	25. a	(19)	35. b	(22)	45. d	(25)
6. d	(5, 8–9)	16. b	(13)	26. d	(19)	36. c	(21)	46. a	(24)
7. c	(5)	17. a	(13, 15)	27. b	(20)	37. c	(21–22)	47. c	(23–24)
8. a	(8)	18. c	(13, 15)	28. c	(20)	38. a	(21–22)	48. b	(26)
9. c	(5)	19. d	(15)	29. c	(20–21)	39. d	(22–23)	49. a	(26)
10. a	(8)	20. a	(15)	30. a	(21)	40. d	24	50. d	(27)

Fill in the Blanks

1. psychology
2. evolution or evolution by natural selection
3. nature-nurture
4. Wilhelm Wundt
5. introspection
6. William James
7. functionalism
8. structuralism
9. behaviorism
10. Carl Rogers
11. Sigmund Freud
12. Gestalt
13. G. Stanley Hall
14. hedonism
15. teleology
16. holism
17. human nature
18. model

19. psychiatrist

20. psychologist

Matching Questions

1. c	6. b	11. h
2. h	7. l	12. i
3. e	8. d	13. o
4. n	9. m	14. j
5. a	10. f	15. k

Do These Mini Projects

1. Call or write to the American Psychological Association in Washington, D.C., and request a copy of the names and descriptions of the 48 divisions and a copy of the ethical guidelines for psychologists. Reading through these documents will give you a greater understanding of the field.

2. Ask your college advisor to share with you catalogs for graduate study in the field of psychology. Looking through such catalogs will give you a better idea of the requirements and courses of study in a variety of areas in the field.

3. Look through your local and state newspapers over the next few weeks and notice how many articles focus on the field of psychology by addressing such topics as managed care insurance issues and the use of psychological experts in court-related matters.

Pull It All Together

1. It must be apparent to you after studying the first chapter that psychology is a diverse field with many areas of study and a variety of viewpoints on how human functioning should be viewed and investigated. In spite of the diversity of areas, models, settings, and philosophies, there are common threads and goals that tie the field of psychology together. Discuss the common threads in the field and the common goals of psychologists.

2. Explain the logic behind psychology having its roots in philosophy and physiology. Give examples of how the earlier schools of thought in psychology are related to current models in the field.

Chapter Outline

Chapter Overview

Chapter 2 describes the scientific method and explains how research in psychology is conducted using the principles of scientific investigation. The author of the text points out early in the chapter that the essential difference between our personal observations and those of researchers is that our observations and conclusions are casual and subjective, whereas those of researchers using the scientific method are precise and objective. It is the application of research methods to the study of psychology that makes the field a science.

Chapter 2 contains six major sections: (1) "The Science of Psychology," (2) "Research Methods," (3) "Research Principles and Practice," (4) "Collecting and Analyzing Data," (5) "Sources of Error," and (6) "Doing It Right:Ethical Considerations."

The first section ("The Science of Psychology") explains that the scientific method assumes that events follow lawful, causal principles and uses objective, systematic observation to determine what those principles are. There are advantages to the scientific approach over casual observation, including these: (1) Science is systematic, formal, and objective in both the design of studies and the interpretation of results. (2) Science strives for simplicity and order, and behavioral scientists expect to find order in behavior. (3) Science is precise, relying on careful measurement and quantifying observations. (4) Scientific knowledge is repeatable, with replication of results ensuring that results are accurate and meaningful. (5) Science provides cumulative knowledge, with publication ensuring that new information and ideas build on an existing foundation.

The author of the text distinguishes between two types of scientific research: basic and applied. Basic research addresses issues or problems that have no immediate practical consequence, whereas applied research addresses immediate, practical problems that need a solution. Basic research is essential because it provides knowledge that is needed for the development of practical applications. The scientific method is used for achieving the goals of scientific psychology, which include description of objectively observable behavior, prediction of behavior before it occurs through hypothesis testing, control of behavior, application of knowledge, and understanding of the causes of behavior. The concepts of theory and research are defined and the relationship between them is explained.

The second section ("Research Methods") describes two methods of research that provide a basis for scientific observation: (1) descriptive and correlational methods and (2) experimental methods. The two methods differ considerably in the kinds of observations that can be made and the kinds of conclusions that are legitimate to draw. The author of the text describes three types of descriptive and correlational methods: the case study, the survey, and naturalistic observation.

To go beyond description, relationships between two variables or characteristics can be examined through the use of correlational techniques. A correlation indicates the degree of relationship between two variables. Although correlations can determine relationships between variables, they do not provide an indication of cause-effect relationships. Cause-effect relationships can be determined through the experimental method. The experiment is a research method involving the manipulation of one or more variables under carefully controlled conditions, and the measurement of its effects on one or more other variables. The use of a control group allows us to reach firm causal conclusions. This section ends with a discussion of quasi-experimental techniques.

The third section ("Research Principles and Practice") describes briefly six standard principles and practices that researchers apply in an effort to assure that the results of research are scientifically sound: (1) Standardization—every aspect of an experiment is applied in a consistent, uniform manner to every participant. (2) Operational definition—specifies procedures or operations used to manipulate, control, or measure a variable. (3) Generalization—formulating broad principles of behavior that generalize beyond the sample studied. (4) Reliability and validity—reliability means stability or consistency (in controlled experiments, results are reliable if they can be repeated in other experiments); validity is the extent to which a measure, procedure, or study does what it is supposed to do. (5) Replication—the repetition of a study to determine whether the same results can be achieved. (6) Programmatic research—a series of systematic, interrelated studies that all move toward the same broad goal of establishing a greater understanding of some particular aspect of behavior.

The fourth section ("Collecting and Analyzing Data") describes methods of data collection and data analysis used in psychological research. Three categories of data collection are discussed: (1) self-report, (2) behavioral approaches, and (3) physiological measures. With self-report, participants in a study provide information about themselves. They may provide the information through an interview, which is a dialogue between an interviewer and an interviewee. Information may be provided in a more formal way through psychological tests, standardized measures, or observation of a person's behavior or performance. Behavioral measures are less subject to distortion than self-report. Physiological measures assess the internal functioning of the body. Moving on to data analysis, also known as statistical analysis, the author of the text provides a brief description of descriptive and inferential statistics.

The fifth section ("Sources of Error") describes three sources of error that can distort research findings: (1) experimenter bias; (2) participant expectancy: the placebo effect; and (3) demand characteristics. Regarding the first source of error, an experimenter's biases can have an impact on the procedures and results of the study and invalidate the findings. Regarding the second source of error, if the participants in the study are biased, their behavior will change and the data will be biased. Regarding the third source of error, demand characteristics are cues in the experimental situation that the participant interprets as indicating the purpose of the study and what is expected. Some participants under these conditions will do what they believe is helpful to prove the hypotheses, thereby biasing the results of the study.

The final section ("Doing It Right: Ethical Considerations") discusses the issues of voluntary participation, deception, confidentiality, and animal research. From an ethical standpoint, voluntary participation as a research subject is preferable to required participation, and most human research is now conducted on that basis. The issue of deception is controversial because, on the one hand, psychologists must protect the rights of individuals participating in experiments, but, on the other hand, some types of investigations could not be performed without minor deceptions because the participants' knowledge could bias results. Confidentiality protects individuals' rights to privacy. Finally, the use of animals as research subjects is ethically controversial and has come under close scrutiny.

How to Master Chapter 2

Refer to These Learning Objectives

You should be able to achieve the following learning objectives after mastering the material in chapter 2:

The Science of Psychology

1. List and explain the major principles underlying the scientific method.

2. Explain the specific advantages of the scientific method over casual observation and personal experience.

3. Discuss the difference between basic and applied research.

4. Describe the characteristics of the following goals of scientific psychology: description, prediction, control, application, and understanding.

5. Discuss the important characteristics of a scientific theory.

Research Methods

6. Describe and give examples of the following nonexperimental methods of research: the case study, the survey, and naturalistic observation.

7. Define correlation and explain how it differs from a cause-effect relationship.

8. List and define the components of the experimental method.

9. Define and discuss the importance of control groups, representative samples, and random sampling to scientific inquiry. Give examples.

10. Explain what is meant by a quasi-experiment.

Research Principles and Practice

11. Define and explain the importance of each of the following research principles and practices: standardization; operational definition; generalization; reliability; validity; replication; programmatic research. Give examples.

Collecting and Analyzing Data

12. Describe and explain the use of three major types of data collection procedures.

13. State the types of information yielded by descriptive and inferential statistics.

Sources of Error

14. Describe and give examples of three sources of error in research, and explain how each of them interferes with obtaining objective results.

Doing It Right: Ethical Considerations

15. Discuss and give examples of the major ethical factors to consider when conducting psychological research.

Debate These Myths

MYTH 1: *The principles of psychology are based more on common sense than on scientific knowledge.*

Strategy:

Describe the scientific method used in psychological research:

Discuss five ways in which the scientific approach to establishing the principles of psychology are superior to casual observation and personal experience:

1.

2.

3.

4.

5.

Describe the goals of scientific psychology and how they are achieved through the development of theories and the implementation of research:

Other statements or examples for debating MYTH 1:

Change MYTH 1 into a true statement:

MYTH 2: *Published research findings are always valid and reliable.*

Strategy:

Although researchers strive to publish valid and reliable findings, there are a variety of sources of error that can distort and even invalidate findings. Describe four sources of error:

1.

2.

3.

4.

Describe several possible mistakes researchers could make in designing a research study:

Describe the important role of replication in psychological research:

Other statements or examples for debating MYTH 2:

Change MYTH 2 into a true statement:

MYTH 3: *The correlation between two variables demonstrates a cause-effect relationship.*

Strategy:

Discuss the definition of correlation and what correlations demonstrate regarding the relationship between two variables:

Discuss the process through which cause-effect relationships can be established:

Other statements and examples for debating MYTH 3:

Change MYTH 3 into a true statement:

MYTH 4: *Conducting research that yields meaningful results can be done only if the participants are unaware of the nature of what is being studied.*

Strategy:

Discuss how demand characteristics can influence research findings:

Discuss the ethical issues of deception and the protection of individual rights:

Discuss how the potential problems of demand characteristics and the ethical issues surrounding deception can be reconciled:

Other statements and examples to debate MYTH 4:

Change MYTH 4 into a true statement:

Test Yourself: Multiple-Choice Questions

Directions: Circle the best response for each of the following questions.

1. As compared with casual observation and personal experience, the scientific approach is more:
    a. intuitive
    c. precise
    b. subjective
    d. common

2. Casual observation is to the scientific method as:
    a. subjective is to objective
    c. temporary is to permanent
    b. detailed is to vague
    d. formal is to informal

3. Important issues that have no immediate practical consequences are:
    a. not studied by researchers in the field of psychology
    b. considered basic research issues
    c. published in only obscure journals
    d. free from sources of error

4. A group of professors at a major university are studying the impact of three different types of psychotherapy in the treatment of panic disorder. These professors are engaging in:
    a. basic research
    c. descriptive research
    b. applied research
    d. experimenter bias

5. The findings of basic research on the process of social development of young children:
    a. are interesting, but impractical
    b. are used primarily by pediatricians
    c. can serve as a basis for applied research on parenting techniques
    d. can be safely generalized across cultures

6. The observation that it took a two-year-old child 30 seconds to begin crying after her mother left her in a room with a stranger is an example of:
    a. prediction
    c. control
    b. understanding
    d. description

7. Promising a ten-year-old that he can watch one hour of television after he finishes all his homework is an example of:
    a. description
    c. control
    b. prediction
    d. correlation

8. An organized set of concepts and propositions designed to help scientists account for, predict, and explain some set of phenomena is known as a:
    a. hypothesis
    c. study
    b. correlation
    d. theory

9. Hypotheses are derived from:
    a. descriptions of behavioral phenomena
    b. theories
    c. performance of participants in a study
    d. surveys

10. It is *not* true that theories:
    a. are equally valid
    c. predict observations
    b. produce hypotheses
    d. can be tested

11. A process of inquiry in which scientists use careful, precise observations to arrive at a better understanding of some phenomenon is called:
    a. survey
    b. research
    c. theory
    d. data

12. Cause-effect relationships in the field of psychology can be established only through:
    a. correlational studies
    b. the experimental method
    c. in-depth case studies
    d. self-report

13. A survey is a device used to assess and predict the views, reactions, or standings of:
    a. participants in a controlled experiment
    b. small segments of the population on practical matters
    c. a large group of people on a limited topic
    d. anyone with a valid opinion

14. Piaget based his theory of cognitive development on in-depth observations of his own children as they were growing up. This method of research is based on:
    a. the experimental method
    b. correlational methods
    c. case studies
    d. surveys

15. In an experiment using three groups, the group receiving no treatment serves as a:
    a. dependent variable
    b. control
    c. predictor
    d. random sample

16. Naturalistic observation studies are conducted:
    a. under controlled conditions
    b. mostly on animals
    c. only in laboratories
    d. almost anywhere

17. A study finds that as adults age, short-term memory deteriorates. This type of finding would be considered:
    a. correlational
    b. experimental
    c. replicable
    d. hypothetical

18. When behavior is observed and measured but not controlled or manipulated, the method being employed is:
    a. basic research
    b. applied research
    c. nonexperimental
    d. experimental

19. The bias of participants reporting what they think the researcher wants to hear is a potential problem most closely associated with:
    a. case studies
    b. surveys
    c. psychological testing
    d. observational studies

20. The principal disadvantage of naturalistic observation is:
    a. remaining objective
    b. getting the participants' consent
    c. the complex statistical procedures
    d. finding representative samples

21. In a study designed to assess the effectiveness of a new technique for teaching children how to read, 150 first-grade students were randomly assigned to one of three groups: one group was exposed to the traditional techniques; a second group was exposed to the new technique; and the third group was exposed to no technique, but sat in a classroom with a teacher interacting with them, as did the other two groups. When treatments were completed, the children's reading ability was tested. In this study, the independent variable is:

   a. the children's scores on reading ability tests

   b. teaching technique

   c. the number of students tested

   d. the number of groups

22. In the study described in question 21, the control group is:

   a. the one exposed to the new technique

   b. the one exposed to the traditional techniques

   c. the one exposed to no technique

   d. cannot be determined from the information provided

23. In the study described in question 21, the dependent variable is the:

   a. technique each group was exposed to

   b. number of students tested

   c. number of groups

   d. children's reading ability after treatment

24. The study described in question 21 would be considered:

   a. a survey
   c. a case study

   b. correlational
   d. experimental

25. Referring back to question 21, the purpose of assigning the children to groups randomly is to:

   a. minimize bias
   c. minimize parents' complaints

   b. maximize reading scores
   d. maximize the children's cooperation

26. Natural variables, such as gender and race, are used as independent variables in:

   a. surveys
   c. quasi-experiments

   b. case studies
   d. controlled experiments

27. A small number of people from a much larger population that have the same relevant characteristics as that population would be considered a:

   a. random sample
   c. a stratified random sample

   b. a representative sample
   d. a biased sample

28. When every aspect of an experiment is applied in a consistent, uniform manner to every participant, the data collection procedures are considered:

   a. reliable
   c. replicated

   b. generalizable
   d. standardized

29. A researcher describes improved eating habits as consuming 1,800 to 2,000 calories per day with foods consumed from the basic food groups according to a table provided to the participants. The researcher's description of eating habits would be considered:

   a. an operational definition
   c. reliable and valid

   b. standardized
   d. generalizable to a larger population

30. The "reliability" of test results refers to their:

   a. validity
   c. stability

   b. standardization
   d. generalizability

31. If the study referred to in question 21 were performed a year later and yielded the same findings, the study would be considered:

    a. replicated   c. valid
    b. operationally defined   d. quasi-experimental

32. If a test that is supposed to measure shyness is actually measuring neurological impairment, the test would be considered:

    a. nonstandardized   c. invalid
    b. unreplicatable   d. unreliable

33. In programmatic research, each study provides:

    a. reliable data   c. information on personality dimensions
    b. small increments of information d. replicated results

34. Of the following, it is most difficult to quantify:

    a. interview data   c. psychological test data
    b. behavioral measures   d. physiological measures

35. Concerning data collection, the most accurate of the following statements is that:

    a. psychological tests are more objective than interviews
    b. physiological measures are the least relevant to the study of behavior
    c. the main disadvantage of interviews is their time-limited nature
    d. behavioral measures are more subject to distortion than self-report

36. A standardized measure of a person's behavior that is used to assess individual differences is the:

    a. structured interview   c. behavioral approach
    b. survey   d. psychological test

37. An advantage of interviews for collecting data is:

    a. standardization   c. richness of data
    b. lack of bias   d. attention to individual differences

38. The skin conductance response is a good measure of:

    a. heart rate   c. blood pressure
    b. arousal   d. hunger

39. The application of mathematical calculations to describe, summarize, and account for the observed variability in numerical data is called:

    a. a controlled study   c. statistical analysis
    b. a quasi-experiment   d. a physiological measure

40. Statistical analyses are used for:

    a. communicating results   c. quantifying observations
    b. summarizing data   d. all of the above

41. Compared to inferential statistics, descriptive statistics are:

    a. less complex   c. more generalizable
    b. more significant   d. less reliable

42. An experimenter is told that although the participants consented to be in the study, they consented reluctantly. Based on this information, the experimenter acts in a guarded manner. This type of situation can produce:

    a. experimenter bias   c. the placebo effect
    b. the Hawthorne effect   d. a double-blind procedure

43. The placebo effect is a source of error in research associated with:
    a. experimenter bias
    c. participant expectancy
    b. demand characteristics
    d. ethical problems

44. A medication containing no significant chemical properties that is used in a controlled experiment is considered a:
    a. controlled substance
    c. standardized measure
    b. violation of rights
    d. placebo

45. In a study on tolerance for frustration, participants were asked to wait a few minutes for the experimenter, but it was deliberately planned that the experimenter would not appear for an hour. In spite of the long waiting period combined with being misinformed, most participants acted in a friendly fashion when the experimenter arrived and expressed no frustration. It is likely that the behavior of these participants was uncharacteristic and are attributable to:
    a. experimenter bias
    c. the placebo effect
    b. demand characteristics
    d. participant expectancy

46. When the experiment referred to in question 45 was completed, the participants were told the real reasons they were kept waiting. This is an ethical consideration known as:
    a. debriefing
    c. confidentiality
    b. voluntary participation
    d. informed consent

47. If the participants in the study described in question 45 were not told what participation would involve and were not allowed to ask questions, they would have been deprived of their right to:
    a. confidentiality
    c. informed consent
    b. voluntary participation
    d. participant expectancy

48. When neither the experimenter nor the participants are aware of which group the participants were assigned to, the experiment is employing:
    a. a double-blind procedure
    c. standardized measures
    b. the placebo effect
    d. descriptive statistics

49. The Hawthorne effect refers to the:
    a. positive effects of any change
    b. negative impact of involuntary participation
    c. source of error caused by experimenter subjectivity
    d. none of the above

50. Confidentiality, which protects an individual's right to privacy, does not apply when a person:
    a. participates in an experiment
    c. reveals ongoing child abuse
    b. condones animal research
    d. works in an industrial setting

Test Yourself: Fill in the Blanks

Directions: Fill in the blanks with the correct term or name.

1. The _____ method assumes that events follow lawful, causal principles and uses objective, systematic observation to determine what those principles are.

2. _____ research is designed to deal with an immediate, practical problem that needs a solution.

3. A _____ is a clear, specific proposition that can be tested to determine whether or not it is true.

4. A _____ is an in-depth analysis of the behavior of a single person, whose thoughts, emotions, personality, attitudes, and life history are subjected to careful, detailed scrutiny.

5. A _____ is a device used to assess and predict the views, reactions, or standings of a large number of people on a limited topic.

6. A correlation indicates the degree of relationship between two _____.

7. An experiment involves the manipulation of one or more variables under carefully _____ conditions, and the measurement of its effects on one or more other variables.

8. In an experiment, the _____ group, otherwise identical to the experimental group, does not receive the treatment.

9. Some independent variables are called _____ variables because they are based on preexisting conditions.

10. Variables measured to see whether they change as a result of experimental manipulation are called _____ variables.

11. The variables manipulated by the experimenter are called the _____ Variables.

12. In a _____-experiment, psychologists study independent variables that they cannot readily control or manipulate.

13. The procedures or operations used to manipulate, control, or measure a variable are specified in a(n) 1. _____.

14. _____ refers to the consistency or stability of test results.

15. _____ refers to the repetition of a study to determine whether or not the same results can be achieved.

16. A _____ is a standardized measure of a person's behavior and is used to assess individual differences.

17. _____ analysis refers to the application of mathematical calculations to describe, summarize, and account for the observed variability in numerical data.

18. _____ statistics are designed to tell us whether our results can be generalized beyond the present experiment.

19. One source of bias in research is called the _____, in which behavior changes merely because the participant expects it to change.

20. The process through which the participant receives information about the purpose and nature of the experiment and has an opportunity to voice concerns about the procedures is called _____.

Test Yourself: Matching Questions

Directions: For each item in column I, select the item in column II that is most closely associated with it.

I	II
_____ 1. case study	a. relationship between two variables
_____ 2. survey	b. manipulated by experimenter
_____ 3. correlation	c. consistency or stability
_____ 4. interview	d. in-depth analysis of an individual
_____ 5. independent variable	e. e.g., SCR or EKG
_____ 6. control group	f. participant expectancy
_____ 7. natural variable	g. uniformity
_____ 8. reliability	h. measures views of a large group
_____ 9. physiological measure	i. informing
_____ 10. confidentiality	j. drawn in an unbiased way
_____ 11. placebo effect	k. a self-report method
_____ 12. standardization	l. determines cause-effect relationships
_____ 13. random sample	m. privacy
_____ 14. experiment	n. e.g., gender or height
_____ 15. debriefing	o. receives no treatment

Test Yourself: Answer Key

Multiple Choice

1. c	(32)	11. b	(35)	21. b	(40–41)	31.a	(48–49)	41. a	(51)
2. a	(32)	12. b	(40)	22. c	(40)	32. c	(48)	42. a	(52)
3. b	(33)	13. c	(37)	23. d	(40–41)	33. b	(49)	43. c	(52)
4. b	(33)	14. c	(37)	24. d	(40)	34. a	(50)	44. d	(53)
5. c	(33)	15. b	(40)	25. a	(43–44)	35. a	(50)	45. b	(53)
6. d	(33)	16. d	(38–39)	26. c	(44)	36. d	(50)	46. a	(56)
7. c	(34)	17. a	(39)	27. b	(43)	37. c	(49)	47. c	(56)
8. d	(35)	18. c	(37)	28. d	(47)	38. b	(51)	48. a	(53)
9. b	(35)	19. b	(38)	29. a	(48)	39. c	(51)	49. a	(54)
10. a	(35)	20. a	(39)	30. c	(48)	40. d	(51)	50. c	(57)

Fill in the Blanks

1. scientific
2. applied
3. hypothesis
4. case study
5. survey
6. variables
7. controlled
8. control
9. natural
10. dependent
11. independent
12. quasi
13. operational definition
14. reliability
15. replication
16. psychological test
17. statistical
18. inferential

19. placebo effect

20. debriefing

Matching Questions

1. d	6. o	11. f
2. h	7. n	12. g
3. a	8. c	13. j
4. k	9. e	14. l
5. b	10. m	15. i

Do These Mini Projects

1. An excellent way to gain a better understanding of the terminology used in chapter 2 is to read and analyze one or two research studies. You will be able to find numerous research studies that are presented in the form of articles in psychology journals, which should be readily available in the college library. Don't be afraid to ask the librarian for help in locating the journals; the librarian is a resource person who can be invaluable to you when you do your own library and research projects in the future. You will notice immediately that there are many journals that cover the full range of specializations in the field of psychology that you learned about in chapter 1. There will be more than one journal per specialization. For the purposes of this mini project, select a journal in an area that you think you will find interesting and read through the table of contents. Select an article based on a research study, and note the following:

    How is the article organized?

    What are the investigators trying to determine?

    Why is this topic important?

    Is this study basic or applied research? How do you know?

    What type of study is it experimental? correlational? survey?

    If it is not an experiment, choose another article and answer the first series of questions in this mini project, and then proceed to answer the following questions:

    What are the independent and dependent variables?

    Describe the treatment groups.

    Is there a control group? Describe it.

    What are the results and conclusions?

2. This mini project involves using the technique of naturalistic observation. Select in advance a person, group of people, or pet to observe in a systematic way. Some ideas for subjects might be people waiting on a long line, people on a commuter train, or your instructor. Decide and write down the behaviors you plan to observe and record. Decide whether you are interested in recording the frequency of these behaviors in a particular time period. Make a list of the targeted behaviors in advance of the observation. You are now ready to observe and record. Remember to stay objective and not interfere with the people or animal being observed. Your job is not to change anything nor to draw inferences, but to be an accurate observer of naturally occurring behavior.

Pull It All Together

1. Now that you have studied the methods psychologists use to do scientific studies, go back to chapter 1 and examine the lists of areas of specialization and APA divisions provided toward the end of that chapter. Do certain areas of specialization and divisions lend themselves to the pursuit of scientific research more than others? If you believe so, which ones? Why? If you believe that scientific studies can be done in any area of the field of psychology, explain your reasoning.

2. How much research on a topic do you think would be required to establish a *fact* in the field of psychology? How would you organize your current knowledge to evaluate whether a fact has been established? In your answer, consider what you have learned regarding the establishment of cause-effect relationships, the use of control groups, methods of data collection, and sources of error.

CHAPTER 3
NEUROSCIENCE: THE BRAIN AND BEHAVIOR

Chapter Outline

Chapter Overview

Chapter 3 describes the complex relationship between the brain and behavior. The author of the text begins the chapter by explaining that psychologists study the brain because all human behavior and mental processes are controlled by the brain and the nervous system. A full understanding of behavior requires understanding how the brain and nervous system function. The study of the relationship between the brain and behavior is the province of neuroscience, which is an interdisciplinary science that pools the expertise and resources of psychology, neurology, zoology, physiology, biochemistry, computer science, and other disciplines.

Chapter 3 contains six major sections: (1) "Neurons and the Nerve Impulse," (2) "The Peripheral Nervous System: Acting and Reacting," (3) "The Central Nervous System: Where You Live," (4) "A Brain Divided: Lateralization of Function," (5) "Immersed in Thought: Brain Biochemistry," and (6) "Breaking the Code: Methods of Brain Study."

The first section ("Neurons and the Nerve Impulse") describes the structure and functioning of neurons, the nature of nerve impulses, neuron interaction, the neuron as a computer, and how the billions of neurons in the human body are linked together. A neuron is defined as a single cell in the nervous system that is specialized to receive impulses from other neurons, process those impulses, and transmit information to yet other neurons. Each neuron has three parts—a cell body or soma, dendrites, and an axon—that work together to receive, process, and transmit information.

Three functional types of neurons (sensory neurons, motor neurons, and interneurons) are described. Glial cells or glia make up the other major structural components of the nervous system and perform important functions. The electrochemical process of neurotransmission is described, including the resting and active states of the neuron, the nature of neuronal firing, and the refractory period that follows firing. Although the axon terminals bring the axon of one neuron very close to the dendritic zone of another, neurons do not physically touch each other. Rather, neurotransmitters, specialized chemicals, carry neural information across synapses, the tiny gaps between neurons. The cumulative process through which multiple impulses influence a postsynaptic call is called summation. Whether or not a neuron fires is a function of the balance between excitatory and inhibitory potentials determined by the soma, which acts as a "computer." Nerves are bundles of axon fibers that travel through the nervous system together.

The second section ("The Peripheral Nervous System: Acting and Reacting") describes the functioning of the peripheral nervous system, which consists of all neural structures outside the brain and spinal cord and serves to carry neural information both to and from those structures. Some of the fiber tracts that make up the peripheral nervous system come directly from the brain, and others come from the spinal cord. The fiber tracts that go directly from the brain to the head, face, and neck are called cranial nerves; the spinal nerves originate in the spinal cord. The peripheral nervous system, which is directly involved in the functioning of both the muscles and the internal organs, is divided into two parts: (1) the somatic (skeletal) nervous system and (2) the autonomic nervous system (ANS). The somatic nervous system consists of all the nerves that carry impulses to the skeletal muscles and all those bringing information from the sensory receptors. The somatic system contains sensory neurons (the axons of which group together to form afferent neurons and carry information from the senses to the central nervous system) and motor neurons (the axons of which form efferent neurons and carry impulses from the central nervous system to the periphery to control the movements of the individual).

The autonomic nervous system (ANS) originates in the hypothalamus and controls the activities of the internal organs and glands, regulating heart rate, respiration rate, digestion, and other processes that are not usually under voluntary control. The autonomic nervous system consists of two subsystems: (1) the sympathetic nervous system, which tends to dominate in times of stress or extreme activity, and (2) the parasympathetic nervous system, which tends to be dominant during periods of relative relaxation. Biofeedback is a technique through which individuals can learn to regulate processes, such as heart rate and blood pressure, that are ordinarily not under voluntary control. This section ends with a description of the endocrine system, a set of glands in various parts of the body that release hormones into the bloodstream to influence physiological and emotional functioning.

The third section ("The Central Nervous System: Where You Live") describes the functioning of the central nervous system, which controls all the other systems, interprets the world around us, and tells us who we are. The central nervous system (CNS) consists of two structures: (1) the brain and (2) the spinal cord. The spinal cord contains sensory and motor nerves and has two main functions: a neural switchboard, carrying messages back and forth between the brain and the peripheral nervous system; and a center for processing reflex behaviors.

The brain is the most complex organ in the human body. It is protected from injury by the bony skull, by three layers of insulation called the meninges, by cerebrospinal fluid, and by the blood-brain barrier. The brain is divided into many parts, each with its own function and each working in interaction with the others in an organized way. The three principal divisions of the brain are (1) the hindbrain, (2) the midbrain, and (3) the forebrain. The hindbrain, which lies just above the spinal cord, is the most primitive part of the brain. The midbrain, which lies above the medulla and the pons, is a further continuation of the spinal cord. The forebrain, the largest and most complex section of the brain, begins just in front of the midbrain and is divided into the subcortical and cortical areas. The gray, unmyelinated cortex performs the most complex brain functions. The subcortex is below it and contains the thalamus, the hypothalamus, the limbic system, and the basal ganglia. The thalamus acts as a relay station that receives sensory information, integrates it, and sends it on to the cortex for further processing. The thalamus is also involved in the processing of certain pain sensations and the organization of the sleep-wake cycle.

The hypothalamus is divided into a number of cell groups and is involved in eating, drinking, the regulation of body temperature, consciousness, the sleep-wake cycle, and sexual behavior. Near it lies the limbic system. The basal ganglia, just below the cortex, are involved in the control of sensory and motor functions. The cerebral cortex, the most complex structure of the brain, is divided into four sets of lobes: (1) the frontal lobes (moving and thinking); (2) the temporal lobes (hearing, emotion, and memory); (3) the occipital lobes (vision); and (4) the parietal lobes (touch and movement). The projection areas of the cortex receive input from the senses and send commands to the muscles; the association areas connect the projection areas together. One of the newest theories of neural activity suggests that although certain functions of the brain are localized, others are spread across several areas of the brain in what are called neural networks, sets of neurons linked to each other at their synapses.

The fourth section ("A Brain Divided: Lateralization of Function") explains that the brain is divided into two hemispheres and that control is contralateral, with the right hemisphere controlling the left side of the body and the left hemisphere controlling the right side. The two hemispheres, which differ in structure and somewhat in function, are connected by a tract of fibers called the corpus callosum. Although individuals can function without a corpus callosum, the lack of communication between the two hemispheres of the brain can create difficulties for them. Regarding specialization of the hemispheres, the left appears to dominate in processing verbal information and the right is better equipped to deal with spatial tasks.

The fifth section ("Immersed in Thought: Brain Biochemistry") explains that there are 100 to 150 neurotransmitters that carry nerve impulses across the synaptic cleft. These neurotransmitters are crucial to the normal flow of activity, and any interference with these substances is likely to create problems. The brain also contains natural opiates, or painkillers, called endorphins, which can be activated through exercise and proper nutrition. This section concludes with an explanation of the impact of nutrition on the functioning of the brain.

The final section ("Breaking the Code: Methods of Brain Study") describes both older and newer methods used for studying the brain. Newer methods include computerized axial topography (CT), magnetic resonance imaging (MRI), positron emission tomography (PET), and single photon emission computer tomography (SPECT). This section concludes with a discussion of Alzheimer's disease, a degenerative neurological disorder that gradually leads to severe loss of memory and skill. This disease is thus far incurable and so difficult to recognize that a firm diagnosis must often await autopsy.

How to Master Chapter 3

Refer to These Learning Objectives

You should be able to achieve the following learning objectives after mastering the material in chapter 3:

Neurons and the Nerve Impulse

1. Define neuroscience, and explain why the study of the brain is important to the understanding of human behavior.

2. Describe a neuron and its component parts.

3. Explain the functions of each part of the neuron.

4. Describe the glial cells and how they function.

5. Explain how neurons transmit neural messages.

6. Explain what is meant by resting potential; action potential; threshold; all-or-none firing; the refractory period.

7. Describe a synapse and its role in neurotransmission.

8. Explain the concept of summation and the importance of this process.

The Peripheral Nervous System: Acting and Reacting

9. Describe the components and functions of the peripheral nervous system.

10. Describe the cranial and spinal nerves and their functions.

11. Describe the afferent and efferent nerves and how they function in the somatic nervous system to control sensation and muscle movement. Give examples.

12. Describe the role of the autonomic nervous system (ANS) in the functioning of internal organs and emotions. Give examples.

13. Describe the sympathetic and parasympathetic nervous systems of the ANS, and how they work both together and separately. Give examples.

14. Describe and give examples of the process of biofeedback. Explain the benefits of biofeedback.

15. Explain the role of the endocrine system in human functioning.

The Central Nervous System: Where You Live

16. Name the parts of the central nervous system. Explain the function of the CNS.

17. Describe the structure and the functions of the spinal cord.

18. Name and describe the structures that protect the brain from injury.

19. Describe the location of the hindbrain, name its component parts, and describe how they function.

20. Describe the location of the midbrain, name its component parts, and describe how they function.

21. Describe the location of the forebrain, name its component parts, and describe how they function.

22. Describe and give examples of the functioning of the hypothalamus, the limbic system, and the basal ganglia.

23. Describe the structure and function of the cerebral cortex.

24. Describe the frontal, temporal, occipital, and parietal lobes and give examples of the roles they play in human functioning.

25. Describe and give examples of the functions of the projection and association areas.

26. Explain what is meant by a neural network.

A Brain Divided: Lateralization of Function

27. Describe the functions of the two hemispheres of the brain, and explain what is meant by lateralization of function.

28. Describe the nature and findings of split-brain research.

Immersed in Thought: Brain Biochemistry

29. Explain and give examples of how neurotransmitters and natural opiates influence human functioning.

Breaking the Code: Methods of Brain Study

30. Describe and give examples of both older and newer methods for studying the brain.

31. Explain the following methods of brain study: ablation; lesioning; electrical stimulation; EEG; CT; MRI; PET; and SPECT.

32. Describe what happens to individuals with Alzheimer's disease and how this disease is diagnosed and treated.

Debate These Myths

MYTH 1: *Knowing the parts of the brain and nervous system and how they function is irrelevant to the practice of psychology.*

Strategy:

Describe the discipline of neuroscience and explain how the functioning of the brain and nervous system interact with human behavior and consciousness:

Name the parts of the brain that influence emotion:

Name the parts of the brain that control the primary drives (e.g., hunger, thirst, sex):

Name the parts of the brain involved in thinking and reasoning:

Explain the roles of neurotransmitters and natural opiates in human behavior:

Other statements and examples to debate MYTH 1:

Change MYTH 1 into a true statement:

MYTH 2: *Each part of the brain and nervous system functions independently.*

Strategy:

Explain how the central and peripheral nervous systems work together:

Explain the relationship between the autonomic and somatic nervous systems:

Explain and give examples of the relationship between the sympathetic and parasympathetic nervous systems:

Name parts of the brain that integrate and coordinate the functioning of other parts of the brain:

Describe the function of the association areas of the cerebral cortex:

Other statements and examples to debate MYTH 2:

Change MYTH 2 into a true statement:

Test Yourself: Multiple-Choice Questions

Directions: Circle the best response for each of the following questions.

1. Neuroscience is an interdisciplinary science that pools the expertise and resources of:
    a. psychology and zoology
    b. neurology and computer science
    c. physiology and biochemistry
    d. all of the above

2. A neuron is a:
    a. single cell
    b. bundle of cells
    c. chemical
    d. cell body

3. Dendrite is to axon as:
    a. positively charged is to negatively charged
    b. structure is to function
    c. receive is to transmit
    d. chemical is to electrical

4. The transmission of neural messages *within* the neuron is achieved through:
    a. an electrical process
    b. osmosis
    c. a chemical process
    d. a mechanical process

5. Neurotransmitters are produced in the part of the neuron known as the:
    a. dendrite
    b. axon terminal
    c. synaptic vesicle
    d. soma

6. More intense stimulation causes all the following *except*:
    a. more frequent firing
    b. repeated firing
    c. larger number of neurons to fire
    d   more intense firing

7. During the refractory period, the activity of the neuron most closely resembles that of a:
    a. racehorse that just crossed the finish line
    b. man in a bar getting ready for a fistfight
    c. child in the middle of a temper tantrum
    d. typist typing 100 words per minute

8. The speed of neuronal transmission is increased by:
    a. greater diameter of the axon
    b. presence of myelin sheathing
    c. neither a nor b
    d. either a or b

9. We are able to distinguish the feel of a drop of water from a steady stream of water because of variation in the neuronal impulses':

a. strength   c. charge

b. frequency   d. speed

10. An action potential will be generated only if the stimulus exceeds:

a. polarization   c. the threshold

b. the response   d. the synaptic cleft

11. An inhibitory postsynaptic potential, or IPSP, hyperpolarizes the neuron, making firing:

a. less likely   c. less intense

b. more likely   d. more intense

12. The somatic nervous system consists of all the nerves that carry impulses to the:

a. brain   c. skeletal muscles

b. spinal cord   d. senses

13. The axons of the motor neurons form efferent nerves that carry impulses from the central nervous system to the periphery to control:

a. emotions   c. sensory input

b. movements   d. thinking

14. Behaviors such as folding a piece of paper and swinging a golf club are controlled by the:

a. somatic nervous system   c. hypothalamus

b. autonomic nervous system   d. spinal cord

15. George was walking down a side street at night when he noticed he was being followed. His heart rate increased, his pupils dilated, and his digestive process slowed down, all due to the action of the:

a. natural opiates   c. cranial nerves

b. sympathetic nervous system   d. parasympathetic nervous system

16. Autonomic is to somatic as:

a. peripheral is to central   c. central is to peripheral

b. involuntary is to voluntary   d. voluntary is to involuntary

17. Which one of the following is the best example of a disorder of the ANS?

a. the inability to walk at a normal pace

b. difficulty concentrating on and retaining written material

c. feeling panicked, even when a situation is not threatening

d. poor fine muscle control when writing

18. Which one of the following individuals would be most likely to benefit from biofeedback?

a. Steve, who wants to break his compulsive gambling habit

b. Kelly, who wants to behave more assertively with her peers

c. Greg, who has a fear of public speaking

d. Lenore, who has suffered with chronic headaches for 20 years

19. Which one of the following is the best example of a reflex?

a. jumping back when the water in the shower is too hot

b. becoming angry when your dog tracks mud in the house

c. a boy jumping up and down when surprised with a new bike

d. becoming anxious when your car won't start before work

20. The percentage of total body weight comprised in the brain is about:
   a. 2 percent
   c. 10 percent
   b. 5 percent
   d. 15 percent

21. The reticular activating system, or RAS, would be particularly involved in controlling which one of the following?
   a. a man's ability to catch his breath after climbing up a mountain
   b. a performer's ability to balance on a tightrope
   c. a child's ability to pay attention in class
   d. a teenager's ability to say no to drugs

22. The graceful movements of a ballet dancer are coordinated by the part of the brain known as the:
   a. superior colliculus
   c. pons
   b. cerebellum
   d. raphe system

23. The muscles of the eyes are controlled by the part of the midbrain known as the:
   a. tegmentum
   c. RAS
   b. tectum
   d. inferior colliculus

24. The substantia nigra, which is involved in neuromuscular control, is located in the:
   a. hindbrain
   c. forebrain
   b. midbrain
   d. cerebral cortex

25. Regarding the thalamus, the lateral geniculate nucleus is to the medial geniculate nucleus as:
   a. hunger is to thirst
   b. hindbrain is to midbrain
   c. visual processing is to auditory processing
   d. thalamus is to hypothalamus

26. The limbic system is involved in the control of:
   a. visual and auditory processing
   b. fine and gross motor activity
   c. sleep and wakefulness
   d. emotion and motivation

27. The neural origin of the ANS is the:
   a. amygdala
   c. hypothalamus
   b. thalamus
   d. RAS

28. Problems such as diabetes, chronic drowsiness, depression, memory loss, extreme overeating, and low body temperature can be caused by disorders of the:
   a. hypothalamus
   c. basal ganglia
   b. cerebellum
   d. medulla

29. A woman with damage to the hippocampus would have difficulty:
   a. remembering people she just met
   b. putting on her makeup
   c. standing on one foot
   d. hearing music being played in another room

30. Damage to the basal ganglia is associated with impairment in:
   a. language production
   c. ability to learn
   b. motor functions
   d. long-term memory

31. The number of neurons contained in the cerebral cortex is approximately:
    a. 10 million
    c. 50 billion
    b. 10 billion
    d. 75 billion

32. The Alternate Uses Test has been used to evaluate problems is cognitive functioning caused by damage to the:
    a. parietal lobes
    c. frontal lobes
    b. occipital lobes
    d. temporal lobes

33. While sitting on a park bench with his father, five-year-old Henry was able to look around the park and name what he saw, including trees, birds, and clouds in the sky. The lobes of his cortex that enabled him to engage in this behavior are the:
    a. parietal
    c. occipital
    b. frontal
    d. temporal

34. When Shirley was introduced to Joe, she noticed that he had a weak and clammy handshake. The lobes of Shirley's cortex that enabled her to draw this conclusion are the:
    a. frontal
    c. temporal
    b. occipital
    d. parietal

35. Jane and her friend Denise, both in second grade, were playing "Name That Tune" by taking turns humming songs while the other guessed the song. Jane had no trouble identifying "Mary Had a Little Lamb." She processed primarily in her:
    a. occipital lobes
    c. parietal lobes
    b. temporal lobes
    d. frontal lobes

36. The projection areas of the brain would be the most involved in which one of the following processes?
    a. interpreting a vague figure in the distance to be your sister
    b. being able to fall asleep and stay asleep for six hours
    c. moving out of the way automatically when a ball is coming at you
    d. knowing when you are hungry and when you are satiated

37. Which one of the following is the best example of the specialization of the left half of the brain?
    a. calming yourself down by taking even breaths
    b. using a road map
    c. memorizing a grocery list
    d. writing the music for a symphony

38. The two hemispheres of the brain are connected by a tract of fibers known as the:
    a. corpus callosum
    c. association area
    b. basal ganglia
    d. lateral geniculate nucleus

39. Research on split-brain patients using the visual half-field technique is associated with:
    a. James Olds
    c. Alois Alzheimer
    b. Jose Delgado
    d. Roger Sperry

40. The differentiation of functioning between the right and left hemispheres of the brain is called:
    a. lateralization
    c. ablation
    b. epilepsy
    d. neurotransmission

41. In a procedure called dichotic listening, individuals are presented with two different messages that are:
    a. each in a different language
    b. spoken simultaneously, one presented to each ear
    c. just below the threshold of normal hearing ability
    d. played on a recorder sequentially in one ear and then the other

42. The number of neurotransmitters that carry nerve impulses across the synaptic cleft is estimated to be:
    a. 25 to 50   c. 100 to 150
    b. 50 to 100   d. 1,000 to 2,000

43. The neurotransmitter dopamine is found primarily in the:
    a. medulla   c. midbrain
    b. raphe system   d. cortex

44. What endorphins and serotonin have in common is that they are both:
    a. involved in the control of pain
    b. neurotransimitters
    c. chemically similar to enkephalins
    d. used to alleviate attention deficit disorder

45. Brain biochemistry is influenced by:
    a. nutritional habits   c. both a and b
    b. exercise   d. neither a nor b

46. The destruction of brain tissue for the purpose of studying how the brain functions is performed through a process known as:
    a. ablation   c. prosopagnosia
    b. electrical stimulation   d. lesioning

47. Jose Delgado has been a pioneer in brain research through the use of:
    a. computerized axial tomography
    b. electrical stimulation
    c. ablation
    d. magnetic resonance imaging

48. The electrical activity of the brain is measured by a technique, first developed in the 1920s, known as:
    a. EEG   c. CT
    b. MRI   d. PET

49. The diagnostic technique using a radioactive tracer emitting only a single photon is a new scanning technique abbreviated as:
    a. SPECT   c. CT
    b. MRI   d. PET

50. All of the following are true regarding Alzheimer's disease *except*:
    a. it affects short-term memory   c. it begins gradually
    b. it is curable   d. it lasts about 10 years

Test Yourself: Fill in the Blanks

Directions: Fill in the blanks with the correct term or name.

1. _____ are short, spidery filaments that receive information from other neurons.

2. _____, which are smaller and more numerous than neurons, remove waste materials when neurons die, help supply neurons with nutrients, and produce the myelin sheaths that surround axons.

3. The principle that the neuron either fires or doesn't fire is called the _____ law.

4. The tiny gap of cleft between the axon terminal of one neuron and the dendritic zone of another is known as a _____.

5. The cumulative process through which multiple impulses influence a postsynaptic cell is called _____.

6. The fiber tracts that make up the peripheral nervous system and go directly from the brain to various structures located primarily in the head, face, and neck are called _____.

7. The axons of the motor neurons form _____ nerves that carry impulses from the central nervous system to the periphery to control the movements of the individual.

8. The peripheral nervous system can be divided into the _____ and _____ nervous systems.

9. The _____ nervous system has sometimes been called the "emergency" nervous system because it tends to dominate in times of stress or extreme activity.

10. The _____ system is a set of glands in various parts of the body that release chemicals into the bloodstream to influence both physiological and emotional functioning.

11. The _____ nervous system consists of the brain and spinal cord.

12. The spinal cord is the center for processing _____ behaviors, automatic behaviors that need not involve the brain.

13. For protection, the brain is surrounded by three layers of ôinsulationö called the _____.

14. The three major subdivisions of the brain from most to least primitive are the: _____, the _____, and the_____.

15. The part of the brain called the _____ is where the ANS originates, is about the size of a peanut, and is involved in many functions including eating, drinking, regulation of body temperature, consciousness, the sleep-wake cycle, and sexual behavior.

16. The _____, which is part of the limbic system, is involved in aggressive behavior, anxiety, and processing emotion.

17. The cerebral cortex is divided into four lobes: the _____ lobes (which influence moving and thinking); the _____ lobes (which influence hearing, emotion), and memory; the _____ lobes (which influence vision); and the _____ lobes (which influence touch and movement sensations).

18. _____ involves the surgical removal of a part of the brain, whereas _____ involves destruction of tissue.

19. The neurotransmitter dopamine has been used with some success to treat _____ disease, which is characterized by muscular tremors, rigidity, and movement problems that become progressively more severe.

20. _____ disease is a degenerative neurological disorder that gradually leads to severe loss of memory and skills.

Test Yourself: Matching Questions

Directions: For each item in column I, *select the item in column II that is most closely associated with it.*

<table>
<tr><td colspan="2" align="center">I</td><td colspan="2" align="center">II</td></tr>
<tr><td>_____</td><td>1. myelin sheath</td><td>a.</td><td>secretes hormones</td></tr>
<tr><td>_____</td><td>2. threshold</td><td>b.</td><td>1 or more milliseconds</td></tr>
<tr><td>_____</td><td>3. RAS</td><td>c.</td><td>processes reflex behaviors</td></tr>
<tr><td>_____</td><td>4. limbic system</td><td>d.</td><td>controls hunger and thirst</td></tr>
<tr><td>_____</td><td>5. endocrine system</td><td>e.</td><td>insulation around brain</td></tr>
<tr><td>_____</td><td>6. refractory period</td><td>f.</td><td>fatty covering</td></tr>
<tr><td>_____</td><td>7. synapse</td><td>g.</td><td>bundle of axon fibers</td></tr>
<tr><td>_____</td><td>8. spinal cord</td><td>h.</td><td>primitive structure</td></tr>
<tr><td>_____</td><td>9. nerve</td><td>i.</td><td>natural painkiller</td></tr>
<tr><td>_____</td><td>10. soma</td><td>j.</td><td>minimal level</td></tr>
<tr><td>_____</td><td>11. hypothalamus</td><td>k.</td><td>natural painkiller</td></tr>
<tr><td>_____</td><td>12. meninges</td><td>l.</td><td>controls emotion</td></tr>
<tr><td>_____</td><td>13. hindbrain</td><td>m.</td><td>cell body</td></tr>
<tr><td>_____</td><td>14. endorphin</td><td>n.</td><td>gap between neurons</td></tr>
<tr><td>_____</td><td>15. action potential</td><td>o.</td><td>control wakefulness</td></tr>
</table>

Test Yourself: Answer Key

Multiple Choice

1. d	(62)	11. a	(68)	21. c	(80)	31. d	(22)	41. b	(89)
2. a	(63)	12. c	(71)	22. b	(78)	32. c	(84)	42. c	(91)
3. c	(63)	13. b	(72)	23. a	(79)	33. c	(84)	43. c	(91–92)
4. a	(63)	14. a	(71)	24. b	(79)	34. d	(84)	44. a	(92)
5. d	(67)	15. b	(72)	25. c	(81)	35. b	(84)	45. c	(93)
6. d	(66)	16. b	(71–72)	26. d	(81)	36. a	(85)	46. d	(96)
7. a	(67)	17. c	(72)	27. c	(82)	37. c	(90)	47. b	(96)
8. d	(67)	18. d	(73)	28. a	(81)	38. a	(88)	48. a	(97)
9. b	(66–67)	19. a	(76)	29. a	(82)	39. d	(88)	49. a	(100)
10.c	(66)	20. a	(77)	30. b	(82)	40. a	(89)	50. b	(101)

Fill in the Blank

1. dendrites
2. glia
3. all-or-none
4. synapse
5. summation
6. cranial nerves
7. efferent
8. somatic, autonomic
9. sympathetic
10. endocrine
11. central
12. reflex
13. meninges
14. hindbrain, midbrain, forebrain
15. hypothalamus
16. amygdala
17. frontal, temporal, occipital, parietal
18. ablation, lesioning

19. Parkinson's

20. Alzheimer's

Matching Questions

1. f	6. b	11. d
2. j	7. n	12. e
3. o	8. c	13. h
4. l	9. g	14. i
5. a	10. m	15. k

Do These Mini Projects

1. Using a pencil (so that you can erase and make corrections, if necessary), draw to the best of your ability a diagram of a neuron. Include in your diagram the following parts of the nueron: dendrites; soma (or cell body); axon; myelin sheath;and axon terminals. Label the parts of the nueron on your diagram. Don't be concerned about the quality of your artwork. The important part of this project is your ability to recreate the structure of the neuron accurately. Do this project without referring to the diagram in the text. When you have completed this project, compare your diagram to figure 3-2 in the text. Correct any errors.

2. Fill in the blanks in the following paragraph:
    The central nervous system is composed of the _____ and the _____ . The peripheral nervous system is composed of the _____ and the _____ . The autonomic nervous system is composed of the _____ and the _____ . The _____ nervous sytsem activates under stress. The _____ nervous sytsem maintains body functions.
    When you have filled in all the blanks, check your answers against figure 3-7 in the text. Correct any errors.

3. Imagine as clearly as possible that you are being chased by a bear in the woods. Write down your observations, and include the following: changes in your breathing pattern; any sensations in your stomach or chest; changes in your heart rate or strength of heartbeats; subjective thought; emotions. What part of the nervous system would be engaged if you were being chased by a bear in the woods? Bring your notes to class for sharing.

Pull It All Together

1. Chapter 3 is the third chapter in a row that describes the field of psychology in scientific terms. In chapter 1, the author of the text explained how psychology has roots in physiology. In chapter 2, the author described how psychologists use the scientific method to study human behavior. What is your current understanding of the scientific nature of the field of psychology based on your studying chapters 1, 2, and 3?

2. Explain and give examples of the relationship between the functioning of the brain and human behavior. Based on your own life experience and observations, how is human behavior affected by the food we eat, other chemicals we consume on our own, and different types of medication?

CHAPTER 4
SENSATION AND PERCEPTION

Chapter Outline

More Senses, More Perceptions: Touch, Movement, and Balance

Somesthesis: The Skin Senses

Proprioception: Perceiving Movement and Balance

Chapter Overview

Chapter 4 covers the topics of sensation and perception. The distinction between these two processes is made in the beginning of the chapter: We detect stimuli in the environment through the process of sensation, and we recognize and interpret these stimuli through the process of perception. The author of the text then refines this distinction by stating that whereas *sensation* refers to the process of taking in an image and preparing it for transmission to the brain, *perception* refers to the active process of interpretation through which we come to understand the meaning of the image.

Now that the important distinction between sensation and perception has been made, the heart of the chapter covers these processes sense by sense. Chapter 4 contains six major sections: (1) "Sensation and Perception: Characteristics, Methods, and Theories," (2) "Vision: The Sense of Sight," (3) "Visual Perception: Knowing What You See," (4) "Audition: Sensing and Perceiving Sound," (5) "The Chemical Senses: Taste and Smell," and (6) "More Senses, More Perceptions: Touch, Movement, and Balance."

The first section ("Sensation and Perception: Characteristics, Methods, and Theories") begins by explaining that we need our senses for survival, and that in addition to the five senses of vision, audition (hearing), olfaction (smell), gustation (taste), and somesthesis (touch), there are also the kinesthetic (movement) and vestibular (balance) senses. The process of neural transmission of sensory input is described. Psychophysics, the study of the relationship between a physical stimulus and the sensory experience it produces, and the concept of threshold are then discussed. The psychophysical laws regarding thresholds developed by Weber, Fechner, and Stevens, and Swets's signal detection theory, are described and their applications are considered. This section ends with a discussion of the processes of interpretation and categorization, which help us know what we sense, and the evolution of sensory and perceptual mechanisms, including the evolved mechanism of sensory adaptation.

The second section ("Vision: The Sense of Sight") explains the nature of light (the visual stimulus) and describes the structure of the eye, the transduction of the light stimulus, the neural processing of the sensation to permit perception, and color vision. After explaining the nature of light, the structure and function of the eye is described in detail with a focus on the retina, the window to the brain. The process through which the retina sends messages to the brain via the optic nerve and the functioning of the receptor cells of the retina, the rods, and cones are described, followed by a discussion of visual adaptation and the main pathways traveled by the nerve impulses from the retina to the brain. In the visual cortex sensation becomes perception, a process facilitated by specialized nerve cells called feature analyzers. The section concludes with discussions of the properties of the color stimulus, three theories of color vision, and color blindness.

Whereas the second section of the chapter dealt with the process of visual sensation, the third section ("Visual Perception: Knowing What You See") covers the process of visual perception, the interpretation of the sensation. Interpretation is a subjective process and can be influenced by a variety of factors involving the stimulus and the observer. Perception involves two types of processing, bottom-up processing and top-down processing. Gestalt psychology emphasizes the importance of top-down processing and depicts perception as an active process in which the brain imposes organization and interpretation on incoming stimulus information. According to Gestalt theory, we perceive objects as whole; and the whole is greater than the sum of the part. Gestalt theory includes the principles of figure-ground, simplicity, proximity, good continuation, similarity, common fate, and closure.

The next visual phenomenon discussed in this section is perceptual constancy, the tendency to perceive objects as being consistent in size, shape, lightness, and other characteristics under a wide variety of circumstances. The perception of depth and movement are then discussed, followed by a description and explanation of optical illusions, or distorted perceptions. The section on visual perception concludes with a discussion of the role of mental imagery in our perception of objects.

The fourth section ("Audition: Sensing and Perceiving Sound") covers the topics of hearing and interpretation of what is heard. The auditory stimulus consists of sound vibrations, which have the characteristics of amplitude, loudness, frequency, and purity. A description of the structure and function of the ear is followed by an explanation of how vibration becomes information as sensory input travels through auditory pathways to the primary auditory cortex of the temporal lobe. The text describes the major theories of auditory perception and concludes with a discussion of how we localize sounds in space and a description of hearing disorders.

The fifth section ("The Chemical Senses: Taste and Smell") covers gustation and olfaction. Regarding gustation, the sense of taste, taste buds, taste qualities, and the process of taste perception are described. Regarding olfaction, the sense of smell, the sensation and perception of this sense are described.

The sixth section ("More Senses, More Perceptions: Touch, Movement, and Balance") considers the sensation and perception of the senses of touch, movement, and balance. Regarding somesthesis, the skin senses, the sensory receptors are described and perceptions of touch, pressure, temperature, and pain are considered. The receptors involved in movement and balance are called proprioceptors. Kinesthesis provides neural feedback concerning position and movement. The control of balance is achieved through the vestibular sense, which has been studied extensively. The receptors for rotary motion are contained in the semicircular canals and the vestibular sacs.

How to Master Chapter 4

Refer to These Learning Objectives

You should be able to achieve the following learning objectives after mastering the material in chapter 4:

Sensation and Perception: Characteristics, Methods, and Theories

1. Distinguish between the process of sensation and the process of perception.

2. Define and give examples of threshold, difference threshold, just-noticeable difference, method of limits, method of constant stimuli, and method of average error.

3. Explain the following three laws and psychophysics, including their similarities and differences: Weber's law, Fechner's law, and Stevens's power law.

4. Describe the process involved in signal detection theory.

5. Describe and give examples of sensory adaptation and explain its evolutionary function.

Vision: The Sense of Sight

6. Describe the properties of light, the visual stimulus.

7. Describe the structure of the eye and how the eye functions.

8. Describe the process of neural transmission of visual information via the retina.

9. Distinguish between the rods and the cones, the receptor cells of the retina.

10. Describe the process through which light becomes information.

11. Discuss and distinguish between the three theories of color vision: trichromatic theory, opponent-process theory, and dual-process theory.

Visual Perception: Knowing What You See

12. Explain and distinguish between bottom-up and top-down processing.

13. Describe and give examples of the major Gestalt principles of visual perception.

14. Describe the processes and functions of perceptual constancy and depth perception.

15. Explain how we experience movement.

16. Describe the major optical illusions and how they operate.

17. Discuss how mental imagery affects visual perception.

Audition: Sensing and Perceiving Sound

18. Describe the nature of the auditory stimulus, the structure of the ear, and how the ear functions.

19. Discuss and distinguish among the following major theories of auditory perception: place theory, frequency theory, and place plus frequency theory.

20. Describe the nature and treatment of hearing disorders.

The Chemical Senses: Taste and Smell

More Senses, More Perceptions: Touch, Movement, and Balance

21. Describe the receptors, process of sensation, and process of perception for the following senses: gustation (taste), olfaction (smell), somesthesis (skin senses), and proprioception (movement and balance).

Debate These Myths

MYTH 1: Sensation and perception are basically the same thing.

Strategy:

Define the process of sensation and describe the sensory receptors for vision, audition, gustation, olfaction, somesthesis, and proprioception:

Explain and give examples of how sensory input travels via neural pathways to the brain:

Explain at which point sensations become interpreted:

List and give examples of factors that influence what is perceived:

Distinguish between sensation and perception:

49

Other statements or examples for debating MYTH 1:

Change MYTH 1 into a true statement:

MYTH 2: *Most people perceive the environment in the same way.*

Strategy:

Distinguish between the processes of sensation and perception, as you did in debating MYTH 1:

Give examples from your own experience in which two people perceived a visual stimulus, an auditory stimulus, a taste stimulus, or a smell stimulus differently:

Discuss the factors that contribute to differences in perception among individuals and within an individual at different times:

Other statements or examples for debating MYTH 2:

Change MYTH 2 into a true statement:

Test Yourself: Multiple-Choice Questions

Directions: Circle the best response for each of the following questions.

1. In the study of sensation, a distal stimulus is an object or event:

    a. that can be detected in another room
    c. in the real world
    b. received by a sensory organ
    d. too far below threshold to detect

2. Somesthesis refers to the sense of:

    a. touch
    c. pain
    b. pressure
    d. all of the above

3. The process of converting physical stimulus energy into electrochemical messages for transmission as nerve impulses to the brain is called:

    a. transduction
    c. psychophysics
    b. signal detection
    d. sensory adaptation

4. Psychophysics studies the relationship between a physical stimulus and:

    a. a sensory experience
    c. its durability
    b. its limits
    d. adaptation

5. Jan turned up the volume on the car radio slowly. The point at which she could first detect that it was on would be considered the:

    a. difference threshold
    c. point of sensory adaptation
    b. absolute threshold
    d. signal detection

6. Allen, a seven-year-old, was pouring soda into two glasses for himself and his brother, and he wanted the amounts of soda to be exactly the same. He poured slightly more into one glass and then overcompensated by pouring slightly too much into the other glass. He kept trying to even out the amounts when he could just barely notice that he had poured too much. Allen's strategy is an example of:

    a. Fechner's law
    c. sensory adaptation
    b. the method of constant stimuli
    d. the method of average error

7. According to Weber's law, if the fraction for the middle range of detecting the difference in weight in pounds between two suitcases were hypothetically 1/20, then if a suitcase weighed 40 pounds, you would just notice a difference in weight between this suitcase and one that weighed:

    a. 20 pounds
    c. 42 pounds
    b. 41 pounds
    d. 44 pounds

8. The psychophysical law using a method called magnitude estimation that applies to stimuli across all senses was developed by:

    a. Fechner
    c. Weber
    b. Stevens
    d. Swets

9. Signal detection theory differs from other psychophysical theories by incorporating the factor of:

    a. subjectivity
    c. visual acuity
    b. pitch
    d. the JND

10. Sensory adaptation is an example of:

    a. a Gestalt law
    c. an evolved mechanism
    b. detection through olfaction
    d. a theory of color vision

11. On a hot summer day, at first Barbara found the sound of a window fan distracting as she tried to do her homework. Within a few minutes, she hardly noticed the sound due to the process known as:

   a. signal detection
   c. magnitude estimation
   b. constant stimuli
   d. sensory adaptation

12. The transparent sac that serves to focus objects at varying distances is called the:

   a. fovea
   c. pupil
   b. lens
   d. cornea

13. The image of a cat on the retina would appear on the retina as:

   a. an upside-down cat
   b. a black and white cat, no matter the cat's real color
   c. a blurry image
   d. a much larger cat than it really is

14. The rods are receptor cells that would be most involved for which of the following examples?

   a. seeing well when driving a car at 11 P.M.
   b. appreciating the colors in a rainbow
   c. creating the sharpest possible vision
   d. being able to detect distance

15. It is *not* true that feature analyzers:

   a. are also occipital neurons
   c. are also feature detectors
   b. were discovered by Hubel and Wiesel
   d. are essential for detection of pitch

16. Bob was able to read the complex patterns formed by the words on a menu in an expensive Italian restaurant with the help of his:

   a. adaptive mechanism
   c. feature analyzers
   b. organ of Corti
   d. monocular cues

17. Animals that function primarily during the day have a predominance of:

   a. rods
   c. feature analyzers
   b. cones
   d. ganglion cells

18. Hue is to saturation as:

   a. wavelength is to purity
   c. purity is to wavelength
   b. amplitude is to purity
   d. purity is to amplitude

19. The length of time it takes the rods to adapt to darkness is approximately:

   a. a few seconds
   c. an hour
   b. 10 minutes
   d. two hours

20. After processing in the lateral geniculate nucleus, visual information is passed directly to the:

   a. parietal cortex
   c. temporal cortex
   b. occipital cortex
   d. frontal cortex

21. All of the following are theories of color vision *except*:

   a. signal detection theory
   c. opponent-process theory
   b. dual-process theory
   d. trichromatic theory

22. All of the following are true concerning bottom-up processing *except* that it:
    a. begins with processing features such as lines and edges
    b. is useful for deciphering words from individual letters
    c. is strongly influenced by anticipations
    d. is analagous to putting a puzzle together
23. Gestalt psychologists believe that the basis for organizing parts into wholes:
    a. is learned in infancy   c. varies from culture to culture
    b. is innate   d. is gender specific
24. When observing a horse race, we tend to perceive the horses out in the front as one group, and the horses further behind as belonging to a separate group based on the Gestalt principle   known as:
    a. closure   c. similarity
    b. common fate   d. perceptual constancy
25. When you look at *hhhh hhhh hhhh,* you see three groups each containing four letters, rather than a single row of letters, because of the Gestalt principle known as:
    a. simplicity   c. figure-ground
    b. closure   d. proximity
26. According to the principle of perceptual constancy:
    a. a rectangular table looks rectangular, even at an angle
    b. a car viewed from the top of a skyscraper would be mistaken for a toy car
    c. both a and b
    d. neither a nor b
27. Late at night, in the darkness, your silver-colored car will be perceived by you as:
    a. white   c. silver
    b. black   d. gold
28. Retinal disparity is considered a:
    a. visual problem   c. depth cue
    b. Gestalt law   d. theory of color vision
29. Convergence is a depth cue that is useful in perceiving depth up to a distance of:
    a. one foot   c. a city block
    b. ten feet   d. about a mile
30. Being able to perceive a figure as female based on the pattern of movement of that figure is a phenomenon of real movement called:
    a. sensory adaptation   c. the autokinetic effect
    b. stroboscopic motion   d. biological motion
31. The Müller-Lyer illusion is an example of inaccurate application of the principle of:
    a. illusory movement   c. shape constancy
    b. induced movement   d. size constancy
32. Optical illusions are misperceptions caused by the:
    a. application of inappropriate perceptual assumptions to misleading cues
    b. human tendency toward inattentiveness to appropriate sensory cues
    c. misapplication of the figure-ground concept
    d. lack of compensation for poor vision

33. When Nancy was driving home at nightfall, she spotted something brown and crumpled on the side of the highway and perceived what was actually a brown paper bag as a dead animal. Her misperception was most likely due to:
    a. an optical illusion
    b. poor adaptation of her cones
    c. her expectations
    d. the moon illusion

34. The span of human hearing is quite wide, ranging from about:
    a. 10 dB to 100 dB
    b. 20 dB to 20,000 dB
    c. 20 Hz to 20,000 Hz
    d. 20 Hz to 100,000 Hz

35. The malleus, incus, and stapes are located in the:
    a. auditory canal
    b. middle ear
    c. cochlea
    d. organ of Corti

36. The primary transducers of sound preparatory to the transmission of the signal to the brain are the:
    a. hair cells on the inner side of the organ of Corti
    b. tiny bones located in the middle ear
    c. fluids in the cochlea
    d. fibers of Reissner's membrane

37. Place plus frequency theory combines two opposing theories of the processing of:
    a. sound frequency
    b. wavelengths
    c. color
    d. olfactory stimuli

38. As we age, we experience hearing loss, particularly:
    a. if we are men
    b. at higher frequencies
    c. both a and b
    d. neither a nor b

39. Conduction deafness is caused by all of the following *except*:
    a. wax accumulation in the auditory canal
    b. a defect in the eardrum
    c. damage to the ossicles of the middle ear
    d. damage to the hair cells of the cochlea

40. Olfaction refers to the sense of:
    a. taste
    b. smell
    c. balance
    d. touch

41. Across-fiber pattern theory tries to account for complexities in the detection of:
    a. tastes
    b. smells
    c. sounds
    d. movements

42. The number of sensory receptors in each nasal passage is about:
    a. 100
    b. 10,000
    c. 100,000
    d. 100 million

43. The olfactory bulb is part of the:
    a. lateral geniculate nucleus
    b. limbic system
    c. retina
    d. frontal cortex

44. We are able to feel being tickled because of our sense of:
    a. olfaction
    b. kinesthesis
    c. somesthesis
    d. proprioception

45. Pacinian corpuscles and basket cells are found in the:
   a. nose   c. skin
   b. tongue   d. retina

46. The two-point threshold refers to the detection of two different stimuli sensed by the:
   a. cochlea   c. tongue
   b. skin   d. olfactory epithelium

47. If you place your hand in a bowl of hot water, allow it to adapt, and then place it in a bowl of warm water, the hand that was in the hot water will now feel:
   a. hot   c. cold
   b. cool   d. warm

48. Free nerve endings are simple nerve cells that are located:
   a. just beneath the surface of the skin
   b. primarily in hairless areas
   c. in hairy areas of the body
   d. beneath the pain receptors

49. Proprioceptors are associated with the coordination of:
   a. depth cues   c. movement
   b. taste and smell   d. touch sensations

50. The principal balance apparatus is located in the:
   a. auditory canal   c. middle ear
   b. proprioceptors   d. semicircular canals

Test Yourself: Fill in the Blanks

Directions: Fill in the blanks with the correct term or name.

1. The _____ is the lowest level of stimulus intensity to which a sense will respond.

2. In the method of _____, the researcher gradually reduces a clearly detectable stimulus until the observer can no longer detect it.

3. _____ law states that the smallest detectable increase in the intensity of a stimulus is a constant proportion of the intensity of the original stimulus.

4. _____ is a progressive decrease in sensitivity to continuing or recurrent stimuli.

5. Wavelengths of light are distributed along the _____spectrum.

6. The _____of the eye is considered the window to the brain.

7. _____ are visual receptors that are highly sensitive to light and are involved in night vision.

8. _____ is primarily the psychological interpretation of amplitude.

9. The trichromatic theory of color vision was formulated by _____ and _____ in the nineteenth century.

10. One major approach that emphasizes top-down processing is _____, which insists that perception is an active process in which the brain imposes organization and interpretation on incoming stimulus information.

11. The Gestalt principle of _____ states that we tend to perceive corners as continued along smooth perceptual lines.

12. The tendency to perceive objects as being consistent in size, shape, lightness, and other characteristics under a wide variety of viewing conditions is called_____.

13. _____ results from the differences in the strain on the eye muscles as you view objects that are far away or close up.

14. _____ movement occurs when the actual movement of one object causes the perceived movement of another.

15. The development of place theory, which holds that different areas or places on the basilar membrane respond to sound waves of different frequencies, won a Nobel Prize for _____.

16. The cochlear duct is separated from the vestibular canal by Reissner's membrane and from the tympanic canal by the _____.

17. The sense of taste is technically known as _____.

18. The sense of smell is technically known as _____.

19. _____ are tiny, rounded receptors found primarily in hairless areas of the skin, such as the palms of the hands.

20. _____ provides neural feedback concerning position and movement.

Test Yourself: Matching Questions

Directions: For each item in column I, select the item in column II that is most closely associated with it.

I	II
_____1. pheromones	a. completion
_____2. kinesthesis	b. visual acuity
_____3. somesthesis	c. skin senses
_____4. olfaction	d. sense of taste
_____5. threshold	e. measured in decibels
_____6. perception	f. monocular cue
_____7. fovea	g. sexual attraction chemical
_____8. cones	h. sense of smell
_____9. closure	i. movement sense
_____10. interposition	j. ear membrane
_____11. retinal disparity	k. binocular cue
_____12. stroboscopic motion	l. color receptors
_____13. amplitude	m. stimulus detection
_____14. oval window	n. interpretation
_____15. gustation	o. apparent motion

Test Yourself: Answer Key

Multiple Choice

1. c	(107)	11. d	(112–13)	21. a	(122–24)	31. d	(132–33)	41. a	(145)
2. d	(107)	12. b	(117)	22. c	(126)	32. a	(132)	42. d	(146)
3. a	(107)	13. a	(117)	23. b	(127)	33. c	(134–35)	43. b	(146)
4. a	(107)	14. a	(117)	24. b	(129)	34. c	(139)	44. c	(147)
5. b	(107)	15. d	(119)	25. d	(128)	35. b	(139)	45. c	(148)
6. d	(108)	16. c	(119)	26. a	(129)	36. a	(140)	46. b	(148)
7. c	(108)	17. b	(117)	27. c	(129)	37. a	(142)	47. b	(148)
8. b	(109)	18. a	(120)	28. c	(130)	38. c	(142)	48. a	(148)
9. a	(109)	19. c	(118)	29. b	(130)	39. d	(143)	49. c	(150)
10. c	112)	20. b	(119)	30. d	(132)	40. b	(146)	50. d	(150)

Fill in the Blanks

1. absolute threshold
2. limits
3. Weber's
4. sensory adaptation
5. electromagnetic
6. retina
7. rods
8. brightness
9. Thomas Young, Hermann von Helmholtz
10. Gestalt psychology
11. good continuation
12. perceptual constancy
13. convergence
14. induced
15. Georg von Bekesy
16. basilar membrane
17. gustation
18. olfaction

19. Meissner corpuscles

20. kinethesis

Matching Questions

1. g　　　　　　　　　6. n　　　　　　　　　11. k

2. i　　　　　　　　　7. b　　　　　　　　　12. o

3. c　　　　　　　　　8. l　　　　　　　　　13. e

4. h　　　　　　　　　9. a　　　　　　　　　14. j

5. m　　　　　　　　　10. f　　　　　　　　　15. d

Do These Mini Projects

1. This mini project will help you find and experience your blind spot. Put a postage stamp and a large dot about four inches apart on an index card. Hold the index card at arm's length with your right hand and cover your left eye with your left hand. Then, fixate your uncovered eye on the dot and slowly move the card forward. At some point, the postage stamp will "disappear."

2. This mini project is designed to help you experience an afterimage. Draw an image of any kind in bright red marker on an unlined index card and have a blank, unlined index card handy. Stare at the red image for a few minutes. Then look at the blank card. You should see the color green as an afterimage on the blank card.

3. Examine figures 4–20 through 4–25 in the text, the optical illusions. After looking at each one carefully, see if you can figure out (1) the misleading sensory cues in each illusion, and (2) the inappropriate perceptual assumptions you are using when processing each illusion.

4. Ask a friend to act as your partner for this mini project on the sense of touch. Collect in advance and keep out of sight the following: a feather, a pencil eraser, a cotton ball, an ice cube, and a piece of sandpaper. Ask your partner to close his or her eyes, and state that you will touch his or her fingertips with a series of objects, one at a time. Your partner's task will be to verbalize what each object is, based solely on the sense of touch. When you are both ready, touch your partner's fingertips with one object at a time for about 5 seconds each, giving your partner a chance to verbalize what the object is between touches. Make notes of your partner's responses of your observations. When you have competed the project, share your findings with your partner.

Pull It All Together

1. Chapter 4 is the fourth chapter in a row that describes the field of psychology in scientific terms. In chapter 1, the author of the text explained how psychology has roots in physiology. In chapter 2, the author described how psychologists use the scientific method to study human behavior. In chapter 3, the author explained the relationship between the brain and behavior in the context of neuroscience. What is your current understanding of the scientific nature of the field of psychology based on your studying chapters 1, 2, 3, and 4?

2. Describe in your own words the processes of sensation and perception, how they are related to each other, and how they are distinguished from each other. Give examples from your own life experience that distinguish the processes of sensation and perception from each other.

3. What factors account for the phenomena that different people can perceive the same stimulus differently and that the same person can perceive the same stimulus differently at different times? Have you ever experienced these phenomena?

CHAPTER 5
CONSCIOUSNESS

Chapter Outline

The Nature of Consciousness

The Evolution of Consciousness

Modes of Consciousness

Features of Consciousness

Determinants of Conscious Experience

Selective Attention

The Study of Consciousness

Altered States of Consciousness

"To Sleep, Perchance to Dream"

Stages of Sleep

REM Sleep

Sleep Schedules and Biological Rhythms

Sleep Problems and Disorders

Dreams: Windows to the Unconscious?

More States: Daydreaming, Meditation, Relaxation, and Hypnosis

Daydreaming

Meditation and Relaxation

Hypnosis

Alcohol and Other Psychoactive Drugs

Alcohol Dependence and Abuse

Other Psychoactive Drugs

The Neurophysiology of Consciousness

The Waking State

Sleep and Dreaming

The Sleep-Wake Cycle

Drug Effects

Other Altered States

Chapter Overview

Chapter 5 covers the topic of consciousness, which is described as existing along a continuum from the unconsciousness of deep sleep to the full alertness of intense concentration. The author of the text explains that consciousness occurs in many forms or states, the most common of which are sleep, dreaming, and daydreaming. The concept of altered states of consciousness is introduced. A brief exercise involving the process of introspection and the examination of your stream of consciousness is suggested to provide a flavor of the concept of consciousness.

Chapter 5 contains five major sections: (1) "The Nature of Consciousness," (2) "To Sleep, Perchance to Dream," (3) "More States: Daydreaming, Meditation, Relaxation, and Hypnosis," (4) "Alcohol and Other Psychoactive Drugs," and (5) "The Neurophysiology of Consciousness."

The first section ("The Nature of Consciousness") defines consciousness as awareness of one's own thoughts and of stimuli in the external environment. Consciousness is distinguished from unconsciousness and nonconscious processes. The author of the text discusses the substantial adaptive benefits of human consciousness, the modes of passive and active consciousness, and other features of consciousness. Conscious experience is influenced by both internal factors and environmental factors. Much of the time, the contents of consciousness are a product of selective attention. The text discusses the history of the interest in and study of consciousness from the nineteenth century through the present, and then introduces the concept of altered states of consciousness.

The second section ("To Sleep, Perchance to Dream") discusses the topics of sleeping and dreaming. We spend about a third of each day in the altered state of consciousness known as sleep. The hypnagogic state is a transitional stage between wakefulness and sleep in which thoughts are loose and disorganized and dreamlike images are experienced. There are four stages of sleep. As we proceed from stage 1 through stage 4, we are deeper into the sleep state. Rapid eye movement (REM) sleep occurs during stage 1, with the other three stages referred to as slow-wave or non-REM (NREM) sleep. REM sleep is often referred to as paradoxical sleep because in some ways the sleeper acts like a person who is awake. We experience longer and more intense REM sleep as the night progresses. Although there is considerable variation in sleep schedules, virtually all adults average six to ten hours of sleep a night. Sleep is described as one major part of the circadian rhythm, the biological activities that occur on a daily cycle. Sleep problems are described. The section concludes with a discussion of dreaming and the causes of night terrors and nightmares.

The third section ("More States: Daydreaming, Meditation, Relaxation, and Hypnosis") covers four more states of consciousness. Although the exact causes of daydreaming are not completely understood, it is known that daydreaming takes a variety of forms and can involve any shift of attention away from immediately demanding tasks. Meditation, which can have positive or negative effects, has been defined as a family of techniques that have in common a conscious attempt to focus attention in a nonanalytical way and an attempt not to dwell on discursive, ruminating thought. Relaxation is one of the main benefits of meditation. Hypnosis is a state in which the subject displays heightened suggestibility and distortion of perception or memory. The induction of hypnosis involves relaxation and imagery. Theories and uses of hypnosis are discussed.

The fourth section ("Alcohol and Other Psychoactive Drugs") begins with a discussion of alcohol dependence and abuse. The use of alcohol is described as the largest single drug problem today, other than nicotine. This section contains a variety of statistics regarding alcohol abuse. For example, a 1995 survey shows that 11 million Americans admit to being heavy drinkers. Alcoholism is defined as a disorder in which the individual consumes an excessive amount of ethyl alcohol and is unable to control his or her drinking. Both the biological and the psychological factors underlying alcoholism are discussed. Drugs that alter consciousness and affect the psychological functioning of the individual are referred to as psychoactive drugs. The concepts of tolerance, addiction, withdrawal, and psychological dependence are defined. The types of psychoactive drugs and their effects described in this section include depressants (for example, barbiturates), stimulants (for example, caffeine, amphetamines, and cocaine), hallucinogens (for example, LSD and PCP), marijuana, and the opiates.

The final section ("The Neurophysiology of Consciousness") brings into focus the challenge of the twenty-first century to discover how the brain controls states of consciousness and the patterns of behavior associated with them. Some of the questions that need to be answered include: What neural mechanisms put us to sleep and wake us up? What happens during dreaming? What are the brain states during meditation, relaxation, and hypnotic trance? The role of the reticular activating system (RAS) in the waking cycle is discussed. The mechanisms controlling NREM and REM sleep are described. Finally, the way in which psychoactive drugs achieve their effects in the process of neurotransmission is explained. More research is needed in order to understand these complex processes in more detail.

How to Master Chapter 5

Refer to These Learning Objectives

You should be able to achieve the following learning objectives after mastering the material in chapter 5:

The Nature of Consciousness

1. Define consciousness.

2. Discuss the evolution of consciousness and give examples of its adaptive nature.

3. Distinguish between passive and active consciousness.

4. Describe the four features of consciousness.

5. Define and give examples of the process of selective attention.

6. Discuss changes in the attitudes toward the study of consciousness in the scientific community from the nineteenth century through the present.

"To Sleep, Perchance to Dream"

7. Describe the process of falling asleep, including the hypnagogic state.

8. Describe and distinguish among the four stages of sleep.

9. Define and distinguish between REM and NREM sleep.

10. Describe a typical night's sleep in terms of the stages of sleep and REM periods.

11. Explain the circadian rhythm and its relationship to sleep.

12. Describe and give examples of insomnia, narcolepsy, and sleep apnea.

13. Discuss and contrast Freud's theory of dreaming and the activation-synthesis hypothesis.

14. Discuss the types of factors that influence dream content, and describe the characteristics of lucid dreams, night terrors, nightmares, and anxiety dreams.

More States: Daydreaming, Meditation, Relaxation, and Hypnosis

15. Describe the nature of the states of daydreaming, meditation, and relaxation.

16. Discuss the nature of hypnosis, including theories and uses.

Alcohol and Other Psychoactive Drugs

17. Discuss and give statistics regarding alcohol dependence and abuse.

18. Discuss and give examples of the biological and psychological factors underlying alcoholism.

19. Describe the nature and effects of psychoactive drugs, including depressants, stimulants, hallucinogens, marijuana, and opiates.

The Neurophysiology of Consciousness

20. Explain our current knowledge of the neurophysiology of consciousness, including the sleep-wake cycle and drug effects.

Debate These Myths

MYTH 1: *Dreaming takes place during the deepest stages of sleep.*

Strategy:

Discuss the nature of REM sleep:

Identify the stage during which REM sleep occurs:

Explain why REM sleep is often referred to as paradoxical sleep:

Other statements or examples for debating MYTH 1:

Change MYTH 1 into a true statement:

MYTH 2: *People with a high tolerance for a substance are less likely to become addicted to that substance than people with a low tolerance.*

Strategy:

Define tolerance:

Give an example that distinguishes between high and low tolerance for a substance:

Explain the relationship between tolerance and addiction:

Other statements and examples for debating MYTH 2:

Change MYTH 2 into a true statement:

Test Yourself: Multiple-Choice Questions

Directions: Circle the best response for each of the following questions.

1. The passage of nutrients via the bloodstream to various organs in the body is a process that would be considered:
    a. conscious
    b. unconscious
    c. nonconscious
    d. introspective

2. Paul was sitting in his favorite chair, listening to familiar classical music after a long day. Paul's mode of consciousness in this scenario would be considered:
    a. active
    b. passive
    c. dreaming
    d. nonconscious

3. The study of consciousness was rejected by:
    a. John Watson
    b. Wilhelm Wundt
    c. William James
    d. George Ladd

4. Concerning REM sleep, it is *not* true that:
    a. REM sleep takes place during the deepest stage of sleep
    b. REM sleep is sometimes called paradoxical sleep
    c. REM occupies 20 to 25 percent of total sleep time
    d. Dream recall is very high during REM sleep

5. The foreground of consciousness is characterized by:
    a. personal identity
    b. a moving spotlight
    c. blurry thoughts
    d. passing reactions

6. The stream of consciousness takes place during the feature of consciousness known as:
    a. focus
    b. attributes
    c. flow
    d. structure

7. When Janet was repairing her toaster, her focus was on locating the source of the problem. Her feeling confident about her ability to complete the task would be part of the:
    a. background of consciousness
    b. nonconscious
    c. passive consciousness
    d. subconscious

8. The ability to intentionally focus on a relatively narrow aspect of the environment is a product of:
    a. the nonconscious
    b. external factors
    c. selective attention
    d. passive consciousness

9. Helen was focused on reading a magazine that she had hidden on her lap during algebra class when she suddenly heard the teacher call her name. This is an example of:

   a. a hypnagogic state c. meditation

   b. perceptual set d. selective attention

10. Turning your head toward the sound of screeching brakes is an example of:

    a. perceptual set c. a hypnagogic state

    b. selective attention d. active consciousness

11. At a rally, Mary was engrossed in a conversation with Sue. When she heard her name mentioned in a group nearby, she switched her focus due to a phenomenon known as:

    a. the cocktail party effect c. perceptual set

    b. stream of consciousness d. passive consciousness

12. The study of self-awareness is most closely associated with:

    a. Wilhelm Wundt c. Carl Rogers

    b. John Watson d. William James

13. The Experience Sampling Method (ESM) has been used mostly for the study of:

    a. selective attention c. perceptual set

    b. self-awareness d. sleep patterns

14. Of the following, the best example of the Experience Sampling Method (ESM) would be:

    a. selecting subjects at random for a survey on self-awareness

    b. having subjects report thoughts, behaviors, and moods at steady intervals

    c. waking subjects during REM sleep to record their dreams

    d. studying a subject's stream of consciousness in a laboratory setting

15. After Alan was in bed for a few minutes, he felt sleepy and began to have distorted, dreamlike thoughts and images about the day's events. It is most likely that Alan was in:

    a. a REM cycle c. a hypnagogic state

    b. stage 1 of sleep d. a drug-induced state

16. The altered states of sleep and daydreaming are considered:

    a. the most intense in later adulthood

    b. components of passive consciousness

    c. hypnagogic

    d. universal

17. Regarding sleep, bursts of EEG activity lasting from 1/2 to 2 seconds, are called:

    a. sleep spindles c. alpha brain waves

    b. REM cycles d. altered states

18. Sleep spindles occur during:

    a. REM sleep c. stage 2 of sleep

    b. deepest sleep d. night terrors

19. In the middle of the night, Joan heard a sound and tried to wake her husband, who was in a deep sleep. She was finally able to awaken him, but with some effort. Joan's husband was most likely in the stage of sleep known as:

    a. stage 1 c. stage 3

    b. stage 2 d. stage 4

20. Brain waves shift from alpha to theta during:
   a. stage 1 of sleep
   b. stage 2 of sleep
   c. stage 3 of sleep
   d. stage 4 of sleep

21. Bobby's parents were having a midnight snack at the kitchen table when they spotted their four-year-old son walking in his sleep. Bobby was in the stage of sleep known as:
   a. stage 1
   b. stage 2
   c. stage 3
   d. stage 4

22. Delta waves are characteristic of:
   a. stage 1 of sleep
   b. stage 2 of sleep
   c. stage 3 of sleep
   d. stage 4 of sleep

23. Larry spends about 50 percent of his time in REM sleep. Of the following, it is most likely that Larry is how old?
   a. 5 years
   b. 25 years
   c. 2 days
   d. 70 years

24. The most significant feature of REM sleep is the occurrence of:
   a. sleepwalking
   b. dreams
   c. sleep talking
   d. sleep apnea

25. As compared with the first period of REM sleep, the second period of REM sleep during a typical night is:
   a. longer
   b. lighter
   c. deeper
   d. shorter

26. When Sheila sleeps, she tends to change position or move in some way every 10 or 20 minutes. According to the research on sleep, Sheila is most likely to:
   a. dream less than people who don't move around during sleep
   b. feel refreshed upon wakening
   c. have higher sleep spindles than those who don't move around
   d. walk in her sleep

27. Jay is a morning person, whereas his friend Len is a night person. This difference between Jay and Len most likely reflects differences in their:
   a. biological rhythms
   b. tendency toward insomnia
   c. REM sleep patterns
   d. EEG patterns

28. When Jennifer arrived in London after a seven-hour flight from New York, her experience of jet lag was most likely due to:
   a. sleep loss
   b. a disturbance of the normal circadian rhythm
   c. a disruption of REM sleep
   d. shorter sleep cycles

29. The number of Americans who suffer from some form of insomnia at any give time is estimated to be:
   a. 5 million
   b. 10 million
   c. 30 million
   d. 50 million

30. An example of a factor that would predispose an individual to insomnia is:
   a. muscle tension
   b. napping
   c. worry about sleep
   d. death in the family

31. A person who falls asleep suddenly, during the day, with little or no warning, while engaging in an activity may be suffering from:
    a. sleep apnea   c. hypersomnia
    b. parasomnia   d. narcolepsy

32. Manifest content is to latent content as:
    a. story is to symbol   c. unconscious is to conscious
    b. male is to female   d. delayed is to immediate

33. After a few nights of interrupted REM sleep, typical reactions include:
    a. irritability   c. heightened anxiety
    b. agitation   d. all of the above

34. The activation-synthesis hypothesis of dreaming suggests that dreaming is a product of:
    a. unconscious thought processes
    b. problem-solving activities
    c. neurological processes
    d. none of the above

35. An individual can establish an awareness of dreaming and some conscious control over the content of the dream in a process known as:
    a. daydreaming   c. lucid dreaming
    b. cognitive dreaming   d. none of the above

36. The process of meditation is associated with all of the following *except*:
    a. poor attentional control   c. a state of relaxation
    b. conscious effort   d. opening up

37. Hilgard's theory of hypnosis is based primarily on the concept of:
    a. motivation   c. role playing
    b. dissociation   d. suggestibility

38. Other than nicotine, the largest drug problem today is the abuse of:
    a. marijuana   c. cocaine
    b. alcohol   d. barbiturates

39. The percentage of males that become diagnosable alcoholics at some time in their lives is:
    a. 5%   c. 20%
    b. 10%   d. 30%

40. Drunk driving is responsible for the following percentage of teenage deaths:
    a. 5%   c. 10%
    b. 20%   d. 40%

41. In most European countries and most U.S. states, a person is legally intoxicated when the blood alcohol level reaches:
    a. .01   c. 10
    b. 1.00   d. 10.00

42. It is *not* true that alcoholics:
    a. often suffer from B-complex deficiency
    b. are unable to control their drinking
    c. are genetically predisposed to the problem
    d. are more prevalent in the homeless population

43. Predisposing biological factors for alcoholism are found:
   a. during fetal development
   b. for both men and women
   c. both a and b
   d. neither a nor b

44. Behavior theory suggests that drinkers might become alcoholics because of:
   a. the tension-reducing effects of alcohol
   b. expectations regarding the effects of alcohol
   c. unsatisfied dependency needs
   d. a deficiency of norepinephrine

45. Cocaine is classified as a:
   a. depressant   c. stimulant
   b. opiate   d. hallucinogen

46. Alcohol is classified as:
   a. a hallucinogen   c. a stimulant
   b. a depressant   d. an opiate

47. Seconal and nembutal are examples of:
   a. barbiturates   c. both a and b
   b. depressants   d. neither a nor b

48. The effects of marijuana typically last up to:
   a. 15 minutes   c. 4 hours
   b. an hour   d. a full day

49. The primary subcortical mechanism involved in REM sleep is the small area of the lower pons called the:
   a. RAS   c. posterior nucleus
   b. neural network   d. locus coeruleus

50. Cocaine blocks the reuptake of:
   a. epinephrine   c. dopamine
   b. serotonin   d. all of the above

Test Yourself: Fill in the Blanks

Directions: Fill in the blanks with the correct term or name.

1. _____ can be defined as awareness of one's own thoughts and of stimuli in the external environment.

2. In _____ consciousness, you typically seek information from either external or internal sources and prepare to act on this information.

3. The process of _____ involves intentionally focusing on a relatively narrow aspect of the environment.

4. _____ defined psychology as "the science of mental life, both of its phenomena and their conditions."

5. A _____ state is a transitional stage between wakefulness and sleep in which thoughts are loose and disorganized and dreamlike images are experienced.

6. REM stands for _____ sleep.

7. REM sleep is often referred to as_____ sleep because in some ways the sleeper acts almost like a person who is wide awake.

8. A _____ rhythm is a roughly 24-hour cycle involving consistent biological changes.

9. _____ is a disorder characterized by sudden attacks of sleep.

10. A sleep disorder in which the sleeper stops breathing for a short time, awakens slightly, emits a loud gasp and loud snore, and then falls asleep again is known as _____

11. According to Freud, in our dreams, unacceptable, repressed desires are translated into symbolic form as the _____ content.

12. According to Alan Hobson and Robert McCarley's _____ hypothesis, a biological clock mechanism in the brain stem periodically activates neural circuitry in a random fashion during sleep.

13. In a _____ dream, the sleeper becomes aware of the fact that she is dreaming and establishes an almost conscious degree of control over the content of the dream.

14. _____ is a family of techniques that have in common a conscious attempt to focus attention in a nonanalytical way and an attempt not to dwell on discursive ruminating thought.

15. _____ would be considered the first hypnotist.

16. Drugs that alter consciousness and affect the psychological functioning of the individual are referred to as _____ drugs.

17. _____ dependence involves coming to need a drug to maintain a comfortable level of emotional functioning.

18. Drugs that inhibit the activity of the central nervous system are called _____.

19. _____ is the process by which the neurotransmitter is reabsorbed into the axon terminals of the presynaptic neuron.

20. An _____ is a drug that attaches to a postsynaptic receptor but cannot produce the same effects as the neurotransmitter.

Test Yourself: Matching Questions

Directions: For each item in column I, select the item in column II that is most closely associated with it.

I	II
_____1. mesmerism	a. nicotine
_____2. tolerance	b. hypnosis
_____3. placebo	c. maintains NREM sleep states
_____4. depressants	d. maintains waking state
_____5. barbiturate	e. adaptation
_____6. stimulant	f. stage 3 of sleep
_____7. crack	g. morphine
_____8. hallucinogen	h. inert substance
_____9. PCP	i. concentrated cocaine
_____10. opiate	j. preexisting expectation
_____11. RAS	k. seconal
_____12. serotonin	l. angel dust
_____13. locus coeruleus	m. inhibitors
_____14. perceptual set	n. LSD
_____15. delta waves	o. involved in REM sleep

Test Yourself: Answer Key

Multiple Choice

1. c	(156)	11. a	(158)	21. d	(161)	31. d	(166)	41. c	(178)
2. b	(157)	12. c	(159)	22. c	(161)	32. a	(167)	42. d	(179-80)
3. a	(159)	13. b	(159)	23. c	(161)	33. d	(168)	43. c	(180-81)
4. a	(161–3)	14. a	(159)	24. b	(162)	34. c	(168)	44. a	(181)
5. d	(157)	15. c	(160)	25. a	(162)	35. c	(168)	45. c	(181)
6. c	(157)	16. d	(159)	26. b	(163)	36. a	(171)	46. b	(183)
7. a	(157)	17. a	(161)	27. a	(163)	37. b	(174)	47. c	(183)
8. c	(158)	18. c	(161)	28. b	(164)	38. b	(177)	48. c	(186)
9. d	(158–9)	19. d	(161)	29. c	(164)	39. c	(177)	49. d	(188)
10. b	(159)	20. a	(161)	30. a	(164)	40. b	(178)	50. d	(189)

Fill in the Blanks

1. consciousness
2. active
3. selective attention
4. William James
5. hypnagogic
6. rapid eye movement
7. paradoxical
8. circadian
9. narcolepsy
10. sleep apnea
11. latent
12. activation-synthesis
13. lucid
14. meditation
15. Anton Mesmer
16. psychoactive
17. psychological
18. depressants

19.   reuptake

20.   antagonist

Matching Questions

1. b	6. a	11. d
2. e	7. i	12. c
3. h	8. n	13. o
4. m	9. l	14. j
5. k	10. g	15. f

Do These Mini Projects

1.   This mini project is designed to help you appreciate the nature of stream of consciousness. Spend 3 minutes writing down, or recording on a cassette tape, all your thoughts as they occur. Write or record everything that comes to mind, no matter how silly it seems or how seemingly unrelated to what you were just thinking. Try to hold nothing back so that you can capture the stream of consciousness as it is actually flowing. Notice that this is not an easy task and that thoughts can be quick and fleeting. Notice how some thoughts are in words and others are in images.

2.   Keep track of your sleep-wake cycle for one week by recording the time you go to bed, the time you actually fall asleep, and the time you wake up every day. Include nap times as well. What do you notice about your sleep-wake cycle? Are you consistent or inconsistent in the times when you go to bed, fall asleep, and wake up? How do naps affect your sleep-wake cycle? How do you deal with insomnia, if you experience it?

3.   Keep track of your daydreaming for one week. Record the time of day and circumstances under which you daydream, the length of daydreaming time, and the contents of your daydreams. Does your daydreaming serve a useful or a dysfunctional purpose? How is your state of consciousness during daydreaming different from when your are focusing your attention on the environment?

Pull It All Together

1.   How does chapter 5, on consciousness, fit in with the first four chapters of the text, which focused on psychology as a science? Discuss the topic of states of consciousness in scientific terms.

2.   Chapter 5 discusses (1) states of consciousness that occur as a function of everyday life, such as wakefulness, sleep, dreaming, and daydreaming; (2) states of consciousness that can be induced through natural means, such as meditation and hypnosis; and (3) states of consciousness that are induced by alcohol and other psychoactive drugs. What do these three types of states of consciousness have in common? In what ways do they differ?

3.   How do biological and psychological factors work together to influence the states of consciousness that occur as a function of everyday life, such as wakefulness, sleep, dreaming, and daydreaming? How do biological and psychological factors work together to influence individuals to use alcohol and other psychoactive drugs to alter their state of consciousness?

Chapter Outline

Classical Conditioning: Ivan Pavlov

Pavlov's Classic Studies

Components of Classical Conditioning

Classical Conditioning Processes

Beyond Pavlov: Modern Developments in Classical Conditioning

Applications of Classical Conditioning

Operant Conditioning: B. F. Skinner

Edward L. Thorndike: The Law of Effect

B. F. Skinner: Consequences Determine Behavior

Operant Conditioning Processes

Principles of Reinforcement

Schedules of Reinforcement

Positive and Negative Reinforcement

Evolution at Work: Biological Preparedness

Applications of Operant Conditioning

The Current Status of Operant Psychology

Cognitive Factors in Learning

Cognitive Maps

Cognitive Elements in Classical Conditioning

"Aha!": Insight Learning

Observational Learning: Albert Bandura

Four Basic Processes

The Role of Reinforcement

Human Social Behavior

The Neurophysiology of Learning

Evolution: Learning as an Adaptive Mechanism

The Lowly Aplysia

Learning in More Complex Brains

Chapter Overview

Chapter 6 covers the topic of learning. The author of the text begins the chapter by making the important point that learning is a part of almost every aspect of psychology, from developmental psychology to social psychology to abnormal psychology. Learning has evolved over the course of genetic history as a set of adaptive mechanisms that allows us to acquire new behaviors and modify old ones. Learning is more specifically defined as a set of relatively permanent changes in behavior that result from prior experience.

Chapter 6 contains five major sections: (1) "Classical Conditioning: Ivan Pavlov," (2) "Operant Conditioning: B. F. Skinner," (3) "Cognitive Factors in Learning," (4) "Observational Learning: Albert Bandura," and (5) "The Neurophysiology of Learning."

The first section ("Classical Conditioning: Ivan Pavlov") summarizes Pavlov's theory and research in classical conditioning. To accomplish classical conditioning, we arrange two events in such a way that the learner can form an association between them. Pavlov's experiments in classical conditioning contained several important elements: (1) the unconditioned stimulus (UCS), any stimulus that evokes a response without prior conditioning; (2) the unconditioned response (UCR), the unlearned reaction to the UCS; (3) the conditioned stimulus (CS), a previously neutral stimulus that comes, through association with the UCS, to evoke a response very similar to the UCR; and (4) the conditioned response (CR), the newly learned response to the CS. Pavlov's studies involved dogs who learned to salivate (CR) because of the association between the sound of the bell (CS) and the meat powder (UCS). Classical conditioning includes five processes, which are explained in the text: (1) acquisition, (2) extinction, (3) spontaneous recovery, (4) stimulus generalization, and (5) stimulus discrimination.

Modern developments in classical conditioning include (1) the debate as to whether the important association is between the CS and the CR or between the CS and the UCS—views on this issue have shifted over time; and (2) the debate regarding equipotential versus biological preparedness, which deals with whether any response of an organism can be conditioned to any stimulus it can perceive, or whether there are species-specific genetic predispositions to form certain learned associations over others. The section concludes with a discussion of applications of classical conditioning in everyday life.

The second section ("Operant Conditioning: B. F. Skinner") begins with a discussion of Thorndike's law of effect, which was the precursor to Skinner's theory and research. Thorndike's experiments demonstrated instrumental learning and the law of effect, which states that a behavior is more likely to be repeated when it is followed by satisfaction and reward. Skinner believed that consequences determine behavior and hypothesized that behaviors are acquired primarily through operant conditioning. Through his experiments with pigeons in a Skinner box, Skinner demonstrated the power of reinforcement, which occurs when the consequences of a response increase the likelihood or probability that the response will be repeated. Skinner's thesis that psychology should study only directly observable behavior and ignore internal, mentalistic constructs like thinking and consciousness is called behaviorism.

The processes of operant conditioning, the principles of reinforcement, and schedules of reinforcement are discussed in detail. Operant conditioning processes include (1) acquisition and behavioral shaping; (2) extinction and spontaneous recovery; and (3) stimulus control—discrimination and generalization. Principles of reinforcement include the experimental analysis of behavior (EAB), the Premack principle, and primary and secondary reinforcers. Schedules of reinforcement are divided into continuous and partial reinforcement, which differ in the ease with which the acquired behavior can be extinguished. Partial reinforcement schedules can be powerful in maintaining behavior. Positive reinforcement involves a reinforcer that produces pleasure or satisfaction; negative reinforcement involves one that removes displeasure or dissatisfaction. Punishment involves a consequence that follows a response and decreases its probability. Escape and avoidance learning are explained. This section concludes with discussions of the role of biological preparedness in operant conditioning, applications of operant conditioning to everyday life, and the current status of operant conditioning in the field of psychology.

The third section ("Cognitive Factors in Learning") explains how cognitive processes—those involved in thought and in acquiring, modifying, and acting on knowledge—affect learning. Edward Tolman, a pioneer in cognitive psychology, argued that learning is based in cognitive or thought processes, not merely in the formation of associations. In his experiments on maze learning in rats, he hypothesized that rather than learning by association, the rats were developing cognitive maps as they repeatedly negotiated the mazes. Tolman concluded from his studies that the rats demonstrated latent learning—learning that is not apparent when it takes place. More recent developments in cognitive psychology indicate that classical conditioning is not necessarily a mechanical process, but that the stimuli in classical conditioning have meaning for the learner. Three aspects of cognitive elements in classical conditioning are examined: blocking, rule generation, and forming complex associations. The section concludes with a discussion of the Gestalt concept of insight learning, which is characterized by sudden resolution or action after a period of study during which there is no action or apparent understanding. The behaviorists and cognitive psychologists do not agree on the best explanations for the process of learning.

The fourth section ("Observational Learning: Albert Bandura") explores the topic of observational learning, which takes place when the ability to perform a behavior is acquired or modified by observing others. Those performing the behavior and being observed are called models. Bandura's research suggests that both animals and humans learn through observation, which is divided into four processes: attention, retention, reproduction, and motivation. Although reinforcement can have an impact on observational learning, this type of learning can occur without reinforcement. Bandura argues that observational learning is the basis for the development of most human social behaviors.

The final section ("The Neurophysiology of Learning") explains that the learning process produces changes in the brain. The author of the text examines the evolutionary basis for learning processes, changes that take place at the synapses when learning occurs, the major brain structures involved in learning, and the neurochemistry of response acquisition. Evolution has favored learning as an important survival tool in the context of natural selection, as discussed in chapter 1. The nervous system of the aplysia, a simple invertebrate, is used to illustrate the neurophysiology of learning in two simple forms—habituation and sensitization. Learning in more complex brains is being researched. Research findings on the functioning of the hippocampus, cerebellum, and cerebral cortex are discussed.

How to Master Chapter 6

Refer to These Learning Objectives

You should be able to achieve the following learning objectives after mastering the material in chapter 6:

Classical Conditioning: Ivan Pavlov

1. Define learning and explain its relevance to the field of psychology.

2. Describe Pavlov's methods of experimentation.

3. Define classical conditioning and its elements—the unconditioned stimulus (UCS), the unconditioned response (UCR), the conditioned stimulus (CS), and the conditioned response (CR)—and how they work together to create classical conditioning. Give examples.

4. Define and give examples of the following processes of classical conditioning: acquisition; extinction; spontaneous recovery; stimulus generalization; stimulus discrimination.

5. Discuss biological preparedness and other modern developments in classical conditioning.

6. Give examples of applications of classical conditioning.

Operant Conditioning: B. F. Skinner

7. Define and give examples of Thorndike's concept of instrumental learning and the law of effect.

8. Explain what is meant by consequences determining behavior.

9. Define operant conditioning and distinguish between elicited and emitted responses. Give examples of each.

10. Describe a Skinner box and Skinner's methods of experimentation.

11. Define behaviorism and its roots.

12. Describe the processes of operant conditioning, including acquisition, autoshaping, superstitious behavior, extinction, spontaneous recovery, stimulus control, stimulus discrimination, and stimulus generalization. Give examples of each.

13. Define reinforcement and explain how it maintains behavior.

14. Explain the experimental analysis of behavior (EAP), the Premack principle, primary reinforcer, and secondary reinforcer. Give examples.

15. Describe and give examples of continuous versus partial reinforcement, the effects of partial reinforcement, and the following four schedules of reinforcement: fixed ratio (FR), variable ratio (VR), fixed interval (FI), and variable interval (VI).

16. Define, distinguish among, and give examples of positive reinforcement, negative reinforcement, and punishment, and explain how they are applied.

17. Define and distinguish between escape learning and avoidance learning, and describe how they are studied.

18. Discuss the application of biological preparedness to operant conditioning.

19. Discuss the current status of operant conditioning and give examples of applications of operant conditioning, including the study of depression through learned helplessness and behavior modification.

Cognitive Factors in Learning

20. Discuss and give examples of cognitive factors in learning.

21. Explain what is meant by blocking, rule generation, and the Rescorla-Wagner model of forming complex associations.

22. Discuss and give examples of the process of insight learning.

Observational Learning: Albert Bandura

23. Discuss the theory and research of Albert Bandura and observational learning.

The Neurophysiology of Learning

24. Discuss research on the neurophysiology of learning.

Debate These Myths

MYTH 1: Conditioning really applies to animals, not humans.

Strategy:

Describe and give examples of the processes of classical and operant conditioning in terms of the role of stimuli, responses, reinforcement, generalization, and discrimination:

Give examples of how these processes and concepts can be applied to animal learning:

Give examples of how these processes and concepts can be applied to human learning in childhood in the context of family, school, and peer interaction:

Give examples of how these processes and concepts can be applied to adult human learning in the context of family relationships, the workplace, the use of drugs, eating habits, self-image, and other areas of human functioning:

Other statements or examples for debating MYTH 1:

Change MYTH 1 into a true statement:

MYTH 2: *If we are products of conditioning, we are not unique as individuals.*

Strategy:

Define and distinguish between primary and secondary reinforcers and give examples:

Explain the diversity in the types of secondary reinforcers that help maintain behavior:

Discuss the variations in people's environments and in people's responses to their environments:

Discuss the cognitive factors that influence conditioning:

Discuss the role of observational learning in human functioning:

Other statements or examples for debating MYTH 2:

Change MYTH 2 into a true statement:

Test Yourself: Multiple-Choice Questions

Directions: Circle the best response for each of the following questions.

1. The changes in behavior caused by the learning processes are considered to be:
    a. strongest in children under age 3
    b. deeper if based on a cognitive process
    c. the most difficult to achieve when under stress
    d. relatively permanent

2. The processes of classical conditioning were established through the research of:
    a. B. F. Skinner   c. Ivan Pavlov
    b. Edward L. Thorndike   d. John B. Watson

3. In an experiment in classical conditioning, a dog learns to salivate when a 60-watt light is turned on. In order to establish the dog's learning, the 60-watt light was presented 1/2 second before the presentation of meat over many trials. After the behavior was firmly established, the 60-watt light was presented many times without the meat, and eventually the dog stopped salivating. In this experiment, the meat would be considered the:
    a. unconditioned stimulus (UCS)   c. previously neutral stimulus
    b. conditioned stimulus (CS)   d. generalized stimulus

4. Referring to the experiment in question 3, the dog's salivation to the meat would be considered:
    a. a conditioned response (CR)   c. stimulus discrimination
    b. an unconditioned response (UCR)   d. spontaneous recovery

5. Referring to the experiment in question 3, the dog's salivation to the 60-watt light would be considered:
    a. a conditioned response (CR)   c. stimulus discrimination
    b. an unconditioned response (UCR)   d. spontaneous recovery

6. Referring to the experiment in question 3, the 60-watt light would be considered:
    a. an unconditioned stimulus (UCS)   c. a previously neutral stimulus
    b. a conditioned stimulus (CS)   d. both b and c

7. Referring to the experiment in question 3, if the dog salivated to a 50-watt light, this phenomenon would be considered:

    a. stimulus generalization c. spontaneous recovery

    b. stimulus discrimination d. biological preparedness

8. Referring to the experiment in question 3, the dog's failure to salivate when the light was no longer paired with the meat is an example of:

    a. spontaneous recovery c. extinction

    b. an unconditioned response (UCR) d. a conditioned response (CR)

9. Referring to the experiment in question 3, if the dog were presented with the light after not seeing it for several days, and the salivation CR were once again present, this phenomenon would be considered:

    a. extinction c. an unconditioned response (UCR)

    b. spontaneous recovery d. stimulus generalization

10. Referring to the experiment in question 3, the temporal arrangement of stimuli was:

    a. standard c. backward

    b. delayed d. simultaneous

11. The point of Watson and Rayner's 1920 classical conditioning of Little Albert to fear rats was to demonstrate:

    a. the importance of the temporal arrangement of the UCS with the CS

    b. that it is the connection between the two stimuli, not the connection between stimulus and response, that underlies learning

    c. the conditioning of a reflexive behavior

    d. how emotional responses are learned

12. The fact that more people are afraid of snakes than of eggs supports the theory of:

    a. equipotential c. biological preparedness

    b. response acquisition d. stimulus contiguity

13. Thorndik's law of effect states that behavior is:

    a. more likely to be repeated when it is followed by satisfaction or reward

    b. established through the repeated pairings of a CS with a UCS

    c. established through trial-and-error learning

    d. imitated when it is observed in others

14. Skinner called elicited responses, such as the salivation, eye blinking, and fear in classical conditioning studies:

    a. operants c. respondent behaviors

    b. emitted behaviors d. reinforced behaviors

15. Teaching a dog to roll over by reinforcing successive approximations to the desired behavior until the dog rolls over is an example of:

    a. stimulus control c. stimulus discrimination

    b. shaping d. partial reinforcement

16. A baseball player licks his lips three times before entering the field because in previous games his team won when he engaged in this behavior. His licking his lips is an example of:

    a. a respondent behavior c. stimulus control

    b. a superstitious behavior d. spontaneous recovery

17.   B. F. Skinner would consider ignoring a child who is having a tantrum:

   a.   overly punitive   c.   an effective way to extinguish the behavior
   b.   a form of stimulus control   d.   a form of negative reinforcement

18.   Joey's parents allowed him to have a bowl of ice cream only if he ate his peas, which he disliked but they considered good for him. Joey's parents were using:

   a.   the principle of primary reinforcement
   b.   a partial reinforcement schedule
   c.   the Premack principle
   d.   an interval schedule

19.   Money is an example of a:

   a.   primary reinforcer   c.   partial reinforcer
   b.   secondary reinforcer   d.   continuous reinforcer

20.   Gambling behavior is maintained on a reinforcement schedule based on a:

   a.   fixed interval   c.   variable interval
   b.   fixed ratio   d.   variable ratio

21.   For every one hundred dollars Madeline charged on her credit card, she earned 20 points toward a bonus gift. Her credit card company had the credit card holders on the type of reinforcement schedule known as:

   a.   fixed interval   c.   fixed ratio
   b.   variable interval   d.   variable ratio

22.   Paul was working on a writing project and allowed himself a 5-minute break every 45 minutes. Paul had placed himself on the type of reinforcement schedule known as:

   a.   fixed interval   c.   variable ratio
   b.   variable interval   d.   fixed ratio

23.   Ellen disliked the sound made by her car when she did not fasten her seat belt. The sound would stop as soon as she fastened her seat belt. The stopping of the annoying sound is an example of:

   a.   positive reinforcement   c.   negative reinforcement
   b.   stimulus control   d.   avoidance learning

24.   In negative reinforcement, the aversive stimulus occurs:

   a.   during punishment   c.   after the response
   b.   with the response   d.   before the response

25.   When Justin's mother yells at him for using bad language, he uses bad language even more. Instead of being an effective punishment, the yelling is acting as a:

   a.   positive reinforcer   c.   negative reinforcer
   b.   primary reinforcer   d.   partial reinforcer

26.   Two-process theory has been proposed to explain:

   a.   escape learning   c.   the value of punishment
   b.   avoidance learning   d.   the power of negative reinforcement

27.   In the process of instinctive drift, the acquisition of an operant response is impaired by:

   a.   classical conditioning   c.   inborn predispositions
   b.   learned helplessness   d.   a terrifying event

28.   Depression has been linked to the behavioral concept of:

   a.   spontaneous recovery   c.   punishment
   b.   learned helplessness   d.   biological preparedness

29. Programmed instruction and token economies are examples of applications of the principles of:
    a. classical conditioning   c. operant conditioning
    b. cognitive learning   d. observational learning

30. The latent learning demonstrated by the rats in Tolman's studies supported his view of:
    a. classical conditioning   c. operant conditioning
    b. observational learning   d. cognitive maps

31. On your first day on a new job, you have to devise a route to work. As you repeat the same route, you develop a mental map of how to get there. The type of learning involved in this process was studied by:
    a. Edward L. Thorndike   c. B. F. Skinner
    b. Edward Tolman   d. Leon Kamin

32. The phenomenon of blocking—interfering with the association between a CS and a UCS—was studied by:
    a. Edward L. Thorndike   c. B. F. Skinner
    b. Edward Tolman   d. Leon Kamin

33. That animals learn an expectancy that allows them to predict a second event when the first event occurs was demonstrated by:
    a. the Premack principle   c. the Recorla-Wagner model
    b. the law of effect   d. Mowrer's two-process theory

34. Insight learning involves:
    a. problem solving   c. the use of models
    b. instinctive drift   d. habituation

35. In Bandura's classic study, the children watching the film learned and imitated the aggressive behavior they saw based on:
    a. observation   c. both a and b
    b. reinforcement   d. neither a nor b

36. It is *not* true that observational learning:
    a. can be achieved by chickens   c. requires reinforcement
    b. affects social behavior   d. involves the process of attention

37. In Bandura's study of observational learning, the children in the control group:
    a. displayed the modeled behavior toward the toy
    b. developed cognitive maps to help them learn
    c. were influenced by the principles of operant conditioning
    d. displayed no new behaviors

38. All of the following are included as processes of observational learning *except*:
    a. attention   c. retention
    b. association   d. reproduction

39. After John watched his father stretch out his arms and let out a sigh in the morning, John began to engage in the same behavior. Bandura would consider John's behavior to have been learned through the process of:
    a. observation   c. association
    b. insight   d. conditioning

40. Emily' mother would express fear and avoidance every time she saw a cat. Soon, Emily became afraid of cats. Emily's fear of cats was most likely based on:
    a. learning through association   c. observational learning
    b. insight learning   d. biological preparedness

41. Attention, retention, reproduction, and motivation are four processes basic to:

    a. learning through insight   c. learning through conditioning

    b. the neurophysiology of learning   d. observational learning

42. It is more common for people to develop a phobia about spiders or heights than about trees or the color blue because phobias are:

    a. genetically predisposed   c. learned

    b. culture-specific   d. based on preference

43. Behaviors that have adaptive value help us:

    a. be better parents   c. process information

    b. survive   d. not fear danger

44. An experiment in the 1920s that tested the idea that babies, left to their own devices, would eat a balanced diet found that:

    a. the babies sought food needed by their bodies

    b. most of the babies developed vitamin D deficiencies

    c. most babies preferred sweets to any other type of food

    d. there were not enough parents willing to let their babies participate in the study

45. It is likely that the declining levels of lactase beyond infancy reflect:

    a. cultural differences   c. an evolved mechanism

    b. the process of habituation   d. food preferences

46. In his experiments on the aplysia, a sea snail, Kandel found that simple forms of learning were reflected:

    a. at the synapses between sensory and motor neurons

    b. at the hippocampus

    c. in the temporal cortex

    d. in the tail of the animal

47. Habituation is to sensitization as:

    a. decrease in responding is to increase in responding

    b. classical conditioning is to operant conditioning

    c. emitted response is to elicited response

    d. simple brain is to complex brain

48. In Kandel's study of the aplysia, sensitization involved:

    a. a decrease in the release of neurotransmitter at the synapse

    b. an increase in the release of neurotransmitter at the synapse

    c. no change in the release of neurotransmitter at the synapse

    d. a delay in the release of neurotransmitter at the synapse

49. Research on long-term potentiation (LTP) have found that learning takes place, in part, by:

    a. increasing the electrical activity of the cerebral cortex

    b. creating lesions in the temporal lobe

    c. habituating the action of neurons

    d. modifying synapses in areas of the hippocampus

50. Research on the neurochemistry of learning suggests that complex discrimination learning requires involvement of the:

    a. cerebellum   c. temporal cortex

    b. medulla   d. aplysia

Test Yourself: Fill in the Blanks

Directions: Fill in the blanks with the correct term or name.

1. _____ is usually defined as a set of relatively permanent changes in behavior that result from prior experience.

2. _____ conditioning has also been called learning by association.

3. The _____ stimulus is any stimulus that evokes a response without prior conditioning taking place.

4. The _____ response is the newly learning reaction to the CS.

5. In classical conditioning, _____ is the reduction is responding that occurs whenever the CS is repeatedly presented without the UCS.

6. In classical conditioning, _____ is the weakened return of the CR following the passage of time without exposure to the CS.

7. The phenomenon called _____ is the species-specific genetic predisposition to form certain learned associations and not others.

8. The law of _____ states that a behavior is more likely to be repeated when it is followed by satisfaction or reward.

9. _____ occurs when the consequence of a response increases the likelihood or probability that the response will be repeated.

10. Shaping a desired response without reinforcement is known as _____.

11. In operant conditioning, the gradual reduction in responding to the absence of reinforcement is known as _____.

12. In operant conditioning, stimulus _____ occurs when the organism responds to a stimulus that differs to some degree from that originally involved in the acquisition of the response.

13. Skinner developed an approach called _____ in which the experimenter follows a behavior with a stimulus that is a potential reinforcer. If it increase the probability of the response, it is defined as a reinforcer.

14. _____ reinforcers are those that become reinforcers as a result of being associated with primary reinforcers.

15. In operant conditioning, high resistance to extinction is caused primarily by the_____ effect.

16. _____ reinforcement involves the removal of displeasure or dissatisfaction.

17. _____ refers to a consequence that follows a response and decreases its probability.

18. In operant conditioning, _____ learning involves responding in a way that prevents an aversive stimulus from occurring.

19. In cognitive learning, _____ learning is learning that is not apparent when it first takes place.

20. _____ learning is characterized by sudden resolution or action after a period of study during which there is no action or apparent understanding.

Test Yourself: Matching Questions

Directions: For each item in column I, select the item in column II that is most closely associated with it.

I	II
_____1. E. L. Thorndike	a. the equipotential view
_____2. Martin Seligman	b. classical conditioning
_____3. Ivan Pavlov	c. insight learning
_____4. B. F. Skinner	d. law of effect
_____5. Edward Tolman	e. blocking
_____6. Wolfgang Kohler	f. observational learning
_____7. Robert Rescorla	g. early philosopher
_____8. O. H. Mowrer	h. instinctive drift
_____9. Albert Bandura	i. learned helplessness
_____10. Eric Kandel	j. conditioned Little Albert
_____11. John Watson	k. operant conditioning
_____12. Gregory Kimble	l. two-process theory
_____13. Leon Kamin	m. neural mechanisms of learning
_____14. K. and M. Breland	n. animals rehearse mentally
_____15. Francis Bacon	o. cognitive maps

Test Yourself: Answer Key

Multiple Choice

1. d (196)	11. d (199)	21. c (212)	31. b (217–18)	41. d (222)
2. c (197)	12. c (201)	22. a (212)	32. d (218)	42. a (225)
3. b (197–98)	13. a (205)	23. c (213)	33. c (219)	43. b (225–26)
4. b (197–98)	14. c (206)	24. d (213)	34. a (220)	44. a (225–26)
5. a (197–98)	15. b (208)	25. a (213)	35. a (221–22)	45. c (226)
6. d (197–98)	16. b (208)	26. b (215)	36. c (222)	46. a (227)
7. a (200)	17. c (208)	27. c (215)	37. d (222)	47. a (226)
8. c (200)	18. c (210)	28. b (215–16)	38. b (222)	48. b (227)
9. b (200)	19. b (211)	29. c (216)	39. a (223)	49. d (228)
10. a (199)	20. d (212)	30. d (217)	40. c (223)	50. c (228)

Fill in the Blanks

1. learning
2. classical
3. unconditioned
4. conditioned
5. extinction
6. spontaneous recovery
7. biological preparedness
8. effect
9. reinforcement
10. autoshaping
11. extinction
12. generalization
13. experimental analysis of behavior or EAB
14. secondary
15. partial reinforcement
16. negative
17. punishment
18. avoidance

19. latent

20. insight

Matching Questions

1. d	6. c	11. j
2. i	7. n	12. a
3. b	8. l	13. e
4. k	9. f	14. h
5. o	10. m	15. g

Do These Mini Projects

1. This mini project is designed to help you practice the operant conditioning technique of shaping. If you have a pet dog or cat, or if you have a family member or friend with a pet dog or cat that you could borrow for this project, you can practice shaping a behavior. Decide on a behavior that you want the animal to learn. Make sure it is a behavior the animal does not already know but is capable of doing. Have reinforcement ready. Your approving voice might be sufficient, but treats would be better. Then, while in close proximity to the animal, watch it as it acts naturally, and reinforce immediately any action that resembles the start of the response you want the animal to learn. When that behavior is repeated, reinforce it again. Then, reinforce behaviors that more closely approximate the desired behavior. Through the method of successive approximations, you can gradually shape the behavior you want. Remember to reinforce desired responses immediately.

2. Make note of behaviors that you engage in every day that are the product of classical and operant conditioning. What types of associations have created and maintained some of your behavior patterns through classical conditioning? What types of primary and secondary reinforcers on what types of reinforcement schedules have created and maintained your behavior patterns through operant conditioning? To what extent can you override the impact of conditioning through the use of cognitive processes?

3. Make a list of appliances and objects in your own home and office that play a role in conditioning your behavior. How does this process work?

Pull It All Together

1. Why do you think the author of the text chose to place the chapter on learning at this point in the text? How does the information on the processes of learning build on the material on consciousness in chapter 5?

2. At this point, you may realize that information on neuroscience relates to just about everything in the field of psychology. How is the behavior of learning related to the neurochemical processes of learning, and why is knowing about this connection relevant to the study of psychology?

3. Based on the information you have mastered in the text up to this point, how do you think the information on the processes of learning will further your understanding of future topics in the text, such as child development, personality, and abnormal behavior?

Chapter Outline

Human Memory: Origins and Basic Processes

Sensory Memory

Short-Term Memory

Long-Term Memory

Forgetting

The Neurophysiology of Memory

Chapter Overview

Chapter 7 covers the topic of memory. The author of the text points out that memory is a complex process and that there is more than one type of memory. Applying the memory principles discussed along with reading and studying the chapter material is suggested.

Chapter 7 contains six major sections: (1) "Human Memory: Origins and Basic Processes," (2) "Sensory Memory," (3) "Short-Term Memory," (4) "Long-Term Memory," (5) "Forgetting," and (6) "The Neurophysiology of Memory."

The first section ("Human Memory: Origins and Basic Processes") begins with a discussion of the evolution of memory. Evolutionary theory hypothesizes that memory, like learning, arose as a response to environmental demands and serves an adaptive function. The processes of encoding, storage, and retrieval are described. Encoding is the process by which information is converted into a form that allows it to be placed into memory. Storage is the retention of memorized material over a period of time. Retrieval is the process by which previously encoded, stored memories are brought back for current use. Three approaches to the study of memory are described: recognition, recall, and relearning. The three-system model (which includes sensory memory, short-term memory, and long-term memory) is introduced. The elements of the three-system model are covered in the next three sections of the chapter.

The second section ("Sensory Memory") defines a sensory memory as being specific to a particular sensory modality and as very briefly continuing the sensation of a stimulus after that stimulus ends. The two major types of sensory memory are iconic memory and echoic memory. Research on sensory memory is described.

The third section ("Short-Term Memory") defines short-term memory (STM) as a system that retains a limited amount of information for a brief time. The processes of encoding, storage, and retrieval pertain to short-term memory. Encoding in short-term memory is most often acoustic. Storage of information in short-term memory can be enhanced through the processes of chunking and rehearsal. The concepts of total operating space, levels of processing, and working memory are described under storage in short-term memory. Retrieval of information from short-term memory is accomplished by scanning, parallel processing, and serial processing. This section ends with a description of serial position effects (primacy and recency), which influence the processes of retrieval based on the position of items on a list.

The fourth section ("Long-Term Memory") discusses the processes of encoding, storage, and retrieval as they pertain to long-term memory (LTM). The primary form of encoding for information entering long-term memory appears to be semantic, although visual encoding is also used. Semantic encoding is encoding on the basis of meaning; this achieves the greatest depth of storage and the best recall. Prior experience can influence the encoding process by affecting how we formulate or construct the specific memory to be stored. Constructive memory is accomplished through the use of schema—mental representations of a category of objects, people, or events. Although the capacity of long-term memory may be unlimited, there are large individual differences in how much people actually store in long-term memory, and there are different types of long-term memory. The retrieval of information from long-term memory is dependent on the presence of cues associated with the remembered material. Retrieval can be enhanced by the use of priming and mnemonic devices. The section concludes with a discussion of exceptional memories.

The fifth section ("Forgetting") covers availability and accessibility theories of forgetting. Availability theories are based on the concept of information loss, which can occur through trace decay, disuse, interference, or encoding failure. The two major accessibility theories are retrieval failure theory and motivational theory. The retrieval failure theory of forgetting suggests that memories, though stored, cannot be recalled because the appropriate retrieval cues are not present. Motivational forgetting takes the form of selective forgetting of information as the result of repression, an unconscious process in which painful or anxiety-producing information is forced out of the conscious mind. The section ends with a discussion of the controversial topic of false memory syndrome and allegations of sexual abuse.

The final section ("The Neurophysiology of Memory") explores our current state of knowledge of the neural structures in memory, the changes that take place in the brain when a memory is established, retrieved, or forgotten, the biochemistry of memory, and memory pathology. Most recent research confirms that memory storage may involve the synapse, where a number of possible changes could account for it. The hippocampus, other subcortical structures, and the temporal cortex are involved in memory above the neuronal level. According to connectionist models, a memory consists of a set of associations formed through such processes as classical and operant conditioning. Memory is also explained through the process of parallel distributed processing, through which acquiring new information not only establishes or modifies information-specific memory but also alters overall understanding of some general part of your world. The roles of neurotransmitters, proteins, hormones, and RNA are discussed. The chapter ends with a discussion of brain damage and memory loss due to brain injury, the aging process, and alcohol consumption.

How to Master Chapter 7

Refer to These Learning Objectives

You should be able to achieve the following learning objectives after mastering the material in chapter 7:

Human Memory: Origins and Basic Processes

1. Discuss and give examples of memory as an adaptive process.

2. Define the processes of encoding, storage, and retrieval.

3. Explain how memory is studied through the processes of recognition, recall, and relearning.

4. Explain what is meant by the three-system memory model and list its components.

Sensory Memory

5. Define sensory memory and describe the two types of memories it comprises: iconic and echoic memories. Give examples.

Short-Term Memory

6. Define short-term memory (STM) and the processes of encoding, storage, and retrieval as they relate to STM.

7. Discuss storage capacity in short-term memory and the process of chunking.

8. Describe the processes of rehearsal, levels-of-processing theory, working memory, and what the Brown-Peterson paradigm tells us about storage in short-term memory.

9. Explain the process of scanning as it pertains to retrieval in short-term memory.

10. Distinguish between parallel and serial processing and between the primacy effect and the recency effect. Give examples.

Long-Term Memory

11. Describe the processes of encoding in long-term memory (LTM), including the definitions of semantic and visual encoding.

12. Explain what is meant by dual-coding theory, encoding specificity, constructive memory, schemas, and scripts. Give examples.

13. Discuss what is known about the capacity and permanence of long-term memory.

14. Define and give examples of autobiographical memory, declarative memory, procedural memory, episodic memory, and semantic memory.

15. Discuss and give examples of how cues aid the retrieval of information from long-term memory, and describe the process of forming flashbulb memories.

16. Explain and give examples of how context, physiology, and mood affect retrieval of information from long-term memory.

17. Describe how mnemonics can be used to enhance retrieval.

18. Discuss what is known about exceptional memories and eidetic imagery.

Forgetting

19. Define and distinguish among the theories of forgetting, including availability theories (trace-decay, disuse, interference, and encoding failure) and accessibility theories (retrieval failure and motivational forgetting).

20. Define false memory syndrome and discuss related research findings.

The Neurophysiology of Memory

21. Discuss our current state of knowledge regarding the neurophysiology of memory, including the neural structures in memory, the connectionist models, and the biochemistry of memory.

22. Discuss the major types of memory loss and their causes.

Debate These Myths

MYTH 1: *Eyewitness testimony should be the basis of jurists' decisions in criminal trials because of its reliability.*

Strategy:

Discuss how encoding, storage, and retrieval are involved in eyewitness testimony:

Discuss the role of constructive memory in eyewitness testimony:

Explain the nature of false memory syndrome:

Give examples of how false memory syndrome could interfere with the accuracy of eyewitness testimony:

Give examples of other factors, including context, motivation, and physiological state that could interfere with the accuracy of eyewitness testimony:

Other statements or examples for debating MYTH 1:

Change MYTH 1 into a true statement:

MYTH 2: You have to have a photographic memory to be a good student.

Strategy:

Discuss what is currently known about eidetic imagery (photographic memory):

Given how rare eidetic imagery is, discuss other factors that contribute to making someone a good student:

Give examples of memory strategies that could help improve study skills and grades:

Other statements or examples for debating MYTH 2:

Change MYTH 2 into a true statement:

Test Yourself: Multiple-Choice Questions

Directions: Circle the best response for each of the following questions.

1.   The process through which information is converted into a form in which it can be placed into memory is
        called:
        a.   storage   c.   attention
        b.   encoding   d.   rehearsal

2. The retention of memorized material over a period of time is called:

   a. storage   c. recognition

   b. relearning   d. encoding

3. Bringing back information from memory into current use is known as:

   a. relearning   c. retrieval

   b. recall   d. recognition

4. Bob was shown a series of pictures, which was then removed. He was then shown a longer series and was asked to indicate which of the pictures he had seen in the previous series. This task tested Bob's ability to:

   a. recognize the pictures   c. recall the pictures

   b. relearn the pictures   d. encode the pictures

5. Nancy was asked to memorize a list of words. The next day, she was asked to write down all the words from that list that she could remember. The memory task tapped her ability to:

   a. recognize the words   c. recall the words

   b. relearn the words   d. encode the words

6. Pamela had taken driver's education in high school but did not take a driving test right afterward. When she came home after her first semester of college, she took two more lessons and then passed the test. This example demonstrates:

   a. recall   c. recognition

   b. relearning   d. retrieval

7. Iconic and echoic memories are types of:

   a. sensory memory   c. short-term memory

   b. long-term memory   d. declarative memory

8. Iconic is to echoic as:

   a. visual is to auditory   c. short-term is to long-term

   b. recognition is to recall   d. encoding is to storage

9. Regarding sensory memories, neuroscientists have found that:

   a. sensory icons can last up to 10 seconds

   b. iconic viewing is uncommon in normal visual perception

   c. sensory memories are processed through phonemic encoding in the cortex

   d. there are very brief memory traces in the brain corresponding to sensory memories

10. The focusing of consciousness on a limited range of stimuli or events is the definition of:

    a. encoding   c. attention

    b. elaborative rehearsal   d. parallel processing

11. STM typically hold information for no more than:

    a. 20 to 400 milliseconds   c. 10 minutes

    b. 30 seconds   d. 1 minute

12. The three-system memory model includes short-term memory, long-term memory, and:

    a. eidetic memory   c. sensory memory

    b. constructive memory   d. visual memory

13. The Brown-Peterson paradigm demonstrated that people:

    a. retain information in short-term memory without rehearsal for no more than about 15 to 30 seconds

    b. can retain an icon in sensory memory for about 10 to 400 milliseconds

    c. can relearn information in much less time than the original learning took

    d. can retain information in long-term memory forever

14. Transferring information from short-term to long-term memory is facilitated by the process of:
    a. retrieval   c. elaborative rehearsal
    b. serial processing   d. parallel processing

15. According to the research of Craik and Tulving, the deepest level of processing is:
    a. semantic   c. structural
    b. phonemic   d. visual

16. According to the research of Craik and Tulving, structural encoding relies primarily on:
    a. memory for past events   c. physiological state of the person
    b. attention span   d. physical properties of the stimulus

17. Compared to short-term memory, working memory is more:
    a. superficial   c. visually oriented
    b. complex   d. imagery oriented

18. Judith and Ken were shown the following list of words: *man, bench, sailboat, puppy, restaurant, cave, hospital, telephone, mountain, gallery*. Later, they were each asked to recall as many words as they could from the list. Judith recalled *man, bench,* and *sailboat*. Her recall demonstrated:
    a. semantic encoding   c. the primacy effect
    b. the recency effect   d. serial processing

19. Referring back to question 18, Ken recalled *mountain* and *gallery,* thereby demonstrating:
    a. the recency effect   c. the primacy effect
    b. semantic encoding   d. serial processin

20. Rachel, John, and Adam were asked to memorize a randomly organized list of 30 words that named 10 professions, 10 states in the U.S., and 10 foods. When asked to reproduce the list, Rachel wrote them down according to their categories, which demonstrates:
    a. rehearsal in STM   c. semantic encoding
    b. the serial position effect   d. parallel processing

21. Referring back to question 20, John wrote down more items from beginning of the original list than from the end, which demonstrates:
    a. semantic encoding   c. constructive memory
    b. the recency effect   d. the primacy effect

22. Referring back to question 20, John could remember very few of the items, which demonstrates:
    a. a lack of encoding   c. that he did not pay attention to the list
    b. a lack of rehearsal   d. any of the above

23. Compared with memory for pictures, memory for the labels of pictures is:
    a. worse   c. the same
    b. better   d. unknown

24. Under most circumstances, you could recall more easily the details of a mental image of a dog if you visualized the dog:
    a. sitting next to another dog   c. sitting next to a mouse
    b. standing next to a skyscraper   d. standing next to a tree

25. Leslie's schema of what a typical kindergarten child looks like helped her with:
    a. constructive memory when picking up her friend's child at school
    b. rehearsing the characteristics of typical five-year-olds
    c. maintaining her attentional focus at her child's school play
    d. developing a schema of what a typical third-grader looks like

26. Of the following, constructive memory is affected the most by:

a. the recency effect
c. depth of processing
b. bias
d. STM

27. Research suggests that the capacity of LTM is:

a. determined in infancy
b. determined by individual differences in memory use
c. virtually unlimited
d. unknowable

28. Research on the value of using drugs called "truth serums" in order to study memory has found that under the influence of such drugs:

a. most people can recall childhood events with great accuracy
b. unconscious inhibitions are removed so that the truth can be told
c. most memories provided are no more accurate than those under hypnosis
d. most people strive to please the investigator

29. The electrical stimulation of the brain to reveal memories during surgery was done by:

a. Karl Lashley
c. Hermann Ebbinghaus
b. Wilder Penfield
d. Endel Tulving

30. Remembering that Canada and Mexico are countries that border the United States is an example of:

a. autobiographical memory
c. procedural memory
b. declarative memory
d. flashbulb memory

31. Remembering that you have an appointment with the dentist this Friday is an example of:

a. declarative memory
c. autobiographical memory
b. procedural memory
d. episodic memory

32. Remembering a complex set of activities, such as the rules of chess, would be an example of:

a. semantic memory
c. declarative memory
b. autobiographical memory
d. procedural memory

33. Recalling what you did and how you felt on your first date is an example of:

a. semantic memory
c. declarative memory
b. procedural memory
d. autobiographical memory

34. Episodic is to semantic as:

a. factual is to conceptual
c. short-term is to long-term
b. verbal is to visual
d. serial is to parallel

35. Priming may be especially effective for material that can be:

a. learned quickly
c. organized hierarchically
b. made into images
d. rehearsed elaboratively

36. Recalling information that is on the tip of the tongue is made easier with:

a. rehearsal
c. priming
b. serial processing
d. mnemonics

37. Linda remembers that when she heard about the bombing of the federal building in Oklahoma City, she was drinking a soda at her son's soccer game. Her detailed memory of what she was doing at the time she heard the tragic news is an example of:

a. an episodic memory
c. encoding specificity
b. a flashbulb memory
d. a repressed memory

38. Research has shown that if a person learned new information when under the influence of alcohol, recall was best when the person:
   a. was again under the influence of alcohol
   b. was sober
   c. was aware of having a drinking problem
   d. had a good night's sleep

39. If you learn how to bake a cake using a new recipe when you feel happy, you will later recall most effectively how to bake the same cake when you feel:
   a. sad
   b. happy
   c. angry
   d. any of the above

40. You form associations among otherwise unrelated words or objects, with the result that recalling one word in the list allows you to recall the next word, through the:
   a. method of loci
   b. use of mnemonics
   c. use of priming
   d. link method

41. The researcher who studied memory and forgetting by having people memorize a long list of nonsense syllables and demonstrated a forgetting curve was named:
   a. Karl Lashley
   b. Brenda Milner
   c. Hermann Ebbinghaus
   d. George Miller

42. The trace-decay theory of forgetting is based on the concept of:
   a. availability
   b. motivation
   c. accessibility
   d. retrieval failure

43. If learning a list of French vocabulary words makes it difficult for you to remember a subsequently presented list of Spanish vocabulary words, you are experiencing:
   a. proactive interference
   b. retroactive interference
   c. trace decay
   d. repression

44. Matthew could not remember being spanked as a child even though his sister told him about the repeated spankings he received from his father. The theory of forgetting that most likely accounts for Matthew's forgetting is:
   a. trace theory
   b. motivational theory
   c. interference theory
   d. false memory syndrome

45. Past events are likely to be reported in a distorted fashion when:
   a. misleading information is provided
   b. suggestions about the memories are made by powerful people
   c. both a and b
   d. neither a nor b

46. An early theory on the neural structures in memory was proposed by:
   a. Hermann Ebbinghaus
   b. Karl Lashley
   c. Sigmund Freud
   d. Endel Tulving

47. Synaptic plasticity refers to the fact that synapses:
   a. influence memory
   b. create memory traces
   c. are interrelated in a complex network
   d. change over time

48. At the subcortical level, the neural structure that has been found by researchers to facilitate memory storage and retrieval is the:
   a. hippocampus
   b. hypothalamus
   c. temporal lobe
   d. thalamus

49. According to the connectionist models, a memory consists of a set of associations formed through such processes as:

    a. classical conditioning   c. both a and b

    b. operant conditioning   d. neither a nor b

50. The neurotransmitter that increases in quantity when memory storage takes place and appears to be crucial to the formation of memories is called:

    a. serotonin   c. epinephrine

    b. acetylcholine   d. RNA

Test Yourself: Fill in the Blanks

Directions: Fill in the blanks with the correct term or name.

1. The retention of memorized material over a period of time is called _____.

2. _____ is the process by which previously encoded, stored memories are brought back for current use.

3. _____ means that you are asked to remember something you have previously learned without again seeing the material.

4. The three-system model includes _____ memory, _____ memory, and _____ memory.

5. _____ is a system that retains a limited amount of information for a brief time.

6. _____ concluded from his research on short-term memory that the average person can retain five to nine items in STM.

7. The overall capacity of STM is referred to as _____.

8. _____ rehearsal facilitates the transfer of information from short-term to long-term memory.

9. Based on the levels-of-processing theory, depth of processing is the most superficial when you use _____ encoding, deeper when you use _____ encoding, and the deepest when you use _____.

10. _____ theory holds that memory performance is dependent on both verbal and nonverbal cues.

11. The use of existing knowledge, expectancies, or biases to modify new, incoming information is called _____.

12. A _____ is a mental representation of a category of objects, people, or events.

13. _____ memory is memory for motor, cognitive, and perceptual skills.

14. _____ means giving a person a cue to facilitate recall from LTM.

15. _____ memories are graphic, detailed remembrances of striking events.

16. _____ are organizational memory schemes that help you retrieve information from memory.

17. _____ argued that selective forgetting, the forgetting of certain kinds of information and not other kinds, is due to repression.

18. Karl Lashley suggested that a memory trace, which he called an _____, is left in the brain whenever learning occurs.

19. The distributed neurons for making word associations are interconnected to form a _____, which is a set of neurons linked together through synaptic connections to form a circuit.

20. The occurrence of many simultaneous operations distributed across many locations in the brain is called
_____.

Test Yourself: Matching Questions

Directions: For each item in column I, select the item in column II that is most closely associated with it.

I	II
_____1. icon	a. selective forgetting
_____2. echoic memory	b. cue for aiding retrieval
_____3. recognition	c. involves meaning
_____4. working memory	d. memory trace
_____5. parallel processing	e. brief visual memory trace
_____6. serial processing	f. pseudoforgetting
_____7. semantic encoding	g. brief registration of sounds
_____8. STM	h. examine one at a time
_____9. constructive memory	i. identification
_____10. primacy effect	j. mental representation
_____11. schema	k. information retained 30 seconds
_____12. priming	l. central processor
_____13. encoding failure	m. use of existing knowledge
_____14. repression	n. examine all at once
_____15. engram	o. serial position

Test Yourself: Answer Key

Multiple Choice

1. b (234)	11. b (238–39)	21. d (242)	31. d (248)	41. c (254)
2. a (234)	12. c (236)	22. d (242–43)	32. a (248)	42. a (255)
3. c (234)	13. a (239)	23. a (243)	33. d (248)	43. a (256)
4. a (235)	14. c (240)	24. c (244)	34. a (248)	44. b (258)
5. c (235)	15. a (241)	25. a (245)	35. c (250)	45. c (258–59)
6. b (235)	16. d (240)	26. b (244–45)	36. c (250)	46. b (259)
7. a (237)	17. b (241)	27. c (245)	37. b (250)	47. d (261)
8. a (237)	18. c (242)	28. c (248)	38. a (251)	48. a (261)
9. d (237)	19. a (242)	29. b (248)	39. b (251)	49. c (261)
10. c (237)	20. c (243)	30. b (248)	40. d (252)	50. b (263)

Fill in the Blanks

1. storage
2. retrieval
3. recall
4. sensory, short-term, long-term
5. short-term memory or STM
6. George Miller
7. total operating space
8. elaborative
9. structural, phonemic, semantic
10. dual-coding
11. constructive memory
12. schema
13. procedural
14. priming
15. flashbulb
16. mnemonics
17. Sigmund Freud
18. engram

19. neural network

20. parallel distributed processing or PDP

Matching Questions

1. e	6. h	11. j
2. g	7. c	12. b
3. i	8. k	13. f
4. l	9. m	14. a
5. n	10. o	15. d

Do These Mini Projects

1. Select a significant event—either a news event or a personal event—and record your flashbulb memory of what you were doing at the time the event occurred. Include as much vivid detail as possible concerning your whereabouts and activities at the time of the significant event. If you have flashbulb memories concerning more than one event, you may record those as well. What is it about those significant events that helps us remember information in such detail? In what ways are flashbulb memories adaptive?

2. Go through chapter 7 sequentially and jot down words and phrases that will prime you to recall the information in the chapter. Remember that priming involves selecting cues that will help you retrieve information from long-term memory. Therefore, you must master the material by encoding it and storing it before you are ready to use the priming technique. You can retrieve information only if it is in storage.

3. Devise a mnemonic to help you remember the information on the neurophysiology of memory. You will recall that a mnemonic is an organizational device that can help you retrieve information from memory. For example, the sentence *Every good boy does fine* is a mnemonic for remembering the musical notes E, G, B, D, and F on the staff of written music, because each word in the mnemonic begins with a letter in the sequence to be remembered. Bring your mnemonic to class for sharing.

Pull It All Together

1. Although in the presentation of the material, memory is divided into three distinct entities—sensory memory, short-term memory, and long-term memory—the process of memory is smooth and flowing, with all three aspects of memory working together as integral parts of the three-system model. How do the three components of this model interact to create a smooth process? What are some other processes that you have learned about so far in the field of psychology that have component parts that work together? Consider the chapter on neuroscience and the brain when formulating your answer.

2. Describe and give examples of techniques that you have used throughout your life to remember different types of information, such as written material or the names of people as you are introduced to them. What additional techniques have you learned by studying chapter 7 that you will apply to future memory tasks?

CHAPTER 8
COGNITION AND LANGUAGE

Chapter Outline

Chapter Overview

Chapter 8 covers the interrelated topics of cognition and language. Cognitive processes are closely linked to learning, memory, and intelligence. The process of cognition, or thinking, is among the most complex of all human activities. Cognition means "to know" and refers to the mental activities involved in acquiring, processing, and using knowledge. The process of cognition was largely ignored by the field of psychology until nearly 1960, mostly because behaviorism rejected the study of internal constructs. Today, about 75 percent of psychologists in U.S. colleges and universities identify themselves as cognitive psychologists.

Modern cognitive psychologists are interested in how we gain new knowledge, incorporate that knowledge into existing frameworks, and use information to solve problems, make decisions, and engage in effective behavior. The broader field of which cognitive psychology is a part is cognitive science, the study of the nature, components, and development of thought and knowledge.

Chapter 8 contains five major sections: (1) "Elements of Cognition," (2) "Problem Solving," (3) "Decision-Making and Reasoning," (4) "Language: Its Structure and Function," and (5) "The Evolution and Neurophysiology of Cognition and Language."

The first section ("Elements of Cognition") explains that a specific thought is the end product of a process that involves one or more of several elements, including concepts and propositions. A concept is a mental representation of the central properties of a class of like objects or instances that serves to group or classify them into categories. Concept formation is a cognitive process through which we learn major categories of information and the members of those categories. Many concepts are acquired through experience and are organized into hierarchies. A proposition is a statement that links mental elements in ways that allow us to use those elements for purposes of thought. Without concepts and propositions, we would have no way of organizing information. The section concludes with a brief discussion of metacognition, which is your awareness of your own processing.

The second section ("Problem Solving") defines problem solving as the active effort to resolve a problem that occurs when a barrier blocks the path to a goal. Theories of problem solving and cognition include Gestalt theory, information-processing theory, and connectionism. Gestalt theory centers around the concept of insight, a sudden recognition of the correct solution, usually after a period during which we are not consciously thinking about the problem. Information-processing theory views the brain as a computer, or central processing unit. Cognitive psychology has been joined in recent years by connectionism, which hypothesizes that problem solving and other thought processes take place through the establishment of systems of neural associations, or connections. These connections engage in parallel distributed processing (PDP), which means that multiple cognitive activities can take place at one time.

A number of strategies that people use to solve problems are described. A variety of factors are described that can contribute to the success or failure of the problem-solving process. Experts can solve problems in their areas of expertise because they store information in meaningful chunks, process deeply, and have highly organized bodies of knowledge. The section concludes with a brief discussion of artificial intelligence, the use of computer hardware and software to solve complex problems in ways similar to how humans are thought to solve them.

The third section ("Decision-Making and Reasoning") considers what cognitive psychologists have learned about how we make decisions and engage in the reasoning process. Decision making is the process of evaluating two or more alternatives and choosing one of them. Factors that lead to incorrect decisions are described. Reasoning is the process by which we generate, examine, and evaluate information. Reasoning, which can be based on either illogical or realistic thinking, permits us to adapt to a complex physical and social environment that would otherwise threaten the survival of the species. There are two types of realistic reasoning: deductive and inductive. In deductive reasoning, we use (general) logical relationships to determine the validity or truth of our (specific) conclusions. In inductive reasoning, we move from the specific to the general, the opposite of deductive reasoning.

The fourth section ("Language: Its Structure and Function") covers the topic of psycholinguistics, the study of the psychological nature of language. Language is defined as a structured system of symbols that can be combined according to a set of guidelines to produce virtually infinite messages. Language, which is closely tied to thought, has two essential properties: (1) It is semantic, or meaningful, and (2) it is productive, in that you can produce novel sentences. Whether language reflects thought or creates thought is a controversial issue. The structure of language is described. Syntax is the set of rules that govern the arrangement of words into phrases and sentences. Semantics is the study of the meaning of language and particularly of its individual words and the relationships among them. Noam Chomsky's theory of transformational grammar, now known as government and binding theory, proposes that there are two levels of structure of language: the surface structure of a sentence and the deep structure, or meaning, of a sentence.

The sequence of language development and theories of language acquisition are described. Theories of language acquisition include environmental approaches, biological approaches, and interactionist theories. Both learning and biological explanations have been criticized for not providing a full understanding of language acquisition. Two interactional approaches are described: (1) the cultural-context or social communication perspective of Jerome Bruner, and (2) the cognitive theory of Jean Piaget. The section ends with a discussion of language acquisition and use in animals.

The fifth and final section ("The Evolution and Neurophysiology of Cognition and Language") explains that the evolutionary view of language and its neural basis is an extension of what has been presented about cognition. The two types of research that have yielded valuable information regarding the neurophysiology of cognition involve the electroencephalogram (EEG) and the study of individuals with brain damage. With regard to the neurophysiology of language, the basic form of speech pathology that results from brain damage is aphasia, which involves difficulty in producing or comprehending meaningful speech. Studies of aphasics show that the neural circuits necessary for language and speech functions are located primarily in the left hemisphere. Three types of aphasia are described. The section concludes with a brief discussion of the neural networks for language.

How to Master Chapter 8

Refer to These Learning Objectives

You should be able to achieve the following learning objectives after mastering the material in chapter 8:

Elements of Cognition

1. Define cognition and place it within the context of cognitive science and cognitive neuroscience.

2. Define and give examples of the elements of cognition, including concepts and propositions.

3. Describe the process of concept formation.

Problem Solving

4. Discuss and distinguish among three theories of problem solving: Gestalt theory, information-processing theory, and connectionism.

5. Explain what is meant by parallel distributed processing, and explain it's relationship to problem solving.

6. Define and give examples of the following problem-solving strategies: algorithms, heuristics, working backward, difference reduction, means/ends analysis, and finding analogies .

7. Explain how each of the following factors can contribute to the success or failure of the problem-solving process: representing the problem, using prior skills and knowledge, memory, attending selectively, and planning.

8. Describe and give examples of the following barriers to effective problem solving: functional fixedness, irrelevant information, psychological set, and confirmation bias.

9. Describe the factors that enable experts to solve problems.

10. Explain what is meant by artificial intelligence (AI).

Decision-Making and Reasoning

11. Define decision making and describe the factors that can make decisions difficult or lead to incorrect decisions.

12. Define reasoning and explain the adaptive value of this process.

13. Define and distinguish between deductive and inductive reasoning

Language: Its Structure and Function

14. Define language and describe its nature and function.

15. Define and distinguish between linguistic determinism and linguistic relativism.

16. Explain how language is structured.

17. Describe the nature of semantics and the theory of transformational grammar developed by Noam Chomsky.

18. Explain the government and binding theory.

19. Describe the process of language development.

20. Explain and distinguish among the environmental, biological, and interactionist theories of language acquisition.

21. Explain what is meant by LAD and LASS.

22. Discuss our current state of knowledge of language acquisition and use in animals.

23. Discuss the evolution of cognition and language.

The Evolution and Neurophysiology of Cognition and Language

24. Discuss what research using the electroencephalogram (EEG) and research on brain damage has revealed about the neurophysiology of cognition.

25. Discuss the neurophysiology of language, including aphasia, Broca's area, and Wernicke's area.

Debate These Myths

MYTH 1: *The entire basis of children learning language is listening to their parents talk.*

Strategy:

Discuss environmental theories of language acquisition:

Discuss biological theories of language acquisition:

Describe what is meant by a language acquisition device (LAD) and a language acquisition support system (LASS):

Discuss interactionist approaches to language development:

Other statements or examples for debating MYTH 1:

Change MYTH 1 into a true statement:

MYTH 2: *You either know how to solve problems, or you don't.*

Strategy:

Describe the following problem-solving strategies: algorithms, heuristics, working backward, difference reduction, means/ends analysis, and finding analogies:

Explain how these strategies can be acquired:

Describe the major factors that determine success or failure at problem solving:

Discuss obstacles to problem solving and how they can be overcome:

Other statements and examples for debating MYTH 2:

Change MYTH 2 into a true statement:

MYTH 3: *Certain animals have learned to use language almost at a human level.*

Strategy:

Describe the research on the acquisition and use of language in primates and other animals:

Discuss the nature of the evidence concerning language acquisition and use in primates and other animals:

Other statements and examples for debating MYTH 3:

Change MYTH 3 into a true statement:

Test Yourself: Multiple-Choice Questions

Directions: Circle the best response for each of the following questions.

1. Cognition means to:
    a. achieve
    b. know
    c. learn
    d. solve

2. Cognitive neuroscience is the study of:
    a. the process of language acquisition
    b. learning and memory
    c. the origins and processing of thought in the brain
    d. the elements of cognition

3. Helen Keller was able to learn language once she developed:
    a. the concept
    b. the metacognition
    c. a proposition
    d. problem-solving skills

4.   Two-year-old Charlie's first dog was a cocker spaniel. While walking the dog with his mother, he saw a poodle and a terrier. These examples of dogs helped Charlie develop the concept of dog by serving as:

    a.   hierarchies   c.   propositions

    b.   natural concepts   d.   prototypes

5.   A cantaloupe is a melon. A melon is a fruit. Fruit is a food. This series of statements represent a:

    a.   natural concept   c.   prototype

    b.   concept hierarchy   d.   proposition

6.   Observing a line of traffic for an opening to enter a lane takes place during the stage of information processing known as:

    a.   preparation   c.   judgment

    b.   production   d.   incubation

7.   Dana was working on a puzzle and got stuck. After a ten-minute break, she suddenly saw how the pieces fit together. The break would be considered by information-processing theory as:

    a.   preparation   c.   judgment

    b.   production   d.   incubation

8.   Dana's sudden recognition of how the pieces fit is known as:

    a.   insight   c.   a metacognition

    b.   concept formation   d.   a natural concept

9.   Mediation theory is to hypothesis-testing theory as:

    a.   cognition is to language

    b.   concept acquisition is to concept formation

    c.   passive process is to active process

    d.   inductive reasoning is to deductive reasoning

10.   The statement *Money is freedom* is an example of:

    a.   a proposition   c.   a problem

    b.   difference reduction   d.   a metacognition

11.   Which one of the following is the best example of a metacognition?

    a.   Joe suddenly realizes how to solve the puzzle.

    b.   Meg remembers the words to a song she had forgotten.

    c.   Neil knew he looked nervous on the plane.

    d.   Paula kept trying the same strategies over and over again.

12.   Metacognition always involves:

    a.   mediation   c.   insight

    b.   awareness   d.   hierarchies

13.   The concept of insight is most closely associated with:

    a.   George Miller   c.   Herbert Simon

    b.   George Kelly   d.   Wolfgang Kohler

14.   Information-processing theory considers the brain as the:

    a.   CPU   c.   EEG

    b.   LAD   d.   LASS

15.   James McClelland and David Rumelhart published a two-volume book in 1986 called *Parallel Distributed Processing* in which they present their theory of:

    a.   transformational grammar   c.   connectionism

    b.   information processing   d.   artificial intelligence

16. All of the following are true regarding connectionism *except*:

   a. It hypothesizes the existence of a single central processing unit that analyzes and integrates data, drawing from other units, such as memory.

   b. It conceptualizes the brain as processing information in scattered neural circuits that span the brain.

   c. It hypothesizes the existence of neural networks that engage in parallel distributed processing, allowing multiple cognitive activities to take place at one time.

   d. It was first proposed as a theory in cognitive science in the 1980s.

17. The brain is conceptualized as processing information in scattered neural circuits that span the brain by the theory of:

   a. information processing   c. mediation

   b. hypothesis testing   d. connectionism

18. Mechanical, step-by-step solutions are provided by:

   a. means/ends analyses   c. algorithms

   b. analogies   d. working backward

19. When planning a car trip from New York to California, Jim established subgoals, including stops in Ohio, Kansas, and Nevada. He was using a strategy known as:

   a. difference reduction   c. finding analogies

   b. a rule of thumb   d. working backward

20. Lorna wanted to advance her career from administrative assistant to marketing researcher, but it would mean going back to school for an advanced degree. She decided it was worth it based on a problem-solving strategy known as:

   a. working backward   c. heuristics

   b. means/ends analysis   d. attending selectively

21. Barbara and Harry, both intelligent individuals, looked at computer output from a research study. Barbara immediately knew how to organize and interpret the data, whereas Harry was at a total loss. The most likely explanation is that Barbara:

   a. used a heuristic

   b. used an algorithm

   c. had a psychological set

   d. drew upon prior skills and knowledge

22. Bob's office door kept closing, and he wanted to keep it open. He did not seem to realize that he could use his paperweight as a doorstop, most likely because of:

   a. a memory lapse   c. functional fixedness

   b. selective attention   d. psychological set

23. Mrs. Smith, a kindergarten teacher, repeatedly interpreted Johnny's refusal to sit still in his seat as an act of defiance. She developed a dislike for the child, whose behavior she interpreted as deliberately disruptive. In first grade, testing revealed that Johnny suffered from attention deficit disorder with hyperactivity. Apparently, Mrs. Smith's problem solving regarding Johnny was incorrect due to:

   a. psychological set   c. functional fixedness

   b. confirmation bias   d. irrelevant information

24. A physical trainer was immediately able to see problems in her new client's approach to using exercise by using problem-solving skills known as:

   a. functional fixedness   c. both a and b

   b. psychological set   d. neither a nor b

25. The expert's ability to process more deeply involves the use of:
     a. meaning   c. set
     b. heuristics   d. syntax

26. Which one of the following is the best example of how a researcher in early stages of the field of artificial intelligence developed problem-solving computer programs?
     a. by attaching electrodes on the participant's skull in order to record brain waves
     b. by recording the verbal output of the participant who was solving a problem
     c. by observing children solve problems in a naturalistic setting
     d. by interviewing participants about their problem-solving strategies

27. When the stakes are high and accuracy is of major importance, people tend to approach decisions by using:
     a. anchoring heuristics   c. representative heuristics
     b. algorithmic approaches   d. probability biases

28. Making the assumption that a woman walking around a woman's clothing store with no purse is a salesperson is an example of:
     a. using a representative heuristic   c. both a and b
     b. matching a prototype   d. neither a nor b

29. How you structure questions and pose the issues involved in making a decision is known as:
     a. framing   c. getting organized
     b. concept formation   d. chunking

30. Regarding confidence level and decision making, research has shown that people are generally:
     a. afraid of making the wrong decision   c. functionally fixed
     b. appropriately confident   d. overconfident

31. The process by which we generate, examine, and evaluate information is known as:
     a. reasoning   c. decision making
     b. concept formation   d. the use of heuristics

32. Moving from the specific to the general is a process used in:
     a. deductive reasoning   c. both a and b
     b. inductive reasoning   d. neither a nor b

33. Thinking logically through a process of using premises to reach a conclusion describes:
     a. deductive reasoning   c. estimating probabilities
     b. inductive reasoning   d. concept formation

34. Language has appeared in written form for about:
     a. one million years   c. 1,000 years
     b. three million years   d. 6,000 years

35. The theory that language determines thought is known as:
     a. psycholinguistics   c. linguistic determinism
     b. transformational grammar   d. government and binding theory

36. The hypothesis that language is a reflection of thought processes was proposed by:
     a. John Watson   c. Edward Sapir
     b. Jean Piaget   d. George Miller

37. All of the following research findings support the Sapir-Whorf hypothesis *except*:

a. Because Eskimo languages have more than one word for *snow*, the speakers of these languages think differently about snow than speakers of English do.

b. Chinese speakers have much more difficulty than English speakers in understanding counterfactual reasoning.

c. Although the Dani people of New Guinea have only two words for colors, they were easily able to learn nonsense names for eleven colors.

d. It is easier to think certain thoughts in one language than in another.

38. The number of human languages is estimated to be about:

a. 50
b. 4,000
c. one million
d. three million

39. *Sh, th, h,* and *p* are examples of:

a. phonemes
b. morphemes
c. lexemes
d. syntax

40. The syntax is correct in which of the following sentences:

a. The children came to school on time.
b. The shoe ate the bird.
c. both a and b
d. neither a nor b

41. According to Chomsky, the deep structure of a sentence is essentially its:

a. syntax
b. meaning
c. grammar
d. sequence

42. Chomsky modified his theory of transformational grammar into a new approach known as government and:

a. binding theory
b. context theory
c. syntax theory
d. phoneme theory

43. Children begin to utter meaningful single words, called holophrases, at about age:

a. 6 months
b. 1 year
c. 2 years
d. 3 years

44. Three-year-old Jennie's statement, "He catched the ball," is an example of:

a. inductive reasoning
b. a holophrase
c. overregularization
d. a metacognition

45. Social learning theory suggests that children acquire language primarily by:

a. observing and imitating adults
b. discrimination techniques
c. species uniformity
d. social exchange

46. According to Jerome Bruner, language is acquired from the interaction between:

a. adults and children
b. the LAD and the LASS
c. both a and b
d. neither a nor b

47. In the animal kingdom, the ability to use language is the most highly developed in:

a. dolphins
b. Rhesus monkeys
c. apes
d. Pygmy chimpanzees

48. Research focused on the relationship of the event-related brain potential (ERP) to the processing of information has been performed by:

    a. Emmanuel Donchin   c. Noam Chomsky

    b. David Premack   d. Paul Broca

49. Patients with damage to Broca's area, the frontal lobe of the left cortex, have difficulty:

    a. comprehending the speech of others

    b. producing meaningful speech

    c. singing

    d. hearing the speech of others

50. Damage to the left side of the brain results in aphasia in about:

    a. 50 percent of cases   c. 70 percent of cases

    b. 60 percent of cases   d. 95 percent of cases

Test Yourself: Fill in the Blanks

Directions: Fill in the blanks with the correct term or name.

1. A _____ is a mental representation of the central properties of a class of like objects or instances that serves to group or classify them into categories.

2. _____ is a cognitive process through which we learn major categories of information and the members of those categories.

3. A _____ is a statement that links mental elements in ways that allow us to use those elements for purposes of thought.

4. _____ is a sudden recognition of the correct solution, usually after a period during which we are not consciously thinking about the problem.

5. _____ is the hypothesis that problem solving and other thought processes take place through the establishment of systems of neural associations.

6. A _____ is a problem-solving shortcut or rule of thumb.

7. _____ is the failure to realize that an object can have a use other than the one with which it is most commonly associated.

8. A _____ is a tendency to persist in the use of previously successful strategies, even when they may be inappropriate for the current problem.

9. _____ is the tendency to interpret new information as verifying a preexisting hypothesis.

10. _____ refers to the use of computer hardware and software to solve complex problems in much the same way as humans are thought to solve them.

11. _____ is the process of evaluating two or more alternatives and choosing one of them.

12. _____ is the process by which we generate, examine, and evaluate information.

13. In _____ reasoning, we use logical relationships to determine the validity or truth of our conclusions.

14. _____ suggests that language has three major properties: structure, process, and use.

15. _____, meaning that speakers of different languages perceive and experience the world differently, is often called the _____ hypothesis.

16. A _____ is a distinctive speech sound.

17. _____ is a set of rules that govern the arrangement of words into phrases and sentences.

18. The theory of transformational grammar is associated with _____, a famous psycholinguist.

19. Called nativism, Chomsky's biological approach suggests that humans have a built-in _____, an inborn mechanism that encourages and facilitates language learning.

20. The basic form of speech pathology that results from brain damage is _____, which involves difficulty in producing or comprehending meaningful speech.

Test Yourself: Matching Questions

Directions: For each item in column I, select the item in column II that is most closely associated with it.

I	II
_____1. concept	a. structured system of symbols
_____2. cognition	b. shortcut
_____3. metacognition	c. mental representation
_____4. insight	d. speech problem
_____5. connectionism	e. language determines thought
_____6. algorithm	f. means "to know"
_____7. heuristic	g. word
_____8. functional fixedness	h. rigid thinking
_____9. inductive reasoning	i. Chomsky's theory
_____10. language	j. distinctive speech sound
_____11. linguistic determinism	k. awareness of your cognitions
_____12. phoneme	l. parallel distributed processing
_____13. transformational grammar	m. sudden recognition of a solution
_____14. lexeme	n. specific to general
_____15. aphasia	o. step-by-step solution

Test Yourself: Answer Key

Multiple Choice

1. b	(269)	11. c	(271)	21. d	(275–6)	31. a	(284)	41. b	(291)
2. c	(269)	12. b	(271)	22. c	(277)	32. b	(285)	42. a	(291)
3. a	(269)	13. d	(272)	23. b	(278)	33. a	(284)	43. b	(292)
4. d	(270)	14. a	(272)	24. d	(277–78)	34. d	(283)	44. c	(292)
5. b	(271)	15. c	(273–74)	25. a	(278)	35. c	(286)	45. a	(293)
6. a	(273)	16. a	(274)	26. b	(279)	36. b	(286)	46. c	(294)
7. d	(273)	17. d	(274)	27. b	(282)	37. c	(287)	47. d	(297)
8. a	(272)	18. c	(274)	28. c	(280–2	38. b	(287)	48. a	(301)
9. c	(270)	19. a	(274–75)	29. a	(288)	39. a	(287–88)	49. b	(302)
10.a	(271)	20. b	(275)	30. d	(283)	40. C	(290)	50. d	(302)

Fill in the Blanks

1. concept
2. concept formation
3. proposition
4. insight
5. connectionism
6. heuristic
7. functional fixedness
8. psychological set
9. confirmation bias
10. artificial intelligence (AI)
11. decision making
12. reasoning
13. deductive
14. George Miller
15. linguistic relativism, Sapir-Whorf
16. phoneme
17. syntax
18. Noam Chomsky

19. language acquisition device (LAD)

20. aphasia

Matching Questions

1. c	6. o	11. e
2. f	7. b	12. j
3. k	8. h	13. i
4. m	9. n	14. g
5. l	10.a	15. d

Do These Mini Projects

1. This project is designed to demonstrate in a concrete way the methods you use when you solve a problem, as well as the relationship between the processes of language and thought. Select a problem, such as balancing your checkbook, doing a complex puzzle, or planning a vacation. After you choose the problem, speak out loud into a cassette recorder during the problem-solving process. Make sure that you speak the entire time that you spend on the problem so that you can accumulate verbal data for later analysis that will allow you to (1) pinpoint your problem-solving strategies; (2) define your reasoning and decision-making techniques; (3) identify barriers to successful problem solving; (4) identify strategies that worked for you on that particular type of problem; and (5) analyze the relationship between your verbal and thinking processes. Think about the following: Did verbalizing help or hinder you in the problem-solving process? What problem-solving strategies worked? When and why did you change strategies, and from what to what? What were some of the barriers to problem solving, and how did you attempt to overcome them? To what extent were you successful or unsuccessful, and why?

2. In order to see how you organize concepts, define the following concepts: (1) cow; (2) democracy; (3) family; (4) fear. When defining these concepts, write down their attributes and anything at all you can think of that belongs in a good description of each concept, as though you were explaining the concepts to someone who did not know a lot about them. When you are finished, look at what you wrote and notice how you organized your information, the amount of detail, any hierarchies that you produced, and the differences among these concepts in terms of abstraction. Bring your information to class for sharing.

Pull It All Together

1. At the start of chapter 8, the author of the text states that cognitive processes and language are closely linked to learning (chapter 6) and memory (chapter 7). Now that you have mastered the material in chapter 8, in what specific ways are cognitive processes and language linked to the processes of learning and memory that you studied in chapters 6 and 7? What do we do linguistically and cognitively with information and skills that we learn and remember?

2. Which of the problem-solving strategies described in chapter 8 were already familiar to you? Which ones are new? In what ways, if any, will the information on problem solving presented in this chapter help you in your reasoning and problem-solving efforts in the future? In this same vein, to what extent have you been hampered in your problem-solving efforts by the barriers described in this chapter? Now that you recognize strategies that might have held you back in approaching certain problems, what can you do to improve your problem-solving techniques?

3. The author of the text supports an interactionist view of language acquisition that combines both environmental and biological viewpoints. In what other instances in previous chapters has the author supported an interactionist view?

Chapter Outline

Chapter Overview

Chapter 9 covers the topic of intelligence. Although we all have ideas about what intelligence is, there is a great deal of complexity and controversy surrounding this construct. The differences in the facility with which people learn, remember, and process information reflect differences in cognitive ability, which in turn represent differences in intelligence.

Chapter 9 contains six major sections: (1) "Testing...Testing...," (2) "Theories of Intelligence," (3) "Issues in Human Intelligence," (4) "Controversies in Human Intelligence," (5) "The Ups and Downs of Intelligence," and (6) "The Evolution and Neurophysiology of Intelligence."

The first section ("Testing...Testing...") defines a psychological test as a standardized measure of some aspect of the behavior or performance of an individual. Advantages of psychological testing are discussed. In spite of its advantages, intelligence testing is one of the most controversial topics in the field of psychology because of racial and ethnic group differences in scores. Psychological tests must have three characteristics: standardization, reliability, and validity. Standardization means that everyone is given the same items and instructions, and everyone's test is scored in the same way. A test must also have high reliability and yield consistent scores for an individual relative to the group. Validity is the extent to which a test measures what it is supposed to measure. Any test can be highly reliable without being valid, but you can never have a test that is more valid than it is reliable. The text describes four ways of establishing validity.

Experts agree that intelligence is the capacity for adaptive, goal-directed behavior. The intelligence testing movement started over a century ago with Sir Francis Galton, whose eugenics movement focused on the biological side of the intelligence issue. Alfred Binet and his colleague Theodore Simon compared mental age (MA) to chronological age (CA). Lewis Terman revised Binet's test for use with American schoolchildren and called the new test the Stanford-Binet. He adopted the intelligence quotient (IQ), the ratio of MA to CA multiplied by 100. Aptitude tests predict ability to accomplish something if you are given proper educational opportunities. Achievement tests measure not what you can accomplish but what you have already accomplished. David Wechsler developed the Wechsler Intelligence Scales, including the Wechsler Adult Intelligence Scale (WAIS), the Wechsler Intelligence Scale for Children (WISC), and the Wechsler Preschool and Primary Scale of Intelligence (WPPSI). Group tests, like the SAT and ACT, can simultaneously assess the aptitudes of thousands of people.

The second section ("Theories of Intelligence") describes intelligence as a construct, something abstract that we have to infer from observations we make. Some psychologists have theorized that intelligence is best understood as one general capacity, an overall cognitive ability, whereas others have questioned this view and believe that intelligence can be broken down into a number of relatively independent parts called factors. Charles Spearman developed a statistical technique called factor analysis that is used to determine the component parts of intelligence. When Spearman factor-analyzed his data, he found a general intelligence factor that he called g, and a number of specific (or s) factors. Also using factor analysis, Louis Thurstone theorized that intelligence is composed of primary mental abilities. One of the major current theories of how people reason and solve problems is information-processing theory, which suggests that the person is a system for evaluating and acting on information and that the brain, like a computer, provides the highest level of processing. Robert Sternberg has built the information-processing approach into a general theory of intelligence called the triarchic theory of intelligence, which is described.

The third section ("Issues in Human Intelligence") discusses the decline in population aptitude scores over time, gender differences in specific aptitude scores, and the role of heredity and learning in intelligence. Although IQ scores are rising, SAT scores have been falling. Experts believe that factors such as family size and shortcomings in our educational system have contributed to the decline. Gender differences in aptitude test scores most likely reflect differences in social expectations, educational practices, and biological factors. The differential impacts of nature and nurture have been studied extensively in the area of intelligence. The text considers the results of family, twin, and adoption studies. The bottom line is that scientific research leads us to a three-factor model of influences on cognitive functioning: heredity, environment, and the heredity-environment interaction.

The fourth section ("Controversies in Human Intelligence") deals with racial and ethnic differences in intelligence test scores and how to account for these differences. Group differences tell us nothing about any given individual. Following Galton's lead, Henry Goddard favored a genetic view. In the 1960s, Arthur Jensen also argued for an explanation of group differences based on heredity and was supported by William Shockley; both were accused of being racist. Recently, Philippe Rushton advocated a genetic theory of racial differences in intelligence. The environmental viewpoint is that ethnic and racial differences in intelligence test scores are due to economic and educational factors. The evidence is inconclusive regarding the origins of group differences in intellectual functioning. One possible explanation for group differences in test scores is that the tests themselves are biased. Accuracy of prediction can be improved by applying a balanced multiple-criteria approach, rather than relying on test scores alone to place or label individuals.

The fifth section ("The Ups and Downs of Intelligence") considers the extremes of intellect. We used to classify people as mentally retarded entirely on the basis of IQ. In 1959, the American Association of Mental Retardation (AAMR) established a cutoff IQ score of 85, below which anyone was officially considered to be retarded. In 1973, it dropped that cutoff to 70. Some people classified as mentally retarded manage their everyday lives fairly well, while others do not. There are four ranges or subclasses of retardation: mild, moderate, profound, and severe. Despite extensive studies, little is known about the causes of retardation. Organic retardation, which involves a neural defect, can be clearly diagnosed in only about 25 percent of all cases. Overshadowing all other organic causes are those involving genes and chromosomes. The most commonly diagnosed organic cause is trisomy 21 or Down syndrome. The text also discusses other types of genetically based retardation.

Giftedness, or genius, is formally defined as an IQ greater than 130 combined with high test scores in one or more areas of achievement, such as reading or mathematics. Gifted people also have different styles of thinking than people of average intelligence, and they use higher-level abstractions and integrate complex information more readily. The most famous study research on giftedness is that of Lewis Terman. Although there has been a heavy emphasis in our society on educating the retarded, it is only more recently that we have recognized the special needs of intellectually superior children.

The most intelligent people are not necessarily the most creative. Some minimal level of intelligence is required for creative thinking, but beyond that creativity is fairly independent of general intelligence. Creativity is the ability to develop novel ideas that have some value in society. A common way of measuring creativity is in terms of divergent thinking, which involves generating multiple solutions to the same problem. This section ends with a discussion of the research on the relationship between intellect and aging, and a distinction between fluid and crystallized intelligence.

The final section ("The Evolution and Neurophysiology of Intelligence") describes intelligence as clearly based in the structures and neurochemistry of the brain. Hereditary factors determine the basic nature of neural structure and function, and environmental experience introduces modifications. The author of the text traces the evolution of intellect from the first multicellular, oxygen-breathing species that inhabited the earth nearly 4 billion years ago and had no brain at all to current human functioning. Much of what we know about brain structures that may be involved in intelligence comes from studies of learning, memory, and cognition. It is likely that the prefrontal cortex is heavily involved in the complex cognitive processing that we call intelligence. Other areas of the brain involved in intellectual functioning are the temporal cortex, the hippocampus, the cerebellum, the amygdala, and the thalamus. The neurotransmitters involved in intelligence are discussed. Most neuroscientists are convinced that intelligence does not lie in any one small area of the brain, but rather is spread out over a number of structures. Connectionist models explain how these various areas operate in concert through complex neural associations.

How to Master Chapter 9

Refer to These Learning Objectives

You should be able to achieve the following learning objectives after mastering the material in chapter 9:

Testing…Testing…

1. Define psychological test and explain the advantages of testing.

2. Define and give examples of the three characteristics of test construction: standardization, reliability, and validity.

3. Define human intelligence.

4. Discuss the origins of intelligence testing, including the contributions of Sir Francis Galton, Alfred Binet, Theodore Simon, Lewis Terman, and David Wechsler.

5. Describe how IQ is calculated.

6. Define and distinguish between an aptitude test and an achievement test.

7. Describe the intelligence tests developed by David Wechsler.

8. Give examples of and explain the advantages of group tests.

Theories of Intelligence

9. Explain what is meant by a construct, and discuss the major theories of the construct of intelligence, including those of Charles Spearman, Louis Thurstone, and Robert Sternberg.

10. Discuss the role of factor analysis in theories of intelligence.

11. Describe and distinguish among theories of primary mental abilities, information processing, and the triarchic theory of intelligence.

Issues in Human Intelligence

12. Explain why SAT scores have been declining.

13. Discuss the issues of gender differences in intelligence testing.

Controversies in Human Intelligence

14. Explain what studies of families, twins, and adoption have revealed concerning the nature vs. nurture issue and intelligence.

15. Discuss the controversial issue surrounding minority groups having lower average IQ test scores than the majority group.

16. Describe the beliefs of Henry Goddard, Arthur Jensen, William Shockley, Philippe Rushton, Richard Herrnstein, and Charles Murray concerning genetics and intelligence.

17. Discuss environmental factors that could account for group differences in intelligence test scores.

18. Explain the difference between the issue of test bias and the issue of fairness.

19. Discuss appropriate versus inappropriate uses of tests.

The Ups and Downs of Intelligence

20. Define mental retardation and discuss its causes.

21. Describe the research on and educational implications of giftedness.

22. Discuss the issue and components of creativity.

23. Define and distinguish between fluid and crystallized intelligence, and discuss the impact of aging on intelligence.

The Evolution and Neurophysiology of Intelligence

24. Describe the evolution of intellect.

25. Describe the neurological bases of intelligence in terms of the structures of the brain and the chemicals involved in intellectual functioning.

26. Explain what is meant by saying that intelligence is a neural network.

Debate These Myths

MYTH 1: I must decide if intelligence is inherited through the genes or acquired through environmental influences.

Strategy:

Discuss the nature versus nurture issue as it relates to intelligence:

Discuss how views about the influence of genetics and the environment have been studied by researchers and what they have found:

Explain the concepts of genetic predisposition, the three-factor model, and heredity-environment interaction:

Other statements or examples for debating MYTH 1:

Change MYTH 1 into a true statement:

MYTH 2: *Knowing someone's IQ score tells you a lot about that person's ability.*

Strategy:

Discuss the type of testing that yields an IQ score:

118

Discuss the construct of intelligence as being composed of many diverse types of abilities:

Explain the value of knowing an individual's performance on subtests of an intelligence test and on other measures of ability:

Discuss the issue of bias in testing:

Other statements or examples for debating MYTH 2:

Change MYTH 2 into a true statement:

MYTH 3: *Gifted people are more creative than anyone else.*

Strategy:

Define giftedness:

Discuss the definition and components of creativity:

Explain the relationship between intelligence and creativity:

119

Give an example of an individual with average intelligence who has demonstrated more creativity than a gifted person:

Other statements or examples for debating MYTH 3:

Change MYTH 3 into a true statement:

Test Yourself: Multiple-Choice Questions

Directions: Circle the best response for each of the following questions.

1. A psychological test, whether a test of intelligence or of personality, must be:
    a. standardized
    b. reliable
    c. valid
    d. all of the above

2. Comparative statistics that tell us the characteristics of a test and allow us to determine where a given individual stands are called:
    a. norms
    b. IQs
    c. constructs
    d. metacomponents

3. A test is judged to be reliable if the correlation between two testings is above:
    a. .10
    b. 1.0
    c. .80
    d. .50

4. A problem with test-retest reliability is:
    a. cheating
    b. practice effect
    c. poor norms
    d. low validity

5. On the verbal section of the SAT, researchers divided the items in half for the tenth-graders in New York City and then correlated the two halves in order to determine:
    a. group norms
    b. split-half reliability
    c. standardization
    d. predictive validity

6. A test that was intended to measure self-esteem was actually measuring reading ability. This test was lacking:
    a. content validity
    b. concurrent validity
    c. standardization
    d. norms

7. Criterion-related validity is the same as:
    a. content validity
    b. predictive validity
    c. construct validity
    d. concurrent validity

8. Charles Darwin's theory of natural selection was applied to the study of intelligence and intelligence testing by:

    a. Sir Francis Galton   c. Alfred Binet

    b. Lewis Terman   d. Theodore Simon

9. Alfred Binet's intelligence test was revised for use with American schoolchildren and was named the Stanford-Binet by:

    a. Theodore Simon   c. Lewis Terman

    b. David Wechsler   d. Louis Thurstone

10. The correct formula for calculating IQ is:

    a. MA/CA   c. CA/MA x 100

    b. MA/CA x 100   d. CA/MA

11. Based on the formula for calculating IQ, a 10-year-old child with a mental age of 12 would have an IQ of:

    a. 120   c. 83

    b. 100   d. cannot be determined from this data

12. Megan was tested for her knowledge of algebra after taking two years of algebra in high school. She was most likely given:

    a. an aptitude test   c. an achievement test

    b. an intelligence test   d. the American College Test

13. An IQ score of 100 on any of the Wechsler intelligence scales would fall at the part of the normal distribution called the:

    a. mean   c. median

    b. mode   d. any of the above

14. All of the following are true concerning the Wechsler scales *except*:

    a. they are split into verbal and performance scales

    b. they use a standard deviation of 15

    c. the IQ score distribution falls on a bell-shaped curve

    d. they have low reliability and validity

15. Both the SAT and the ACT would be considered:

    a. group tests   c. nonstandardized tests

    b. tests of creativity   d. Wechsler scales

16. Charles Spearman is known for developing:

    a. information-processing theory

    b. the triarchic theory of intelligence

    c. factor analysis

    d. the primary mental abilities approach

17. The concept of global intellect was supported by the work of:

    a. Louis Thurstone   c. both a and b

    b. Charles Spearman   d. neither a nor b

18. The Test of Primary Abilities was developed through a statistical technique known as:

    a. standardization   c. construct validity

    b. factor analysis   d. knowledge-acquisition

19. Binet and Wechsler viewed intelligence as:

    a. an outcome   c. a process

    b. the same as creativity   d. a set of factors

20. The componential, experiential, and contextual aspects of intelligence are considered by:
    a. Thurstone's theory of primary mental abilities
    b. Alfred Binet's theory of global intelligence
    c. Robert Sternberg's triarchic theory of intelligence
    d. Arthur Jensen's genetic theory of intelligence

21. When Cheryl attended school to learn accounting, she did not just read the textbook, but she challenged herself by asking herself in-depth questions about the material in the text. According to the triarchic theory of intelligence, Cheryl's strategy:
    a. was cumbersome and too time-consuming to lead to efficient learning
    b. was an active learning process that would lead to knowledge acquisition
    c. would work only if she had the genetic potential to learn accounting
    d. tapped into her primary mental ability of word fluency

22. According to the triarchic theory of intelligence, the ability to consider each aspect of a problem and form a symbolic, mental representation of it in words or images is known as:
    a. a performance component   c. both a and b
    b. encoding   d. neither a nor b

23. According to the triarchic theory of intelligence, the step at which you relate the mentally derived resolution back to the problem and its possible solutions is the performance component known as:
    a. comparison   c. encoding
    b. application   d. inference

24. In trying to solve a puzzle, Paul discovered that he had to convert each letter to the number that it represented in the alphabet in order to get the answer. According to the triarchic theory of intelligence, Paul was using:
    a. comparison   c. encoding
    b. application   d. inference

25. The contextual component of the triarchic theory of intelligence allows the individual to:
    a. adapt to the existing environment
    b. choose new environments
    c. modify the existing environment
    d. all of the above

26. According to the triarchic theory of intelligence, a highly intelligent person is one who:
    a. has a substantial capacity for processing information
    b. shows variability in the three aspects of the triarchy
    c. displays strength in seven primary abilities
    d. scores two standard deviations above the mean

27. Since the 1930s, IQ test performance has:
    a. declined   c. remained about the same
    b. increased   d. changed in the same direction as SAT scores

28. Regarding gender differences in performance on the SAT, girls have traditionally:
    a. had lower overall scores than boys
    b. scored lower on verbal section than boys
    c. scored lower on the math section than boys
    d. taken the test more frequently than boys

29. Research on the heritability of intelligence has shown:
   a. no differences in intelligence in pairs of identical versus fraternal twins
   b. greater concordance between IQ scores in identical versus fraternal twins
   c. no relationship in IQ for identical twins reared in separate families
   d. too much fraudulent data to make a judgment on twin studies

30. Adoption studies have revealed that:
   a. the IQ scores of adopted children reflect the IQ scores of adoptive parents
   b. after children have lived with their adoptive parents longer, the IQ scores of adopted children correlate more highly with the IQs of their biological parents
   c. the IQ scores of adopted children are closer to the scores of their adoptive than to biological relatives
   d. the IQ scores of adaptive children correlate highly with the IQ scores of their adoptive parents only when the children were adopted at birth

31. Regarding the nature versus nurture issue and intelligence, all of the following are true *except*:
   a. mathematical abilities are highly heritable
   b. enriched environments can increase IQ scores
   c. children raised in rural settings have lower IQ scores than urban children
   d. heredity accounts for about 20 percent of the variance in general intelligence

32. The bottom line conclusion from scientific research on the nature versus nurture issue in intelligence is that:
   a. hereditary factors account for almost all the variance
   b. environmental factors can overcome heredity
   c. intelligence is influenced by heredity, the environment, and their interaction
   d. the interactional factors are stronger than heredity by itself

33. Research on the IQ scores of minority groups has revealed all of the following *except*:
   a. the IQ scores of minority groups are generally lower than the scores of the majority
   b. Asian Americans score higher on IQ tests than African Americans
   c. the differences in IQ test scores among majority and minority groups is influenced by environmental factors
   d. the origins in group differences in intellectual functioning is based almost entirely on genetic factors

34. Group differences in IQ scores reveal:
   a. differences in intelligence among individuals
   b. that IQ tests are unfair
   c. IQ tests should be eliminated
   d. cultural influences

35. The genetic viewpoint that group differences in IQ scores reflect genetic inferiority and superiority was argued by:
   a. William Shockley   c. Arthur Jensen
   b. Philippe Rushton   d. all of the above

36. That the amount of time spent in school can significantly affect IQ scores:
   a. is supported by about 200 studies
   b. holds true only for minority groups
   c. has not been demonstrated
   d. has been demonstrated, but not replicated

37. IQ has been correlated with:

    a. family income

    b. educational environment of the home

    c. both a and b

    d. neither a nor b

38. The SAT test predicts future academic performance:

    a. more accurately for whites than for blacks

    b. more accurately now than in the past

    c. less accurately than IQ tests

    d. equally well for all ethnic groups

39. Research on teacher expectancy effects has revealed that when teachers are told that their students are bright:

    a. parents expect more from their children

    b. the students score higher on IQ tests

    c. the students develop a laid-back attitude

    d. teachers do not work as hard

40. Between 1959 and 1973, the cutoff IQ score for defining mental retardation changed from:

    a. 85 to 70   c. 20 to 50

    b. 70 to 85   d. 50 to 20

41. All of the following are true concerning the majority of retarded people *except*:

    a. they can conduct their lives reasonably well

    b. they rarely develop high levels of skill

    c. they are classified as "severely retarded"

    d. their IQ scores fall between 50 and 70

42. All of the following apply to trisomy 21, or Down syndrome, *except*:

    a. it is the most commonly diagnosed organic cause of retardation

    b. children with Down syndrome tend to be friendly

    c. Down syndrome is caused by maternal alcohol consumption during pregnancy

    d. children with Down syndrome resemble each other facially

43. Children who appear normal at birth, but who have inherited a recessive gene that results in a deficiency of a liver enzyme and causes profound retardation, are suffering from:

    a. trisomy 21   c. fragile X syndrome

    b. Down syndrome   d. PKU

44. The most famous research on giftedness, which involved following the progress of 1,500 California schoolchildren with high IQs, was conducted by:

    a. Sir Francis Galton   c. William Shockley

    b. Lewis Terman   d. Philippe Rushton

45. In the process of searching for a solution to a complex corporate staffing problem, Ms. Jones, the team leader, asked the members of the team to think of as many possible solutions as they could, as she wrote down their ideas on a blackboard. Ms. Jones was encouraging the use of:

    a. divergent thinking   c. metacomponents

    b. fluid intelligence   d. encoding skills

46. Creative skills, risk taking, expertise, and motivation are components of:
   a. divergent thinking
   c. creative intellect
   b. fluid intelligence
   d. crystallized intelligence

47. Research on aging and IQ has revealed that:
   a. crystallized intelligence continues to rise in old age, as long as the person is intellectually active
   b. fluid intelligence peaks at about age 45
   c. verbal intelligence shows a greater decrease than nonverbal intelligence with advanced age
   d. a person over age 70 can perform an unfamiliar problem more quickly than a person age 20

48. It is *not* true that *Homo sapiens:*
   a. diverged into two human species: Neanderthal and Cro-Magnon
   b. lived in cultural groups
   c. appeared about 30 million years ago
   d. were always capable of speech

49. True mammals first lived:
   a. 250 million years ago
   c. 1 million years ago
   b. 75 to 100 million years ago
   d. 130,000 years ago

50. Of the following brain structures, the one most heavily involved in the complex cognitive processing that we call intelligence is the:
   a. thalamus
   c. parietal lobe
   b. amygdala
   d. prefrontal cortex

Test Yourself: Fill in the Blanks

Directions: Fill in the blanks with the correct term or name.

1. The ability of a test to yield consistent scores for an individual relative to the group is known as
_____.

2. _____ is the extent to which a test measures what it is supposed to measure.

3. _____ validity is established by determining the extent to which the test scores are related to a particular theory that underlies the intelligence construct.

4. When his cousin Charles Darwin proposed his natural selection theory of evolution, _____ applied it to his own developing notions about differential proficiency and is credited with coining the term, *nature-nurture.*

5. When the French government required all children to attend school, _____ developed an intelligence test with his colleague _____ that compared mental age with chronological age.

6. _____ developed the Stanford-Binet, which is still one of the major tests of intelligence.

7. An _____ test measures not what you can accomplish but what you have already accomplished.

8. An _____ test predicts your ability to accomplish something if you are given proper educational opportunities.

9. _____ is a statistical technique that is used to determine the component parts of intelligence.

10. Louis Thurstone developed the _____ approach to intelligence testing.

11. _____ theory suggests that the person is a system for evaluating and acting on information and that the brain acts like a computer.

12. Top-level, coordinating components, called metacomponents, are an important feature of the _____ theory of intelligence developed by _____.

13. An assessment of the genetic influence on the variability of IQs is called _____.

14. _____ effects are changes in a teacher's behavior toward a child based on knowledge of test scores.

15. The most commonly diagnosed organic cause of mental retardation is trisomy 21, or _____.

16. _____ is formally defined as an IQ greater than 130 combined with high scores on tests in one or more areas of achievement, such as reading or mathematics.

17. _____ thinking involves generating multiple solutions to the same problem.

18. _____ intelligence is the ability to reason and manipulate information.

19. _____ intelligence is a base of acquired knowledge and skills.

20. Between 130,000 and 40,000 years ago, *Homo sapiens* appeared and diverged into two human species, _____ and _____.

Test Yourself: Matching Questions

Directions: For each item in column I, select the item in column II that is most closely associated with it.

I	II
_____1. standardization	a. MA/CA x 100
_____2. Sir Francis Galton	b. very set procedure
_____3. Lewis Terman	c. acquired knowledge
_____4. IQ	d. inherited on a recessive gene
_____5. aptitude test	e. eugenics
_____6. achievement test	f. developed WAIS
_____7. David Wechsler	g. ability to reason
_____8. construct	h. Stanford-Binet
_____9. factor analysis	i. predicts ability
_____10. Louis Thurstone	j. triarchic theory of intelligence
_____11. Robert Sternberg	k. generating multiple solutions
_____12. PKU	l. primary mental abilities
_____13. divergent thinking	m. inferred from observations
_____14. fluid intelligence	n. measures accomplishments
_____15. crystallized intelligence	o. statistical technique

Test Yourself: Answer Key

Multiple Choice

1. d	(308–8)	11. a	(311)	21. b	(317–18)	31. d	(323)	41. c	(331)
2. a	(308)	12. c	(311)	22. c	(317)	32. c	(326)	42. c	(332)
3. c	(309)	13. d	(313)	23. a	(317)	33. d	(326)	43. d	(332)
4. b	(309)	14. d	(314)	24. d	(317)	34. d	(329)	44. b	(333)
5. b	(309)	15. a	(314)	25. d	(318)	35. d	327	45. a	(334)
6. a	(309)	16. c	(316)	26. a	(318)	36. a	(328)	46. c	(334–35)
7. d	(309)	17. d	(315)	27. b	(320)	37. c	(328)	47. a	(337)
8. a	(310)	18. b	(316)	28. c	(320)	38. d	(330)	48. c	(338)
9. c	(311)	19. a	(315)	29. b	(322)	39. b	(330)	49. b	(338)
10. b	(311)	20. c	(317)	30. b	(322–23)	40. a	(331)	50. d	(339)

Fill in the Blanks

1. reliability
2. validity
3. construct
4. Sir Francis Galton
5. Alfred Binet, Theodore Simon
6. Lewis Terman
7. achievement
8. aptitude
9. factor analysis
10. primary mental abilities
11. information-processing
12. triarchic, Robert Sternberg
13. heritability
14. teacher expectancy
15. Down syndrome
16. giftedness
17. divergent
18. fluid

19. crystallized

20. Neanderthal, Cro-Magnon

Matching Questions

1. b	6. n	11. j
2. e	7. f	12. d
3. h	8. m	13. k
4. a	9. o	14. g
5. i	10. l	15. c

Do These Mini Projects

1. School systems are required to provide education for all children, regardless of types or levels of intellectual ability. To find out how your local school district provides education for children at both ends of the continuum of intelligence, contact the head of special services and inquire about the policies regarding least restrictive environment, mainstreaming, and special programs. If you can, set up an interview with an administrator or special education teacher so that you can get firsthand information on this important issue. Bring the information you gather to class for sharing.

2. To find out more about people's attitudes toward and experiences with aptitude tests, ask family members, friends, or co-workers if any of them has ever taken an aptitude test for entry into an educational program or for employment purposes. Find out under what circumstances the aptitude test was administered, what types of items the test contained, and how it was used. Think back to your own experiences with aptitude tests, and examine these same issues. Bring the information to class for sharing.

Pull It All Together

1. As pointed out by the author in the text at the start of this chapter on intelligence, the previous chapter, chapter 8, dealt with cognition and the processing of information in the brain, drawing on memories acquired (chapter 7) through learning (chapter 6). What was not discussed in chapter 8 is the fact that different people have different capacities for learning, remembering, and processing information. What have you learned in chapter 9 about the factors that account for such differences?

2. Now that you have mastered the material in chapter 9, how would you define intelligence? Have your views or ways of defining intelligence changed in any way since studying this chapter? If so, how and why?

CHAPTER 10
LIFE-SPAN DEVELOPMENT: INFANCY AND CHILDHOOD

Chapter Outline

Life Span Development: The Journey Begins

The Life Span Emphasis

Nature vs. Nurture

Developmental Continuity

Individuality: Are We Unique?

Nature and Nurture in Human Development

Heredity vs. Environment

Genetic Principles: $1/2 + 1/2 = 1$

Behavior Genetics

Evolution and Individual Development

From Zygote to Newborn to Infant: Early Development

Where Danger Lurks: The Uterine Environment

The Newborn: Sensing and Perceiving the World

Responsiveness and Intellectual Development

Learning in the Newborn

Forming Emotional Bonds: Attachment

Cognitive Development in Infancy and Childhood

Jean Piaget: The Child's Approach to the World

Piaget's Stages of Cognitive Development

Beyond Piaget: Cognitive Development in the 1990s

Lawrence Kohlberg: The Development of Moral Reasoning

Personality Development in Infancy and Childhood

Freud's Theory of Psychosexual Development

Erikson's Theory of Psychosocial Development

Are There Discrete Stages?

Contexts of Development: Parent and Child

The Neurophysiology of Development

Prenatal Neural Development

Physiological Maturation

Chapter Overview

Chapter 10 is the first of two chapters on life span development. Chapter 10 covers infancy and childhood, and chapter 11 will cover adolescence and aging. The author of the text begins chapter 10 by stating that we begin life as a single cell, the product of genetic material contributed by our mother and father. From the moment of conception, both heredity and environment interact to produce a human being. This interaction continues throughout infancy and childhood, influencing physical, cognitive, and emotional development.

Chapter 10 contains six major sections: (1) "Life Span Development: The Journey Begins," (2) "Nature and Nurture in Human Development," (3) "From Zygote to Newborn to Infant: Early Development," (4) "Cognitive Development in Infancy and Childhood," (5) "Personality Development in Infancy and Childhood," and (6) "The Neurophysiology of Development."

The first section ("Life Span Development: The Journey Begins") introduces the area of life span development, which covers human development from conception to death. Until the 1970s, the focus of the field of developmental psychology was on infancy and early childhood. Modern developmental psychology examines changes throughout the life span. Three classical issues are discussed: (1) the nature-nurture controversy, (2) the continuity of development, and (3) the uniqueness of the individual. The nature-nurture controversy, which was introduced in chapter 1, is applied to issues in development, and asks the question to what extent human development is a product of heredity, environment, or a combination of the two. The continuity of development issue asks to what extent human development is continuous or discontinuous. Regarding uniqueness, the elements of development are the same in all people, but they may be combined in unique ways in a given individual.

The second section ("Nature and Nurture in Human Development") explores in greater detail the influences of heredity and environment. First, two extreme historical positions are explored: (1) environmentalism, which insists that behavior is learned and that environment largely determines human personality and behavior, and (2) instinct theory, its opposite, proposing that heredity is the source of most behavior. Modern ethologists, researchers who study the origins of complex behavior patterns in animals, remain interested in the study of instinctual bases of behaviors.

The history of the study of genetics is explored, followed by a discussion of genes, chromosomes, dominant and recessive genes, genotypes, phenotypes, mutation, polygenic transmission, and the Human Genome Project. Direct investigation of the heredity-environment interaction has depended heavily on work over the past several decades in the field of behavior genetics. Family studies, twin studies, and adoption studies have been conducted in an attempt to come to grips with the heredity-environment issue. There is research evidence that points to a strong genetic component in human development. However, environmental factors make a significant contribution as well. The process of individual development involves an ongoing interaction between genes and the environment.

The third section ("From Zygote to Newborn Infant: Early Development") begins with a discussion of the one-cell zygote, which develops into an embryo, which develops into a fetus, and which develops into an infant. Dangers that lurk in the uterine environment, including the mother's use of drugs, maternal diseases, and stress, are mentioned. The normal responses and skills of the newborn are described, including early perceptual skills. Responsiveness and intellectual development in the newborn, although dependent on genetic factors, are affected by parental stimulation and responsiveness. Research on classical and operant conditioning of newborns is discussed. The remainder of this section is devoted to the topics of bonding and attachment. Studies on both humans and monkeys reveal the importance of attachment between infant and caregiver in the development of security. The Harlows' results on monkeys were consistent with the evolutionary attachment theory of John Bowlby and Mary Ainsworth, who observed that human infants become distraught when separated from their mothers and hypothesized that attachment is a survival mechanism of the species. Studies have shown that infants can be just as attached to fathers as to mothers.

The fourth section ("Cognitive Development in Infancy and Childhood") examines Jean Piaget's cognitive theory of development, modern information-processing theory, and Lawrence Kohlberg's theory of moral development. Jean Piaget studied the thought processes of children for over 60 years, producing a powerful legacy of scientific observation and theory. Prior to Piaget's work, children had been seen as passive recipients of information provided by parents and other adults. Piaget emphasized learning as an active process and the development of logical thinking as a central feature of the cognitive learning process. According to Piaget, the child has unique ways of approaching and knowing the world that are called schemes or schemas, mental structures that constitute basic units of knowledge. The constant state of change that characterizes the child's schemes involves two processes, assimilation and accommodation, which are described.

Piaget proposed four stages of cognitive development that unfold on the basis of physiological maturation and occur in a set sequence that can be found at about the same ages in all cultures: (1) sensorimotor stage; (2) preoperational stage; (3) concrete operational stage; and (4) formal operational stage. The features of each of these stages are described. Jerome Bruner, a neo-Piagetian developmentalist, has combined Piaget's theory with learning theory to emphasize how the child processes information about the environment and how that environment rewards and punishes specific behaviors. The text discusses other neo-Piagetians and research on Piaget's theory. More recently, cognitive development has been viewed as the development of information-processing ability. Information-processing theory proposes changes in cognitive capacity over time: changes in the capacity to reason logically, in the availability of a body of knowledge, and in learning and memory skills. Factors that create individual differences in cognitive ability are discussed. The section concludes with a discussion of Lawrence Kohlberg's theory of moral development.

The fifth section ("Personality Development in Infancy and Childhood") begins with a definition of personality as a construct used to refer to the complex but reasonably consistent pattern of thinking, feeling, and behavior we see in an individual. Freud's theory of psychosexual development is described. Freud hypothesized that personality development has a biological basis in physiological maturation and that these maturation processes take the individual through a series of psychosexual stages—discrete periods during which events significantly influence specific aspects of personality development. The stages (oral, anal, phallic, latency, and genital) occur sequentially as the child's inborn sex drive moves from one area of the body to another. Freud's main focus was on the earliest years of life because he believed that personality is developed by school age.

Erik Erikson's theory of psychosocial development emphasizes the social environment as critical in the development of personality. He hypothesizes eight psychosocial stages—the first five span infancy, childhood, and adolescence, and three span the adult years. Each stage involves the resolution of a crisis or conflict, with successful or unsuccessful resolution affecting the outcome of the next stage. The stages are, in order: trust versus mistrust, autonomy versus shame and doubt, initiative versus guilt, industry versus inferiority, identity versus role diffusion, intimacy versus isolation, generativity versus stagnation, and ego integrity versus despair.

The section concludes with a discussion of the role of parents in child development and the influence of the contexts in which the developmental process takes place. Mother-child bonding, the increasing involvement of fathers, and child-rearing practices are discussed. The author considers the differential effects of authoritarian, permissive, and authoritative styles of parenting, as well as how patterns of parenting have changed over the years.

The final section ("The Neurophysiology of Development") examines the neural processes that underlie development, including prenatal neural development, physiological maturation, and critical periods. Maturation is a biological process in which genetic factors direct an orderly sequence of changes that occur with age. The development of the brain is not complete at birth, and considerable neural development takes place during childhood and adolescence. In addition to biological factors, learning can play a role in developmental timing. The role of critical periods is discussed in terms of both animal and human development.

How to Master Chapter 10

Refer to These Learning Objectives

You should be able to achieve the following learning objectives after mastering the material in chapter 10:

Life Span Development: The Journey Begins

1. Explain the concept of life span development.

2. Discuss the three classic theoretical issues in development: nature versus nurture, developmental continuity, and uniqueness.

Nature and Nurture in Human Development

3. Discuss the two opposing historical theories of heredity versus environment: environmentalism and instinct theory.

4. Explain what is meant by preformation theory.

5. Define: gene, dominant gene, recessive gene, chromosome, genotype, phenotype mutation, polygenic transmission, and human genome.

6. Describe the goals and progress of the Human Genome Project.

7. Discuss the field of behavior genetics and the roles of heritability and environmentality in human development.

8. Explain what family studies, twin studies, and adoption studies have revealed concerning the role of the environment and genetics in development.

9. Explain and distinguish between ontogeny and phylogeny and explain how they relate to evolution and individual development.

From Zygote to Newborn to Infant: Early Development

10. Describe the human organism from conception to birth.

11. Discuss the potential dangers to the unborn child.

12. Describe and give examples of the skills of newborns.

13. Discuss the factors that influence responsiveness, intellectual development, and learning in the newborn.

14. Describe the nature and significance of attachment.

15. Describe the work of the Harlows and of Bowlby and Ainsworth on attachment.

Cognitive Development in Infancy and Childhood

16. Describe Piaget's approach to the study of children and their thought processes.

17. Define and give examples of scheme, assimilation, and accommodation.

18. Define and give examples of Piaget's four stages of cognitive development.

19. Discuss the work of the neo-Piagetians.

20. Discuss the information-processing approach to development.

21. Define and give examples of Kohlberg's stages of moral development and how moral reasoning affects behavior.

22. Discuss criticism of Kohlberg's theory.

Personality Development in Infancy and Childhood

23. Explain the meaning of personality.

24. Describe Freud's theory of psychosexual development, including the series of stages proposed by Freud.

25. Describe Erikson's theory of psychosocial development, including the series of stages proposed by Erikson.

26.   Discuss the impact of different parenting styles on development and the roles of mothers, fathers, and child-rearing practices.

The Neurophysiology of Development

27.   Discuss the neural processes that underlie prenatal development, and reflex and motor development in infancy, and the nature of critical periods.

Debate These Myths

MYTH 1: *Newborns and infants are passive.*

Strategy:

Discuss the capabilities of newborns and infants:

Discuss Piaget's theory of cognitive development, particularly the sensorimotor stage and the processes of assimilation and accommodation:

Discuss the active nature of learning and information processing from birth:

Other statements or examples for debating MYTH 1:

Change MYTH 1 into a true statement:

MYTH 2: *We are products of our environments.*

Strategy:

Discuss the nature-nurture controversy:

Explain the point of doing family, twin, and adoption studies and what the results of such studies have revealed:

Discuss current thinking in the field regarding the roles of heredity and environment in human development:

Other statements or examples for debating MYTH 2:

Change MYTH 2 into a true statement:

Test Yourself: Multiple-Choice Questions

Directions: Circle the best response for each of the following questions.

1. "The child is father of the man" is a quote from a:
    a. psychologist
    b. psychiatrist
    c. philosopher
    d. poet

2. Developmental psychologists have studied human development throughout the life span:
    a. since the nineteenth century
    b. in the 1950s
    c. in the 1970s
    d. only recently

3. Regarding the issue of uniqueness, it is safe to assume that the elements of development:
    a. are different in all people
    b. make children unique
    c. combine in unique ways in a given person
    d. create uniqueness cross-culturally

4. The historical viewpoint of environmentalism was supported by:
    a. John Watson
    b. Jean Piaget
    c. William McDougall
    d. Sigmund Freud

5. The preformation theory is now considered:
    a. state of the art
    b. inaccurate
    c. as needing more research
    d. a precursor to environmentalism

6. The number of pairs of chromosomes contained in every cell of the human body is:
    a. 20
    b. 21
    c. 22
    d. 23

7. Laura was born with brown eyes, a dominant trait, which means that regarding eye color she inherited:

   a. two dominant genes

   b. one dominant gene and one recessive gene

   c. either a or b

   d. neither a nor b

8. Of the following, polygenic transmission is exemplified by an individual's:

   a. personality

   b. height

   c. both a and b

   d. neither a nor b

9. The mapping of the human genome:

   a. will never be accomplished

   b. is nearly complete

   c. was completed in the 1970s

   d. is expected to be completed by the year 2110

10. When Carol was a baby, she was easygoing, sociable, and adaptable. As an adult, Carol continues to display these qualities and is considered a well-adjusted extravert by her friends. These types of characteristics are most strongly influenced by:

   a. the environment of the uterus

   b. parenting styles

   c. genetic factors

   d. the modeling of sibling behavior

11. The percentage of obsessive-compulsive children who have at least one parent with the same diagnosis has been found to be:

   a. 21 percent

   b. 35 percent

   c. 51 percent

   d. 71 percent

12. As compared with only 4 percent for fraternal twins, the concordance rate for schizophrenia for identical twins is:

   a. 15 percent

   b. 35 percent

   c. 48 percent

   d. 88 percent

13. The research on twins and adopted children has shown that schizophrenia:

   a. has a genetic basis

   b. is hard to diagnose

   c. is a learned pattern of behavior

   d. was prevalent in control groups

14. Ontogeny is to phylogeny as:

   a. individual is to species

   b. nature is to nurture

   c. genotype is to phenotype

   d. zygote is to embryo

15. After conception, the developing organism is referred to as a fetus beginning with the:

   a. tenth day

   b. sixth week

   c. third month

   d. sixth month

16. For a pregnant woman, drug use, smoking, and malnutrition are considered:

   a. anticoagulants

   b. teratogens

   c. phenotypes

   d. manageable risks

17. The percentage of developmental defects for which the cause is unknown is:

   a. 10 percent

   b. 35 percent

   c. 50 percent

   d. 70 percent

18. Children are first able to turn their heads toward the source of a sound:
    a. as newborns
    c. by age 1 month
    b. by age 4 months
    d. at about 1 year

19. Of the following, most babies have the strongest preference for looking at:
    a. a figure eight
    c. the face of someone unknown
    b. seven straight lines in a row
    d. the color red

20. Babies prefer the voices of their mothers to those of other women beginning at age:
    a. 3 days
    c. two weeks
    b. one week
    d. one month

21. Of the following, the best example of the application of operant conditioning to the behavior of infants would be:
    a. withholding the bottle until the infant is willing to show a stronger sucking response
    b. rewarding only strong sucking behavior to facilitate nourishing the infant
    c. keeping the infant awake as long as possible in the evening to establish a healthier sleep pattern
    d. rewarding outgoing behavior and ignoring shyness in order to establish more adaptable personality traits

22. It can be concluded from research on attachment that an infant is most likely to be securely attached when the mother:
    a. expects the infant to reach her or his potential
    b. makes sure the infant sleeps through the night
    c. responds to the crying infant
    d. is the only caregiver

23. The Harlows' research on attachment in monkeys demonstrated that:
    a. attachment is based on the satisfaction of hunger
    b. separation from mother in infancy does irreversible damage
    c. bodily contact and comfort are important elements of attachment
    d. bottle feeding is just as nurturing as breast-feeding

24. John Bowlby and Mary Ainsworth are known for their theory of:
    a. the human genome
    c. cognitive development
    b. evolutionary attachment
    d. social development

25. Which one of the following children demonstrates the *least* evidence of secure attachment?
    a. Kurt, who in third grade waves his hand eagerly to answer questions
    b. Michelle, who in fifth grade prefers reading to sports
    c. Lou, who in preschool separates easily from his mother in the morning
    d. Tina, who in kindergarten yells at her peers to get her way

26. Six-month-old Janie discovered that when she cries one way, nobody responds, but when she cries a different way, her mother comes immediately. Janie is demonstrating the process of:
    a. accommodation
    c. attachment
    b. assimilation
    d. egocentrism

27. Schemes are all of the following *except:*
    a. logical
    c. mental structures
    b. random
    d. patterns

28. When nine-month-old Doug saw his ball roll under the sofa, at which point he could no longer see it, he did not look for it and acted as though the ball had disappeared, because Doug has not yet achieved:
   a. secure attachment
   b. sensorimotor skills
   c. a sense of object permanence
   d. the grasping reflex

29. When three-year-old Susie's parents took her to preschool through the back door, when she was accustomed to entering through the front door, Susie cried, because to her it appeared to be a different school. Susie is:
   a. still egocentric
   b. insecurely attached
   c. delayed in her development
   d. in the concrete-operational stage

30. In Piaget's theory, egocentrism refers to:
   a. selfishness
   b. immature thought
   c. stubbornness
   d. delayed development

31. Megan is beginning to use words to label objects in her environment, and she likes to pretend her teddy bear is alive. It is most likely that Megan is at the beginning of which of the following stages of cognitive development?
   a. sensorimotor
   b. concrete-operational
   c. formal-operational
   d. preoperational

32. In Piaget's theory, conservation is achieved during the:
   a. formal-operational stage
   b. sensorimotor stage
   c. concrete-operational stage
   d. preoperational stage

33. When Kevin was in kindergarten, his teacher took a ball of clay and made it into a sausage shape. Kevin thought the clay had grown, even though no new clay was added, because Kevin:
   a. was egocentric
   b. lacked experience with clay
   c. did not grasp the concept of conservation
   d. was still in the sensorimotor stage

34. Concepts such as *democracy* and *potential* cannot be understood fully before a child reaches the:
   a. sensorimotor stage
   b. preoperational stage
   c. concrete-operational stage
   d. formal-operational stage

35. A neo-Piagetian, Jerome Bruner emphasizes the level of development of the person's:
   a. behavior
   b. sensitivity
   c. thought process
   d. attachment

36. The capacity to reason logically, a change in body of knowledge, and a change in learning and memory are key ingredients in the development of:
   a. formal operations
   b. information processing ability
   c. individual differences
   d. genetic predispositions

37. Lawrence Kohlberg's theory proposes stages of:
   a. social development
   b. cognitive development
   c. psychosexual development
   d. moral development

38. Consider this dilemma. You have a final exam tomorrow, and you know that if you don't study tonight, you will fail. Your best friend calls and says she is depressed and wants you to come over right away. The theorist most likely to be interested in people's reactions to this dilemma would be:
   a. Piaget
   b. Freud
   c. Kohlberg
   d. Erikson

39. Which one of the following is the best example of functioning at the preconventional level of morality?

    a. returning a book you stole from a store out of an attack of conscience

    b. sitting quietly in class after being threatened with time out

    c. studying for a test in order to get your father's approval

    d. giving up your seat to an elderly person because it is the right thing to do

40. Kohlberg's theory of moral development has been faulted for:

    a. disadvantaging women   c. both a and b

    b. bias toward male responses   d. neither a nor b

41. At 35, Ed finds it difficult to part with money, even though he is wealthy. He is inflexible in his thinking and becomes anxious when things pile up on his desk. According to Freud's theory of psychosexual development, Ed is likely stuck in which stage?

    a. oral   c. phallic

    b. latency   d. anal

42. According to Freud, sex drive:

    a. is inborn

    b. increases in a linear fashion throughout development

    c. is strongest between the ages of 6 and 12 years

    d. is virtually nonexistent during the oral stage

43. Erik Erikson's theory of psychosocial development focuses on:

    a. infancy and early childhood   c. adult development

    b. adolescence   d. development throughout the life span

44. Erikson's stage of trust versus mistrust occurs:

    a. during the first year of life   c. throughout the life span

    b. in elementary school   d. in adolescence

45. In Erikson's theory, the first stage of adulthood involves resolving the conflict between:

    a. identity and role diffusion   c. intimacy and isolation

    b. generativity and stagnation   d. autonomy versus shame and doubt

46. When diagnosed with cancer, 89-year-old Vera was able to feel at peace with herself because she felt she had lived her life to the fullest. According to Erikson, Vera is experiencing:

    a. trust   c. autonomy

    b. ego integrity   d. initiative

47. Research on parenting styles has revealed that:

    a. authoritative parents produce children who are self-reliant and friendly

    b. the children of permissive parents are mature but discontented

    c. the children of authoritarian parents are the most loyal

    d. parenting style makes no difference, due to the overriding impact of genetics

48. The thalamus, limbic system, and other subcortical structures are fairly complete and ready to receive axons from the cortex at about:

    a. 2 weeks after conception   c. the day the child is born

    b. 35 days after conception   d. 2 weeks after the child is born

49. At birth, the percentage of children's adult brain weight is about:

    a. 10 percent   c. 50 percent

    b. 25 percent   d. 90 percent

50. Eric Lenneberg has hypothesized that language learning occurs:
   a. through imprinting
   b. subcortically
   c. in early infancy
   d. during a sensitive period

Test Yourself: Fill in the Blanks

Directions: Fill in the blanks with the correct term or name.

1. Your _____ is your basic genetic makeup.

2. A _____ is a long, coiled strand of DNA that carries and organizes genetic information.

3. _____ are segments of deoxyribonucleic acid (DNA) that constitute the basic units of genetic transmission and are found in every cell in the body.

4. Your _____ consists of your actual, manifest characteristics, the expression of the genotype.

5. _____ are modifications of the genetic code that represent errors during DNA replication.

6. The human _____ is the total set of genes and chromosomes.

7. _____ is the proportion of phenotypic variation that can be attributed to environmental variation.

8. _____ is the evolutionary history of the species.

9. _____ is the lifelong growth and development of one person.

10. A _____ is one cell, the union of egg and sperm.

11. _____ refers to the development of lifelong emotional bonds between infants and their mothers or other caregivers.

12. _____ is the Piagetian concept that refers to taking in an aspect of the environment and making it conform to existing schemes.

13. _____ is the Piagetian concept that involves the modification of existing schemes in response to new information from the environment.

14. _____ is the understanding that the quantity, length, weight, number, mass, area, and volume of a substance do not change merely due to a change in the substance's appearance.

15. Being unable to look at things from another person's viewpoint is known as _____.

16. Kohlberg is known for his theory of _____ reasoning.

17. Psychosexual stages of development were proposed by _____.

18. According to Erikson, the conflict of adolescence is the _____ crisis.

19. _____ reflexes are innate, unlearned responses to stimuli.

20. _____ is a biological process in which genetic factors direct an orderly sequence of changes that occur with age.

Test Yourself: Matching Questions

Directions: For each item in column I, select the item in column II that is most closely associated with it.

I	II
_____1. chromosome	a. psychosocial development
_____2. genotype	b. preoperational characteristic
_____3. concordance	c. stages of cognitive development
_____4. phylogeny	d. very brief, singular time
_____5. Bowlby and Ainsworth	e. strand of DNA
_____6. Jean Piaget	f. degree of agreement
_____7. scheme	g. an instinctual tendency
_____8. egocentrism	h. basic genetic makeup
_____9. Lawrence Kohlberg	i. median age
_____10. Sigmund Freud	j. levels of moral development
_____11. Erik Erikson	k. evolutionary attachment theory
_____12. primary reflex	l. psychosocial development
_____13. developmental norm	m. mental structure
_____14. imprinting	n. evolutionary history of the species
_____15. critical period	o. innate response

Test Yourself: Answer Key

Multiple Choice

1. d (345)	11. d (351)	21. b (359)	31. d (365)	41. d (371)
2. d (345)	12. c (353)	22. c (359)	32. c (365)	42. a (371)
3. c (346)	13. a (354)	23. c (360)	33. c (365)	43. d (372)
4. a (347)	14. a (354)	24. b (360)	34. d (365)	44. a (372)
5. b (347)	15. c (355)	25. d (360)	35. a (366)	45. c (373)
6. d (348)	16. b (356)	26. a (363)	36. b (367)	46. b (373)
7. c (348)	17. d (356)	27. b (362–63)	37. d (368)	47. a (376)
8. c (350)	18. a (357)	28. c (364)	38. c (368)	48. b (377)
9. b (350)	19. c (357)	29. a (365)	39. b (368)	49. b (379)
10. c (351)	20. a (357)	30. b (365)	40. c (370)	50. d (380)

Fill in the Blanks

1. genotype
2. chromosome
3. genes
4. phenotype
5. mutations
6. genome
7. environmentality
8. phylogeny
9. ontogeny
10. zygote
11. attachment
12. assimilation
13. accommodation
14. conservation
15. egocentrism
16. moral
17. Sigmund Freud
18. identity

19. primary

20. maturation

Matching Questions

1. e	6. c	11. a
2. h	7. m	12. o
3. f	8. b	13. i
4. n	9. j	14. g
5. k	10. l	15. d

Do These Mini Projects

1. To integrate the information on the impact of heredity and environment on human development, it might be helpful for you to make a list of genetic factors and a list of environmental factors that influence development in infancy and childhood. Look through chapter 10 at the research findings that are relevant to this issue, and organize the information. You may use the following format, or one that you create yourself.

	Genetic Influences	Environmental Influences
Cognitive development:		
Social development:		
Psychosexual development:		

When your summary is complete, write an explanation of how genetic and environmental influences work together to influence the course of development prenatally, in infancy, and in childhood.

2. Make arrangements to visit on or two day-care centers or preschools in your community and observe the following: (1) how children are grouped; (2) the physical nature of the environment; (3) the amount of structure versus permissiveness provided; (4) how children of the same age are similar and different from each other in temperament, introversion-extroversion, skills, and interests; (5) the types of activities provided; and (6) peer interaction among the children. Bring your observations to class for sharing.

3. Do some naturalistic observation of parents with their children in public places, like the grocery store, a restaurant, on the bus, and notice how the parents you observe interact with their infants and children. How do different parents react to a child who disobeys? How do different parents attend to their children's needs?

What tones of voices do you hear? What types of messages do different parents give their children verbally and nonverbally? Do fathers differ from mothers in their behavior with children? Just observe quietly—do not intervene. Bring your observations to class for sharing.

Pull It All Together

1. One of the themes carried through this chapter that has also been carried through the rest of the text thus far is the nature versus nurture issue—the differential effects of genetic and environmental factors and the interaction between them. Go back to chapter 1 and explain the history and significance of this issue in psychology. Then, look through the chapters that you studied subsequently and explain how this debate relates to the various subfields of psychology. What are the findings so far, including those in chapter 10, regarding the impact of nature and nurture?

2. In chapter 10, a variety of famous stage theories of development are presented, including those of Jean Piaget, Lawrence Kohlberg, Sigmund Freud, and Erik Erikson. In any stage theory, how would you explain the transition from one stage to another in terms of the continuity versus discontinuity issue in development? In what ways do you view development as continuous? discontinuous?

3. The issue of uniqueness is brought up in chapter 10. Given the topics you have studied so far in the field of psychology—including development, intelligence, language, cognition, memory, learning, consciousness, neuroscience, and nature versus nurture—to what extent do we all share the same basic mechanisms of functioning, and to what extent are we all unique individuals?

Chapter Outline

Chapter Overview

Chapter 11 covers life span development from adolescence through death. As the author states at the start of this chapter, the process of development and change does not stop with the arrival of puberty. Researchers have found that life beyond childhood shows distinct developmental patterns, best described in terms of the challenges and tasks that must be faced during the various life periods.

Chapter 11 contains five major sections: (1) "Evolution and Adulthood," (2) "Adolescence: Transition to Adulthood," (3) "Adult Development: From Maturity to Old Age," (4) "The Older Adult: Living Longer and Living Better," and (5) "The Biology and Neurophysiology of Aging."

The first section ("Evolution and Adulthood") points out that development throughout the life span continues to be affected by genetic factors that are a product of the evolutionary history of the species. A variety of characteristics, including certain diseases, are genetically based but do not show up until adulthood. Development throughout the life span is studied through the application of three research designs: (1) cross-sectional; (2) longitudinal; and (3) sequential. In cross-sectional studies, comparisons are made between groups of different ages. In longitudinal studies, a single group is followed over time. Sequential studies combine both techniques.

The second section ("Adolescence: Transition to Adulthood") describes the biological, social, emotional, and cognitive changes that take place over this rapid transitional time. One of the major tasks of adolescence is to deal with the remarkable physical changes that occur in rapid succession. The issues of teen pregnancy and AIDS are discussed. Regarding personality development during adolescence, this point in development is characterized by the crisis of identity versus role confusion, according to Erik Erikson. Expectations and physical and social pressures can combine to create an identity crisis. As part of resolving the identity crisis, adolescents must deal with the classic tug-of-war between their peers and their parents, the issues of gender roles and gender identity, and ethnicity.

The third section ("Adult Development: From Maturity to Old Age") covers the portion of the life span that begins when maturity is reached. Three types of maturity are considered: biological, psychological, and social. Erikson's three stages of adult development are intimacy versus isolation (young adulthood), generativity versus stagnation (middle adulthood), and ego integrity versus despair (age 45 on, especially old age). Biological changes, including menopause, are discussed, as are cognitive, personality, and social development. Issues of marriage, family, divorce, parenthood, empty nest, career development, and unemployment are concerns in adult development.

The fourth section ("The Older Adult: Living Longer and Living Better") discusses the aging process and how aging has changed in our society, due in part to longer life expectancy. Ageism is a form of prejudice and discrimination based on age. Cognitive changes during the aging process are discussed. Studies show a slowing of motor processes and a reduction in physiological functions in older adults, and a decline in verbal learning ability and memory, particularly after age 65. However, the majority of older people do not experience a decline in intelligence. Regarding personality, stability is still the rule, probably because of genetic factors. The vast majority of older people are in good mental health, although the frequency of depression is higher in the elderly. Other changes that are considered during this stage of development are family and social changes, retirement, grandparenthood, and widowhood.

Three types of death are defined: clinical death, brain death, and social death. The meaning of death and stages of death are discussed, including the stages of dying outlined by Elisabeth Kübler-Ross: (1) denial and isolation; (2) anger and resentment; (3) bargaining; (4) depression; and (5) acceptance.

The final section ("The Biology and Neurophysiology of Aging") discusses why we age (one of the principal questions underlying gerontology), and the study of the aging process and its effects. All human beings are subject to primary aging, the inevitable biological process of gradual and continuing changes in various bodily organs and systems that will eventually result in death. Primary aging is complicated by secondary aging, aging that is at least partially under the individual's control. Family longevity, environmental support, life satisfaction, and health practices may contribute to long life. Life span is the maximum length of life that is biologically possible, which is currently estimated at between 100 and 140 years.

Cellular theories attribute the aging process to genetic mechanisms that operate at the level of the individual cell to cause the symptoms of aging. One such theory suggests that changes in and damage to the DNA molecules are responsible. An alternative cellular theory suggests a direct genetic predisposition toward eventual destruction of cells. Physiological theories suggest that aging takes place not so much in individual cells as in organ systems, perhaps the gradual decline of the endocrine system. The chapter ends with a discussion of the dying brain. The ongoing neural decline most likely accounts for some of the functional physiological deterioration commonly seen with aging.

How to Master Chapter 11

Refer to These Learning Objectives

You should be able to achieve the following learning objectives after mastering the material in chapter 11:

Evolution and Adulthood

1. Discuss heredity and adulthood and the ongoing nature of evolution.

2. Describe and give examples of how cross-sectional, longitudinal, and sequential designs are used to study developmental processes and changes.

Adolescence: Transition to Adulthood

3. Explain why adolescence is considered a transitional time.

4. Describe the biology of puberty and the hormonal changes that occur during adolescence.

5. Discuss the issues of teen pregnancy and AIDS.

6. Explain the crisis of identity versus role confusion and the identity crisis.

7. Discuss the roles of peers and parents during adolescence.

8. Define gender role and gender identity, and discuss gender schema theory and ethnicity.

Adult Development: From Maturity to Old Age

9. Distinguish among biological, psychological, and social maturity in adulthood.

10. Discuss Erikson's stages of adult development.

11. Describe the biological and cognitive changes of adulthood.

12. Discuss the personality and social issues of adulthood.

13. Describe the nature of marriage, divorce, parenthood, and career development during adulthood.

The Older Adult: Living Longer and Living Better

14. Describe the statistics on life expectancy.

15. Explain the myth of "elderly."

16. Describe and give examples of changes in cognition during the aging process.

17. Discuss personality change during the aging process.

18. Discuss the issue of aging and psychopathology.

19. Describe and give examples of family and social changes that typically occur during the aging process.

20. Define death, the meaning of death, and the stages of dying.

21. Distinguish between primary and secondary aging.

22. Define the life span.

23. Describe the theories of aging, including cellular and physiological theories.

The Biology and Neurophysiology of Aging

24. Describe the nature of physiological deterioration of the brain during aging.

25. Describe the nature of antioxidants and free radicals.

Debate These Myths

MYTH 1: *Most teenagers reject their parents' values.*

Strategy:

Discuss the task of teenagers to develop an identity:

Describe the pressures on teenagers during the classic tug-of-war between their peers and their parents:

Discuss research findings regarding the advice-seeking behavior of teens and the role of parents in instilling values in teens:

Other statements and examples for debating MYTH 1:

Change MYTH 1 into a true statement:

MYTH 2: *After adolescence, there are hardly any changes in cognitive development.*

Strategy:

Describe the nature of cognitive development during adulthood, including postformal thought:

Discuss changes that take place in cognitive functioning during the aging process:

Other statements and examples for debating MYTH 2:

Change MYTH 2 into a true statement:

MYTH 3: *Almost everyone fears death.*

Strategy:

Discuss the nature of death and dying:

Explain Erikson's concept of ego integrity versus despair:

Discuss how despair can be avoided or overcome:

Discuss the stages of dying described by Kübler-Ross, including the last stage, acceptance:

Other statements and examples for debating MYTH 3:

Change MYTH 3 into a true statement:

Test Yourself: Multiple-Choice Questions

Directions: Circle the best response for each of the following questions.

1. Evolutionary theorists hypothesize that the human tendency toward social cooperation:
    a. has a partially hereditary basis
    b. has evolved over the centuries
    c. promotes survival and reproduction
    d. all of the above

2. A study in which the fluid intelligence of a group of 16-year-olds is compared to the fluid intelligence of a different group of 56-year-olds would be considered:
    a. cross-sectional
    b. longitudinal
    c. sequential
    d. invalid

3. The results of the study described in question 2 might be difficult to interpret due to:
    a. ageism
    b. the placebo effect
    c. cohort effects
    d. practice effects

4. In order to study continuities and discontinuities in intelligence, a group of researchers gave a battery of tests to 500 three-year-olds, factor-analyzed the data, and then tested the same children at ages 4 years, 5 years, 7 years, 9 years, and 12 years. The researchers correlated the factors isolated at each level with each other. This study would be considered:
    a. longitudinal
    b. cross-sectional
    c. sequential
    d. experimental

5. The biggest potential problem with interpreting the data of the study described in question 4 would be:
    a. cohort effects
    b. practice effects
    c. social changes
    d. expense

6. All of the following apply to longitudinal studies *except:*
    a. practice effects
    b. cohort effects
    c. single group of participants
    d. slow to conduct

7. Sequential studies combine:
    a. cross-sectional and longitudinal designs
    b. cohort and practice effects
    c. correlations and comparisons
    d. hereditary and environmental factors

8.   Currently, the age range of adolescence is considered to be:

   a.   12 to 18   c.   13 to 18
   b.   12 to 20   d.   13 to 21

9.   The adolescent growth spurt begins, on the average, at:

   a.   age 13 in girls and age 15 in boys
   b.   age 13 in boys and age 15 in girls
   c.   age 11 in girls and age 13 in boys
   d.   age 11 in boys and age 13 in girls

10.   As compared with girls who lived during the early part of the nineteenth century, girls today experience menarche:

   a.   3.5 years sooner   c.   1.5 years sooner
   b.   2.5 years sooner   d.   2.5 years later

11.   Initial sperm production occurs in about 50 percent of boys by age:

   a.   13   c.   15
   b.   14   d.   16

12.   All of the following are secondary sex characteristics *except:*

   a.   underarm hair growth in boys
   b.   underarm hair growth in girls
   c.   breast development in girls
   d.   initial sperm production in boys

13.   It is estimated that 50 percent of boys have had sexual intercourse by age:

   a.   13   c.   15
   b.   14   d.   16

14.   It is estimated that 50 percent of girls have had sexual intercourse by age:

   a.   14   c.   16
   b.   15   d.   17

15.   The rate of teen pregnancy has dramatically increased mostly because:

   a.   teenage girls are becoming increasingly fertile
   b.   romantic relationships among teens are lasting longer
   c.   many teens lack knowledge about contraception
   d.   contraception is less effective during adolescence

16.   Of the total number of cases of AIDS estimated by the World Health Organization, the number reported for people between the ages of 13 and 24 is:

   a.   21   c.   2,100
   b.   210   d.   21,000

17.   The noted turn-of-the-century psychologist who believed that adolescence is basically one long crisis is named:

   a.   G. Stanley Hall   c.   Erik Erikson
   b.   John Watson   d.   Daniel Levinson

18.   The crisis of adolescence known as identity versus role confusion was proposed by:

   a.   G. Stanley Hall   c. Erik Erikson
   b.   Sigmund Freud   d. Leonard Hayflick

19.   In 1994, single parents accounted for:
       a.   10 percent of all white parents and 50 percent of all black parents
       b.   25 percent of all white parents and 65 percent of all black parents
       c.   10 percent of all black parents and 50 percent of all white parents
       d.   25 percent of all white parents and 25 percent of all black parents

20.   The most accurate conclusion that can be drawn from research on the turmoil of adolescence is that most teenagers:
       a.   are not in crisis   c.   have poor mental health
       b.   hate their parents   d.   do not use contraception

21.   Research on the influence of peers versus parents during adolescence has revealed that:
       a.   parents are more responsible than peers for juvenile delinquency
       b.   more teenagers seek parental over peer advice
       c.   both a and b
       d.   neither a nor b

22.   Drinking parents influence their children to abuse alcohol and drugs by:
       a.   modeling the behavior
       b.   adding stress to their children's lives
       c.   failing to monitor their children's behavior
       d.   all of the above

23.   Boys and girls begin to learn the components of their gender roles:
       a.   at preschool age   c.   around fourth grade
       b.   around age 12   d.   during adolescence

24.   Believing that grown men should not cry is an example of:
       a.   formation of gender identity
       b.   gender-role stereotyping
       c.   gender schema theory
       d.   an androgynous belief

25.   An adolescent boy who considers working toward nursing as a career realizes that certain behaviors and choices are:
       a.   biological   c.   androgynous
       b.   postformal   d.   Sturm and Drang

26.   Of the following examples of maturity, the one that would be reached earliest in development is:
       a.   being able to carry a pregnancy to full term
       b.   functioning as an established part of a large organization
       c.   being capable of commitment and emotional intimacy
       d.   dealing with change effectively

27.   Social maturity arrives when we:
       a.   begin to think through the implications of our actions
       b.   plan our careers
       c.   establish stable family and work roles
       d.   become capable of reproduction

28. Daniel Levinson's theory of adulthood has been criticized for:

    a. emphasis on the widespread occurrence of a midlife crisis

    b. emphasis on the biological changes in adulthood

    c. neglecting to delineate clear-cut stages of adult development

    d. neglecting to include old age as a stage of adulthood

29. Menopause begins at an average age of:

    a. 31   c. 51

    b. 41   d. 61

30. Which one of the following statements regarding menopause is the most accurate?

    a. Women are particularly fertile at the beginning stages of menopause.

    b. The majority of women experience few of no emotional symptoms when menopause begins.

    c. The increased estrogen levels during menopause can contribute to the development of osteoporosis.

    d. "Hot flashes" only occur after a woman no longer experiences any menstrual periods.

31. As compared with formal operations, postformal thought would be best described as more:

    a. absolute and at its peak during adolescence

    b. complex and at its peak in adulthood

    c. situation-specific and dynamic

    d. integrated and used primarily within the individual's area of expertise

32. In terms of personality development, it is likely that an extroverted young adult will become:

    a. more introverted with age   c. more extroverted with age

    b. more independent with age   d. an extroverted older adult

33. Leiben is to Arbeiten as:

    a. love is to work   c. young is to old

    b. heredity is to environment   d. adolescent is to adult

34. Between 1955 and 1992, statistics reveal that the percentage of unmarried people of ages 25 to 29 increased from:

    a. 10 to 30 percent for men   c. 14 to 41 percent for women

    b. 10 to 44 percent for men   d. 30 to 54 percent for women

35. The percentage of people who get married again after divorce is:

    a. 35   c. 65

    b. 45   d. 85

36. Reasons for the increase in the rate of divorce include:

    a. more acceptance of divorce in society

    b. genetic factors

    c. both a and b

    d. neither a nor b

37. Research on career development has found that:

    a. now that many women work, husbands are doing half the housework

    b. gifted women are impressed with the availability of role models

    c. women are exposed to a wide variety of networking skills

    d. jobs interfere with family life more than the other way around

38. Adults who reach age 75 should live another:

   a. 3 years
   b. 5 years
   c. 8 years
   d. 11 years

39. Forcing a physically and mentally healthy person to retire at the age of 65 is an example of:

   a. ageism
   b. gender identity
   c. gerontology
   d. androgynous behavior

40. Which one of the following represents the most likely difference in functioning between a man at age 30 and the same man at age 70?

   a. At age 70, he would be slower to react to the unexpected when driving a car.
   b. At age 70, he would have a more difficult time recalling the plot of a novel he just read.
   c. At age 30, he was better able to attend selectively to conversations.
   d. At age 30, his long-term memory was more accurate.

41. Of the following aspects of human functioning, the most stable over time is:

   a. cognitive functioning
   b. social development
   c. personality
   d. neuronal functioning

42. Of the following types of psychopathology, research has found that the most commonly occurring one in the elderly is:

   a. anxiety
   b. depression
   c. obsessive-compulsive disorder
   d. aggressive tendencies

43. A study on the styles of grandmothers revealed that the symbolic grandmother:

   a. emphasizes the personal aspects of grandparenting
   b. has strict moral standards
   c. is very involved with her grandchildren
   d. assumes full-time care of the grandchild

44. Bereavement, yearning, disorganization, and reorganization are stages in the adjustment to:

   a. aging
   b. job loss
   c. dying
   d. widowhood

45. Clinical death occurs when:

   a. breathing stops
   b. there is no spontaneous heartbeat
   c. both a and b
   d. there is a flat EEG

46. According to Elisabeth Kübler-Ross, anger and resentment:

   a. constitute the second stage of dying, after denial and isolation
   b. can be avoided when facing death if the individual has never been depressed
   c. are part of the fourth stage of dying, immediately preceding acceptance
   d. are rarely expressed to loved ones when we face death

47. The process of primary aging is characterized by:

   a. chronic disease
   b. being under one's control
   c. inevitability
   d. abusive practices

48. Leonard Hayflick's theory of aging suggests:

   a. that DNA molecules of genes within the cell become damaged by chemicals
   b. a direct genetic predisposition toward eventual destruction of cells
   c. a gradual decline in the functioning of the endocrine system
   d. a progressive loss of neurons in the brain

49. Vitamin C, vitamin E, and beta carotene are all considered:
   a. antioxidants
   b. as increasing the life span
   c. free radicals
   d. part of the diets of most aging adults

50. All of the following are true concerning free radicals, *except* that they:
   a. have been associated with heart disease
   b. promote aging
   c. can be destroyed by antioxidants
   d. are abundant in fruits and vegetables

Test Yourself: Fill in the Blanks

Directions: Fill in the blanks with the correct term or name.

1. In a _____ study, comparisons are made between groups of different ages.

2. In _____ studies, a single group of participants from the same cohort is followed for a long period of time.

3. The sequential study, which involves the cross-sectional comparison of two or more groups of subjects who are followed longitudinally over time was developed by _____.

4. In girls, the onset of _____ is signaled by the menarche.

5. Pubic and underarm hair growth in both sexes, breast development in girls, and a lowering of voice pitch and growth of facial hair in boys are all considered _____ characteristics.

6. The result of the combined physical, psychological, and social pressures is the _____ crisis that characterizes adolescence.

7. Some people engage in gender role _____ and believe that certain behaviors and only those behaviors are appropriate for members of a given gender.

8. _____ theory holds that gender identity acts as a central focus around which children and adolescents organize social perceptions of themselves and others.

9. _____ maturity arrives when stable family and work roles are established.

10. With _____ maturity, we begin to routinely engage in such adult behaviors as planning, thinking through the implications of our actions, adapting more readily to new situations, and becoming involved in _____ relationships.

11. _____ is the point at which the ovaries cease to produce estrogen, menstrual periods end, and the woman is no longer fertile.

12. _____ is known for emphasizing a midlife crisis for men.

13. For the _____ thinker, reality consists of numerous, integrated dynamic systems that are interdependent, and knowledge thus depends on context.

14. _____ is a form of prejudice and discrimination based on age.

15. _____ death is characterized by a flat electroencephalogram (EEG), showing no cortical activity, a complete lack of reflexes, and a total failure to respond to stimuli or to breathe without a respirator.

16. _____ death occurs when there is no longer a spontaneous heartbeat and when breathing stops.

17. _____ is known for proposing five stages of dying: denial and isolation; anger and resentment; bargaining; depression; and acceptance.

18. _____ aging is the inevitable biological process of gradual and continuing changes in various body organs and systems that will eventually result in death.

19. _____ aging is aging that is at least partially under the individual's control.

20. _____ refers to the maximum length of life that is biologically possible.

Test Yourself: Matching Questions

Directions: For each item in column I, select the item in column II that is most closely associated with it.

I	II
_____1. menarche	a. capable of reproduction
_____2. puberty	b. first menstrual period
_____3. androgynous	c. chemicals that damage tissues
_____4. gender identity	d. body technically alive
_____5. biological maturity	e. sexual maturity
_____6. social maturity	f. vitamins that destroy free radicals
_____7. menopause	g. flat EEG
_____8. empty nest	h. the study of aging
_____9. ageism	i. appear in either sex
_____10. clinical death	j. stable family, work roles established
_____11. brain death	k. self-perception as male or female
_____12. social death	l. no spontaneous heartbeat; no breathing
_____13. gerontology	m. departure of last child
_____14. antioxidants	n. ovaries stop producing estrogen
_____15. free radicals	o. a form of prejudice

Test Yourself: Answer Key

Multiple Choice

1. d	(385)	11. c	(388)	21. c	(393–94)	31. b	(397)	41. c	(406)
2. a	(386)	12. d	(388)	22. d	(394)	32. d	(397)	42. b	(407)
3. c	(386)	13. d	(388)	23. a	(394)	33. a	(397–98)	43. b	(408)
4. a	(386)	14. d	(388)	24. b	(394–95)	34. c	(398)	44. d	(408)
5. b	(387)	15. c	(390)	25. c	(395)	35. d	(399)	45. c	(409)
6. b	(386–87)	16. d	(391)	26. a	(396)	36. c	(399)	46. a	(409)
7. a	(387)	17. a	(391)	27. c	(396)	37. d	(401)	47. c	(413)
8. d	(387)	18. c	(392)	28. a	(396–97)	38. d	(404)	48. b	(414)
9. c	(387)	19. b	(392)	29. c	(397)	39. a	(404)	49. a	(414)
10. a	(387)	20. a	(392)	30. b	(397)	40. a	(405)	50. d	(414)

Fill in the Blank

1. cross-sectional
2. longitudinal
3. Warner Schaie
4. puberty
5. secondary sex
6. identity
7. stereotyping
8. gender schema
9. social
10. psychological, intimate
11. menopause
12. Daniel Levinson
13. postformal
14. ageism
15. brain
16. clinical
17. Elisabeth Kübler-Ross
18. primary

19. secondary

20. life span

Matching Questions

1. b	6. j	11. g
2. e	7. n	12. d
3. i	8. m	13. h
4. k	9. o	14. f
5. a	10. l	15. c

Do These Mini Projects

1. Interview an adolescent regarding the identity crisis. The adolescent can be a family member or the family member of a friend, schoolmate or co-worker. Make sure you formulate and write down your questions in advance and that your questions focus on the information you want to know without being overly personal or threatening. Issues you may want to get at in your interview include: the adolescent's current interests; the pressures on teens today; the origins of those pressures (parents, teachers, schoolwork, peers, uncertain future, self); current goals; values, e.g., what qualities she or he considers important in a person; problems with society today. Try to make your questions appropriate to the age of the adolescent you interview. After you collect your data, summarize what you found out about where this adolescent stands in resolving the crisis of identity versus role confusion.

2. Make arrangements to visit a local nursing home by calling the head administrator and setting up an appointment for a tour. Let the person you speak with know that you want to visit as part of a school project. Make note of whatever you find interesting or unexpected. Find out about the daily routines and activities available to the residents. Find out about the level of cognitive, emotional, and social functioning of the population. Bring the information you gather to class for sharing.

Pull It All Together

1. Chapter 11 is really the second half of chapter 10, in that chapter 10 covered development from the womb through childhood, and chapter 11 covers development from adolescence through death. In what ways does psychology deal with development after adolescence differently from the way it deals with earlier development? Why do you think that stage theories form such an integral part of the presentation of early development as compared with later development?

2. The life span theory of Erik Erikson is carried through chapters 10 and 11. Review the crises and conflicts he describes from infancy through dying.

3. What are the most stable aspects of human development throughout the life span and how can you account for the stability of those aspects? What are the least stable aspects of development, those that change the most from infancy through old age?

CHAPTER 12
MOTIVATION

Chapter Outline

Chapter Overview

Chapter 12 addresses the question why people behave the way they do. Whereas some behaviors are motivated by physiological needs, the motivations underlying other behaviors are more difficult to explain. The author of the text defines motivation as referring to processes that energize and maintain goal-directed behavior. Motives are defined as the needs and desires the goal-directed behavior attempts to satisfy. The author of the text acknowledges that there is no universal agreement on the definition of motivation. Motivation is closely linked to the topic of emotion, which will be covered in chapter 13.

Chapter 12 contains five major sections: (1) "Theories of Motivation," (2) "Hunger Motivation," (3) "Sexual Motivation," (4) "Achievement and Social Motivations," and (5) "The Neurophysiology of Motivation."

The first section ("Theories of Motivation") begins by stating that the motivational issues addressed by theories of motivation can be summarized in three major questions: (1) What are the major motive systems and how do they motivate behavior? (2) How do these systems relate to each other? and (3) What are the underlying psychological, environmental, and physiological causes of motivated behavior and how do they interact? Seven theories of motivation are covered: (1) instinct theory; (2) drive theory; (3) incentive theory; (4) optimal arousal theory; (5) Maslow's need hierarchy; (6) cognitive theory; and (7) evolutionary theory.

According to instinct theory, some behaviors are driven by instincts, which are innate, biological motives that are present in all members of a species and are expressed in a consistent way. William McDougall hypothesized that human behavior is also motivated by instincts, and he compiled a long list of automatic, inborn behavior patterns. Instinct theories fell into disrepute because they could not explain the variability in human behavior that was influenced by learning. Today, instinct theory takes the form of ethology, the study of the species-specific behaviors of animals, including humans, in their natural settings.

Drive theory, developed by Robert S. Woodworth and Clark Hull, proposes that the concept of a drive, one of the most widely used concepts in theories of motivation, denotes a condition of arousal or tension that motivates behavior aimed at reducing that tension. Drive theories typically hypothesize that a set of physiological survival drives, including hunger, thirst, sleep, pain, and sex, motivate behavior. Hull and other drive theorists have suggested that a drive results from the activation of a need or from intense stimuli. The deficiency or stimulus disrupts homeostasis, a state of equilibrium or stability that the body strives to maintain. Drive theory continues to guide a considerable amount of research. Incentive theory accounts for individual differences in behavior by assessing the value an incentive has for a specific individual. An incentive is any external object or event that motivates behavior. Whereas drive theory bases motivation on internal states, incentive theory emphasizes external stimuli.

Optimal arousal theory hypothesizes that everyone has a physiological need for stimulation and that we constantly strive to maintain an optimal or ideal level of arousal by seeking or avoiding stimulation from the environment. Functioning at an optimal level of arousal maximizes your behavioral efficiency or performance on a variety of tasks. This inverted-U function (the relationship between arousal and performance) was first studied by R. M. Yerkes and J. D. Dodson and is called the Yerkes-Dodson law.

Abraham Maslow theorized that some motivational forces are distinctly human and that human behavior is motivated by a number of competing needs that can be arranged in a hierarchy. The need hierarchy is a systematic listing of needs in priority order, such that the needs farther up the hierarchy can be met only after more basic needs have been satisfied. At the lowest level of the hierarchy are physiological needs, such as hunger and thirst. The very highest need is the need for self-actualization, each individual's need to fulfill his or her potential. Maslow's theory has been very influential both in practical applications and in generating research. Cognitive theories of motivation emphasize the role of thought processes in initiating, maintaining, and guiding behavior. Motivation can come from outside or inside the person. External motivation comes from the outside and takes the form of rewards. Intrinsic motivation comes from within you and causes you to engage in behaviors for no apparent reward.

From an evolutionary perspective, motives are seen as mechanisms that have evolved to ensure the survival and reproduction of the species. Both physiological and social motive systems represent adaptations that solved specific environmental problems over the course of evolutionary history.

The second section ("Hunger Motivation") focuses on hunger as a form of motivation, beginning with the roles of the stomach and the hypothalamus. Recent studies have confirmed early theories that the stomach has a role in hunger. Receptors in the stomach and upper intestine let us know when we are hungry, help determine our appetites for specific foods, and influence the size of the meal we consume. However, even without a stomach, people will still feel hungry.

Three areas of the hypothalamus associated with hunger are discussed: the lateral hypothalamus (LH); the ventromedial hypothalamus (VMH); and the paraventricular nucleus (PVN). The glucostatic theory suggests that specialized hypothalamic neurons function as glucostats and monitor blood glucose. Others have suggested that the hypothalamus might monitor lipids (fats) in the blood rather than glucose. The set point theory proposes the lipostatic hypothesis. A set point is a biologically based weight at which your body tends to remain. Taste is a powerful determinant of what and how much we eat. Taste preference is both innate and learned and has adaptive functions that provide essential nutrients.

Research has shown that the tendency to become obese is inherited and that people with this genetic tendency store fat more efficiently and consume more food. In addition, heredity might affect metabolic rate, fat cells, a weight set point, and the hypothalamus. However, you cannot gain weight by eating alone. People are affected by external cues, emotional arousal, bad eating habits, and dietary restraints. Reasons for the difficulties experienced by overweight people in their attempts to lose weight and maintain weight loss are explored. This section concludes with a brief discussion of the eating disorders anorexia nervosa and bulimia nervosa.

The third section ("Sexual Motivation") explains that sex, like hunger, is a physiological drive that is necessary for the survival of the species. This section begins with a discussion of evolved differences in sexual behavior in men and women. Sexual arousal is described as a complex process that occurs in a fairly consistent, cyclical pattern. The human sexual response proceeds through four stages. Sexual arousal is also described as a product of biology modified by environment. Neurological and hormonal influences are described. Sexual behavior is also a product of psychological processes and is influenced by learning and the physical attractiveness of a partner. Homosexuality (which has been found in every society since the beginning of recorded history) involves the preference for same-gender sexual partners. Public and professional attitudes toward homosexuality, and the causes of homosexuality, are discussed, and both biological and psychological explanations of homosexuality are explored. This section concludes with a discussion of sexual dysfunction and its treatment.

The fourth section ("Achievement and Social Motivations") considers motives that involve complex cognitive and social elements that appear to be basic to their operation as motivational systems. These clearly human motives include achievement motivation and the needs for affiliation and power. Achievement motivation, a uniquely human drive, is defined as a striving to overcome challenges, improve oneself, attain excellence, and accomplish more than others. This motive is learned and is measured by the Thematic Apperception Test (TAT). This motive also involves the tendencies to achieve success and to avoid failure. Building on this concept, the dynamics-of-action theory hypothesizes that the individual is constantly in a state of activity, rather than a state of equilibrium or rest. Expectancy-value theory focuses on the interplay of the motives to achieve success and avoid failure as they interact with the expectancy of success or failure and the incentive value of the goal to be achieved. Research on achievement motivation has focused on sex differences, the development of achievement motivation, and minority group differences.

Social motives are those that are experienced and satisfied through interaction with other people. The affiliation motive, nearly universal among humans, is a need to associate and interact with other people. The need for power is the need to control or influence the behavior of others. Theory and research on the needs for affiliation and power are described.

The fifth and final section ("The Neurophysiology of Motivation") explains that because little is known about the multitude of neurophysiological factors involved in all the various drives, the discussion in this section is limited to two brain centers that play key roles in motivation: the hypothalamus and the reticular activating system. In addition to its important role in regulating hunger and sex, the hypothalamus is involved in thermoregulation (control of body temperature), thirst, and sleep. Although it plays a significant role, the hypothalamus does not function as a unit in controlling drive states. Mechanisms elsewhere in the brain, such as the reticular activating system (RAS), play key roles. The RAS is a neural center for the coordination of activation or arousal arising from various sources, including sensory input and the cerebral cortex. Research with electrical stimulation has indicated that there may be brain "reward centers" that motivate some behaviors.

How to Master Chapter 12

Refer to These Learning Objectives

You should be able to achieve the following learning objectives after mastering the material in chapter 12:

Theories of Motivation

1. Describe and distinguish among the following seven theories of motivation:
    (1) instinct theory; (2) drive theory; (3) incentive theory; (4) optimal arousal theory;
    (5) a need hierarchy: Abraham Maslow's theory; (6) cognitive theory; and
    (7) evolutionary theory.

2. Define and distinguish between instinct and drive, and give examples of each.

3. Explain the concept of homeostasis.

4. Explain what is meant by the inverted-U function and how the Yerkes-Dodson law is applied to optimal arousal theory.

5. Discuss Maslow's concept of self-actualization.

6. Define and distinguish between extrinsic and intrinsic motivation and give examples.

Hunger Motivation

7. Explain the role of the stomach in hunger motivation.

8. Explain the role of the hypothalamus, in particular the LH, VMH, and PVN in controlling hunger.

9. Describe the glucostatic theory and the lipostatic hypothesis.

10. Explain and give examples of the roles of taste and learning in hunger motivation.

11. Describe the nature of obesity and the genetic and environmental factors that contribute to obesity.

12. Explain and give examples of how eating on cue, stress, emotional arousal, and bad eating habits contribute to obesity.

13. Distinguish between restrained and unrestrained eaters.

14. Describe the mechanisms that make it difficult for overweight people to lose weight and to maintain weight loss.

15. Define anorexia nervosa and bulimia nervosa and describe the nature of eating disorders.

Sexual Motivation

16. Discuss evolved differences in sexual behavior and gender differences in sexual behavior.

17. Describe biological factors in sexual arousal, including neurological and hormonal influences.

18. Discuss psychological and sociocultural factors that influence sexual behavior.

19. Discuss the nature, prevalence, and causes of homosexuality.

20. Describe the nature of sexual dysfunction and its treatment.

Achievement and Social Motivations

21. Define achievement motivation and described how this motive has been studied.

22. Describe the major theories of achievement motivation and research findings.

23. Discuss social motivation, in particular the need for affiliation and the need for power.

The Neurophysiology of Motivation

24. Explain what is currently known about the neurophysiology of motivation, particularly the roles of the hypothalamus and the reticular activating system.

Debate These Myths

MYTH 1: *As human beings, what motivates our behavior is completely different from what motivates the behavior of animals.*

Strategy:

Discuss and give examples, from the theories of motivation described in the chapter, of motives that we share with animals and those that are distinctly human:

Discuss the physiological mechanisms in drive theory that motivate both animal and human behavior:

Other statements and examples for debating MYTH 1:

Change MYTH 1 into a true statement:

MYTH 2: *The reason overweight people don't get thin and stay thin is that they lack will power.*

Strategy:

Describe the genetic factors that contribute to obesity:

Discuss the mechanism of hunger cues and the nature of eating habits and how these differ in overweight and normal-weight people:

Discuss the roles of metabolism and craving in the battle to maintain weight loss when a person is overweight:

Other statements and examples for debating MYTH 2:

Change MYTH 2 into a true statement:

MYTH 3: *Homosexuality is a learned behavior.*

Strategy:

Define homosexuality and indicate to what extent it has been found in society:

Discuss the research findings regarding the causes of homosexuality:

Explain what has been found concerning the influence of the X chromosome, androgen deficiency, and the hypothalamus:

Discuss what is known about the influence of the environment on sexual preference:

Other statements and examples for debating MYTH 3:

Change MYTH 3 into a true statement:

Test Yourself: Multiple-Choice Questions

Directions: Circle the best response for each of the following questions.

1.   Innate, biological motives that are present in all members of a species and are expressed in a consistent way are known as:

     a. drives   c. desires

     b. instincts   d. needs

2.   Instinct theory was developed by:

     a. William McDougall   c. Clark Hull

     b. Robert S. Woodworth   d. Bernard Weiner

3.   Which one of the following is most likely to be of interest to an ethologist?

     a. teaching a group of cocker spaniels to jump through a hoop in a fixed sequence

     b. studying the hunting stance of a group of German shorthairs

     c. observing a group of kindergarten children playing with their parents

     d. providing interventions for children with attention deficits

4.   In an experiment on motivation, a rat was deprived of food for 48 hours and was then placed in a Skinner box in which the rat was reinforced with food pellets whenever the rat pressed a lever. This type of study would be performed by:

     a. instinct theorists   c. drive theorists

     b. incentive theorists   d. optimal arousal theorists

5.   In the experiment described in question 4, the rat was pressing the lever in order to achieve:

     a. homeostasis   c. optimal arousal

     b. species-specific behavior   d. control

6.   Referring back to question 4, the hunger drive that resulted from deprivation can be satisfied by consuming food, which produces:

     a. the activation of a need   c. optimal arousal

     b. inborn behavior patterns   d. drive reduction .

7. Drive is to incentive as:

   a. learned is to innate
   c. instinct is to need
   b. push is to pull
   d. arousal is to homeostasis

8. As compared with drive theory, incentive theory is more:

   a. fully researched
   c. environmental
   b. widely accepted
   d. internally based

9. Gregory, age 5, knew that if he behaved himself all week, his parents would take him to see a movie on the weekend, but that if he misbehaved, he would not get to go to the movies. Gregory behaved himself because he wanted to see the movie. In this example, Gregory's incentive is:

   a. his behavior
   c. the movie
   b. his parents' approval
   d. his drive to behave appropriately

10. Tom likes to take apart his classic 1965 Chevy, whether or not it needs to be repaired. The interest and enjoyment he derives from this task can be best explained by:

    a. optimal arousal theory
    c. drive theory
    b. instinct theory
    d. incentive theory

11. The relationship between arousal and performance was first studied by:

    a. Hans Eysenck
    c. Clark Hull and Robert S. Woodworth
    b. R. M. Yerkes and J. D. Dodson
    d. Abraham Maslow

12. Students with no anxiety or with high anxiety do not perform as well on tests as students with a moderate level of concern, a finding that indicates that the relationship between arousal and performance is:

    a. difficult to predict
    b. based on drive reduction principles
    c. based on Maslow's hierarchy of needs
    d. an inverted-U function

13. It is *not* true that the need for stimulation:

    a. decreases with age
    c. is neurologically based
    b. has been observed in animals
    d. varies from individual to individual

14. According to Hans Eysenck, introverts avoid the intense stimulation of interpersonal interactions   because:

    a. they are shy
    c. their internal level of arousal is very high
    b. they are reactive
    d. their tendency to take risks is very low

15. The recording of heart rate, respiration rate, blood pressure, oxygen consumption rate, and the electrical activity of the brain is usually done in experiments designed to test:

    a. drive theory
    c. instinct theory
    b. arousal theory
    d. evolutionary theory

16. Proposing that some motivational forces are distinctly human is what makes Abraham Maslow's need hierarchy theory different from:

    a. drive theory
    c. incentive theory
    b. optimal arousal theory
    d. all of the above

17. The needs at the very top of Maslow's hierarchy are:

    a. growth needs
    c. deficiency needs
    b. basic needs
    d. security needs

18. According to Maslow's theory, feelings of helplessness, inferiority, and incompetence result from the failure to satisfy the:
   a. deficiency needs
   b. survival needs
   c. esteem needs
   d. social needs

19. Maslow believed that the percentage of people who achieve self-actualization is:
   a. about 98 percent
   b. about 50 percent
   c. about 10 percent
   d. less than 1 percent

20. Applications to the world of business, education, nursing, consumer economics, and elder care are common for:
   a. incentive theory
   b. Maslow's theory
   c. drive theory
   d. the Yerkes-Dodson law

21. Elaine's decision to ask her husband to participate with her in marriage counseling was based on her perception that without help, she and her husband would end up divorced. Elaine's motivation to talk with her husband and call a counselor can be best explained by:
   a. instinct theory
   b. optimal arousal theory
   c. drive theory
   d. cognitive theory

22. Whenever Janet got a good grade on a test or paper, she believed her success was due to her hard work, whereas when Karen did well, she believed the test was easy or the teacher gave her a break. According to cognitive theory, Janet and Karen differ on the dimension of:
   a. locus
   b. controllability
   c. stability
   d. decision-making

23. Seven-year-old Roy believes that if he is a "good boy," his dad will pay more attention to him, whereas Roy's eight-year-old brother John believes that his dad will not pay attention to him no matter what he does or doesn't do.   According to cognitive theory, Roy and John differ on the dimension of:
   a. locus
   b. controllability
   c. stability
   d. decision-making

24. A psychology student reads everything she can find about the neurological bases of behavior even though no extra credit is offered for her efforts. Her behavior is based on:
   a. her need for homeostasis
   b. external motivation
   c. intrinsic motivation
   d. her need to control her environment

25. The theory of motivation based on the adaptive value of physiological and social motives for the survival of the species is known as:
   a. evolutionary theory
   b. instinct theory
   c. drive theory
   d. Maslow's theory

26. Research has shown that people whose stomachs have been surgically removed:
   a. continue to have gastric activity
   b. lose their major hunger receptors
   c. have no appetite
   d. still feel hunger

27. When the lateral hypothalamus (LH) of an animal is electrically stimulated, the animal:
   a. stops eating almost entirely
   b. eats
   c. triples in weight
   d. dies

28. Of the following parts of the brain, the one considered to be a satiety center is the:
   a. lateral hypothalamus
   b. ventromedial hypothalamus
   c. thalamus
   d. paraventricular nucleus

29. When you walk past the dessert tray in a restaurant, the part of your brain that triggers your desire for dessert is the:

    a. hypothalamus   c. amygdala

    b. thalamus   d. RAS

30. Signals to the glucostats in the VMH and LH come from the:

    a. kidneys   c. heart

    b. pancreas   d. liver

31. Regardless of how frequently Rita dieted, as soon as she resumed her normal eating habits, her weight returned to between 132 to 135 pounds, which would be considered her:

    a. set point   c. glucostat

    b. lipostat   d. metabolic rate

32. The set point concept is based on the:

    a. Yerkes-Dodson law   c. lipostatic hypothesis

    b. hierarchy of needs   d. work of early ethologists

33. The largest single factor in obesity is:

    a. heredity   c. lack of will power

    b. learning   d. need for affiliation

34. According to research on eating behavior, an overweight person is more likely than an average weight person to eat when:

    a. it is a time when a meal is normally consumed, like noon or 6 P.M.

    b. a beautifully decorated buffet is presented

    c. food tastes good, whether feelings of hunger exist or not

    d. all of the above

35. It is characteristic of restrained eaters to:

    a. actively try to regulate their eating

    b. think about food constantly

    c. feel hungry much of the time

    d. all of the above

36. One of the characteristics of a successful diet is:

    a. restricted caloric intake   c. special foods that burn calories

    b. staying on it for one year   d. it must work for everyone

37. A 16-year-old girl who is 5 feet 6 inches tall weighed 85 pounds and complained that she couldn't stand to look at her fat thighs. This girl was most likely suffering from:

    a. bulimia nervosa   c. both a and b

    b. anorexia nervosa   d. neither a nor b

38. Bulimia nervosa is characterized by:

    a. bingeing   c. self-induced purging

    b. laxative abuse   d. all of the above

39. The brain mechanisms involved in sexual behavior include:

    a. the hypothalamus   c. both a and b

    b. the limbic system   d. neither a nor b

40. All of the following are important hormonal influences for women *except*:

    a. estradiol   c. testosterone

    b. estrogen   d. progestins

41. Homosexuality (the preference for same-gender sexual partners) and homosexual behavior has been found:

    a. only in Western cultures
    b. only in humans
    c. only in the past 200 years
    d. in every society since the beginning of recorded time

42. One of the major approaches to treating sexual dysfunction was developed by:

    a. Yerkes and Dodson
    c. Abraham Maslow
    b. Masters and Johnson
    d. Alfred Kinsey

43. Elizabeth is a high school student who strives to overcome challenges, tries to improve herself and increase her knowledge base, and wants more than anything to be the valedictorian. It appears that Elizabeth is driven by:

    a. achievement motivation
    c. the need for affiliation
    b. the need for power
    d. survival needs

44. The Thematic Apperception Test (TAT), developed by Henry Murray in 1938 is the principal measure of the need for:

    a. power
    c. affiliation
    b. achievement
    d. self-esteem

45. The basic assumption of the dynamics-of-action theory, also referred to as the McClelland-Atkinson theory, is that the individual is constantly:

    a. seeking homeostasis
    c. in a state of activity
    b. taking long breaks to work efficiently
    d. seeking to be near other people

46. The strength of the motive to achieve success, the strength of the motive to avoid failure, the subjective belief that success or failure will occur in the situation, and the perceived value of the goal to be achieved are the four components of:

    a. expectancy-value theory
    c. dynamics-of-action theory
    b. cognitive theory
    d. the Yerkes-Dodson law

47. Stanley Schachter found in his research that high-anxiety participants demonstrated a high need for:

    a. achievement
    c. affiliation
    b. power
    d. social approval

48. In women, a high need for power is associated with:

    a. lower dream recall
    c. a high need for affiliation
    b. concerns about diet and appearance
    d. all of the above

49. All of the following are true about the hypothalamus *except* that it:

    a. is involved in thermoregulation
    b. is involved in sleep
    c. is involved in thirst
    d. functions as a unit to control drive states

50. The reticular activating system appears to be activated by two major forms of input, which are information about:

    a. sensory stimulation and the cerebral cortex
    b. muscle movement and the cerebral cortex
    c. sensory stimulation and the limbic system
    d. muscle movement and the limbic system

Test Yourself: Fill in the Blanks

Directions: Fill in the blanks with the correct term or name.

1. _____ refers to processes that energize and maintain goal-directed behavior.

2. _____ are innate, biological motives that are present in all members of a species and are expressed in a consistent way.

3. A _____ is a condition of arousal or tension that motivates behavior aimed at reducing that tension.

4. A _____ is a physiological deficiency that creates a condition of disequilibrium within the body.

5. _____ is a state of equilibrium or stability that the body strives to sustain.

6. _____ theory hypothesizes that everyone has a physiological need for stimulation.

7. Abraham Maslow developed a _____, which is a systematic listing of needs in priority order, such that needs further up can be met only after more basic needs have been satisfied.

8. The highest need in Maslow's hierarchy is the need for _____.

9. The study of individual differences in terms of the introversion-extraversion dimension is closely associated with _____.

10. Need hierarchies are associated with the humanist, _____.

11. _____ are a kind of thermostat for monitoring blood glucose.

12. A _____ is a biologically based weight at which your body tends to remain.

13. _____ patients are typically underweight, but they usually binge on huge amounts of food, after which they engage in self-induced purging or in laxative abuse.

14. _____ is a disorder in which the patient is extremely fearful of being fat.

15. The male hormones are androgens, principally _____.

16. Impotence is now referred to as _____.

17. Two major figures in the theory and research on achievement motivation are _____ and _____.

18. The _____ motive is a need to associate and interact with other people.

19. In addition to its important role in regulating hunger and sex, the _____ is involved in thermoregulation, thirst, and sleep.

20. The _____ is a neural center for the coordination of activation or arousal arising from various sources.

Test Yourself: Matching Questions

Directions: For each item in column I, select the item in column II that is most closely associated with it.

I	**II**
_____1. William McDougall	a. biologically based weight
_____2. Clark Hull	b. need to associate with others
_____3. homeostasis	c. role of external dues in eating
_____4. Yerkes-Dodson law	d. instinct theory
_____5. Abraham Maslow	e. equilibrium
_____6. extrinsic motivation	f. fear of being fat
_____7. intrinsic motivation	g. drive theory
_____8. glucostat	h. theory of achievement motivation
_____9. set point	i. inverted-U function
_____10. Richard Keesey	j. bingeing and purging
_____11. Stanley Schachter	k. lipostatic hypothesis
_____12. anorexia nervosa	l. monitor
_____13. bulimia nervosa	m. rewards from environment
_____14. John Atkinson	n. self-actualization
_____15. affiliation motive	o. comes from within

Test Yourself: Answer Key

Multiple Choice

1. b	(422)	11. b	(425)	21. d	(427)	31. a	(431)	41. d	(444)
2. a	(422)	12. d	(425)	22. a	(427)	32. c	(431)	42. b	(447)
3. c	(423)	13. a	(425)	23. b	(427)	33. a	(433)	43. a	(448)
4. c	(423)	14. c	(425)	24. c	(428)	34. d	(435)	44. b	(448)
5. a	(423)	15. b	(425)	25. a	(428)	35. d	(435)	45. c	(450)
6. d	(423)	16. d	(426)	26. d	(430)	36. a	(436)	46. a	(450)
7. b	(424)	17. a	(426)	27. b	(430)	37. b	(438)	47. c	(451)
8. c	(424)	18. c	(426)	28. b	(430)	38. d	(438)	48. b	(451)
9. c	(424)	19. d	(427)	29. c	(431)	39. c	(443)	49. d	(453)
10. a	(424)	20. b	(427)	30. d	(431)	40. c	(443)	50. a	(454)

Fill in the Blanks

1. motivation
2. instincts
3. drive
4. need
5. homeostasis
6. optimal arousal
7. need hierarchy
8. self-actualization
9. Hans Eysenck
10. Abraham Maslow
11. glucostats
12. set point
13. bulimia nervosa
14. anorexia nervosa
15. testosterone
16. erectile disorder
17. David McClelland, John W. Atkinson
18. affiliation

19. hypothalamus

20. reticular activating system (RAS)

Matching Questions

1. d	6. m	11. c
2. g	7. o	12. f
3. e	8. l	13. j
4. i	9. a	14. h
5. n	10. k	15. b

Do These Mini Projects

1. Contact a hospital in your county or state that has a program for the treatment of eating disorders and obtain a copy of their brochure and any other written information they have available. Note the symptoms of the various disorders and the forms of treatment offered. Bring the information you gather to class for sharing.

2. Examine Abraham Maslow's hierarchy of needs. Where do you believe you are currently in this hierarchy? Think about a time in your life when you were attempting to fulfill needs lower on the hierarchy. Was there a time that you were higher up, but health concerns, financial concerns, or loss of a loved one forced you back into having to fulfill deficiency and survival needs again? Think about the tasks that are necessary for climbing up the hierarchy after circumstances bring you to a lower level.

3. Choose five of the theories of motivation of the seven discussed in chapter 12, and for each one chosen, write down one or two examples from your own life of each of the types of motivation that you chose. For example, write down one or two instances when you were motivated by drive reduction, one or two instances when you were motivated by incentives.

Pull It All Together

1. As in previous chapters, the issue of genetics versus the environment is a theme in chapter 12. What aspects of motivation are genetically based and what aspects are influenced by the environment? How do hereditary and environmental factors interact in the process of motivation?

2. Thinking back to chapter 3 on neuroscience, and the relationship between the brain and behavior, relate the information in chapter 12 on hunger motivation to the principles you learned in chapter 3. How does hunger motivation reflect the relationship between the brain and behavior?

3. Motivation is a topic that most people can relate to easily. Examining our motives and the motives of others comes naturally. What specifically did you learn from studying chapter 12 on motivation that helped you organize or clarify your thinking on this topic? As a result of studying chapter 12, did you change your thinking about motivation in any way?

Chapter Outline

Chapter Overview

Chapter 13 covers the topic of emotion, which is closely linked to chapter 12's topic, motivation. Although we are all familiar with emotions, one of the problems in the study of emotion has been the difficulty in defining and classifying this human experience. The author lists four components of emotion: a feeling state, cognitive processes, physiological changes, and associated behavior. One problem with defining emotion is distinguishing it from motivation.

Chapter 13 contains five major sections: (1) "Yardsticks for Emotion," (2) "The Structure and Expression of Emotion," (3) "The Experience of Emotion: Major Theories," (4) "Happiness," and (5) "The Neurophysiology of Emotion."

The first section ("Yardsticks for Emotion") discusses a number of measures of emotion. Because emotions are experienced internally, they must be inferred from observable, measurable behavior. Psychologists have developed three main approaches to measuring emotion: self-reports, observation of external correlates of emotion, and psychophysiological measures. Perhaps the most direct way to assess an individual's emotional functioning is to obtain a self-report—a verbal statement by the person of what she or he is feeling. One self-report technique is the interview, used both clinically and in research. Questionnaires administered to larger groups of people are designed to measure specific emotions. The main problem with self-report is that it is impossible to verify the accuracy of accounts. The problem with direct observation is ensuring the reliability of the observations.

Psychophysiology involves the measurement and study of a variety of internal bodily states that reflect the functioning of the autonomic, skeletal, and central nervous systems and typically indicate a person's level of arousal. A variety of devices are described that assess changes in heart rate, blood pressure, muscle tension, respiration rate, brain electrical activity, and electrodermal activity. Difficulties with psychophysiological measures include individual differences and the fact that psychophysiological measurement may not reflect the specific underlying emotional state being investigated.

The second section ("The Structure and Expression of Emotion") discusses the currently influential evolutionary theory of emotion, considers the structure of primary emotions, and examines current theories dealing with the expression of emotion. Evoultion is the common theme running through all these theories. Our current emotions are genetically transmitted products of the adaptation of earlier humans to ancient environments. The exception is the learning theory conceptualization of emotion. The first major theorist to address the issue of how emotions originate was Charles Darwin, who argued that the facial expressions associated with specific emotions are cross-culturally universal and therefore must be innate. Modern theorists have hypothesized that there are just a few primary emotions—basic feeling states that have evolved over the centuries because they are adaptive. Despite criticisms and alternatives, primary emotion theory has survived and continues to be influential.

Robert Plutchik has argued that emotions can be described in terms of different languages and dimensions of intensity, similarity, and polarity. Based on his research, Plutchik concluded that eight basic adaptive reactions serve as prototypes for all emotions and that these adaptive reactions can best be viewed as four pairs of polar opposites, which are described. The facial feedback theory of emotion developed by Silvan Tomkins is based on a Darwinian perspective and proposes that facial expression produces emotion. Tomkins suggests that there are only nine basic, inborn emotions, each activated by specific environmental stimuli and the facial expressions they trigger. Following in Darwin's footsteps, modern-day theorist Carroll Izard suggests that the emotions have evolved in parallel with the evolution of the brain. According to Izard, the neural mechanisms for both facial expressions and the perception of such expressions are innate. Cross-cultural studies and research on newborns support the view that emotional expression is largely innate. However, almost all theorists recognize that learning and experience play at least some role in the expression and acquisition of emotions.

Two views of the role of learning and experience in emotion are discussed: the biological view of experience and the learning theory view of experience. According to the biological theorists, the emotions are inherited givens that emerge as a function of physiological maturation. Although emotions are innate, their expression and activation are influenced by learning and experience. The learning theory view is that emotions are acquired through learning processes, with biology playing only a minor role.

The third section ("The Experience of Emotion: Major Theories") explains that although theories differ in how they approach the issue of emotion, all theorists agree that emotions have several major components. One major set of theories emphasizes the physiological basis of emotion, another the role of cognition, and a third the role of the unconscious. The major approaches that emphasize that emotion is primarily a product of the brain and nervous system are the James-Lange theory, the Cannon-Bard theory, and psychobiological theory. The James-Lange theory, the oldest psychological theory of emotion, was formulated in 1884 by William James and hypothesizes that physiological reactions to a stimulus trigger emotions, not the other way around; that is, your physiological reaction to an emotional stimulus causes you to feel the emotion rather than the emotion causing a physiological reaction. In the 1920s, Walter Cannon and his colleague Phillip Bard proposed that internal or external stimuli lead to sensory impulses that are sent to the cortex of the brain, then to the thalamus, then to the brain stem, and back to the cortex, where the sensation of emotion is produced. A modern psychobiological theory of emotional functioning suggests that the basic emotions are related to specific neural circuits.

Building on the physiological theories, some modern theorists have suggested that cognition or thought has a primary role in generating and guiding emotion. Stanley Schachter's cognitive labeling theory proposes that we use situational cues to help label the emotions we are experiencing. Other cognitive theories hypothesize that thought processes are primarily responsible for triggering both emotional responses and behaviors designed to cope with the emotional situation. This section ends with a brief discussion of Sigmund Freud's psychoanalytic theory, which hypothesizes unconscious processes underlying emotion.

The fourth section ("Happiness") explains that happiness means different things to different people. Surveys have shown that in our society, there is a relatively high degree of happiness. It appears that happiness predicts total adjustment. If you had a reasonably happy childhood and have continued to have predominantly positive emotional experiences, you are likely to have positive long-term affective states. Adaptation level theory proposes that we react to new stimuli on the basis of our present level of adaptation. Solomon's opponent-process theory builds on adaptation theory and suggests that emotions balance toward a neutral point, not only in the long run but also in the short run; every emotion causes an opposite emotion to occur.

The final section ("The Neurophysiology of Emotion") reviews what is known about the roles of the autonomic nervous system, the endocrine system, the amygdala, the limbic system, the cerebral cortex, and neurochemistry. The autonomic nervous system (ANS), a major subdivision of the peripheral nervous system, has two main subsystems—the sympathetic and the parasympathetic nervous systems. The sympathetic nervous system, Cannon's "emergency" system, acts to facilitate the arousal of major functions by producing a widespread neural discharge that mobilizes the body. When we experience an intense emotion, such as fear or anger, the sympathetic nervous system goes into action. The parasympathetic nervous system is dominant during periods of relaxation and acts primarily to conserve and store energy and maintain internal states. The endocrine system consists of a number of glands that produce hormones that are instrumental in heightening levels of such bodily functions as heart rate and blood pressure. The text details how these systems function.

Although the autonomic and endocrine systems play important roles in emotion, it is the brain that recognizes and interprets emotional stimuli, formulates psychological and physiological reactions to those stimuli, and activates the autonomic and endocrine systems. James Papez, a pioneer researcher in the study of brain functions in emotion, proposed the existence of a circuit in the brain, now known as the Papez loop, that mediates emotional responses. Papez's circuit was later named the limbic system. Current work on the limbic system focuses on the amygdala. The roles of the brain stem, the cortex, and the right and left hemispheres are also being researched.

How to Master Chapter 13

Refer to These Learning Objectives

You should be able to achieve the following learning objectives after mastering the material in chapter 13:

Yardsticks for Emotion

1. List four major components of emotion.

2. Describe three self-report techniques that have been used to assess emotions and the pros and cons of these techniques.

3. Explain how direct observation is used as a measure of emotion.

4. Describe the psychophysiological measures of emotion and the pros and cons of using these measures.

The Structure and Expression of Emotion

5. Discuss the common theme that runs through the theories on the structure and expression of emotion.

6. Discuss Charles Darwin's evolutionary theory of emotion, including the issue of innate and universal emotions.

7. Discuss the theories of primary emotions and the pros and cons of these theories.

8. Discuss Robert Plutchik's structure of emotion theory and the theories derived from it.

9. Explain the facial feedback theory of Silvan Tomkins and describe the research on the relationship between facial expressions and emotion.

10. Discuss the research on the heritability of facial expressions.

11. Discuss the role of learning and experience in the expression of emotion.

12. Distinguish between the biological and learning theory views of experience.

The Experience of Emotion: Major Theories

13. Discuss and compare the theories of emotion that emphasize the physiological basis of emotion, including the James-Lange theory, the Cannon-Bard theory, and psychobiological theory.

14. Discuss and compare the cognitive theories of emotion, including Schachter's cognitive labeling theory, misattribution theory, transfer of excitation theory, and cognitive appraisal theories.

15. Discuss the nature of research and the research findings for the various cognitive theories of emotion.

16. Discuss the nature of the unconscious in emotion, according to psychoanalytic theory.

17. Summarize the conclusions that can be drawn from the theories of emotion presented in the chapter.

Happiness

18. Discuss the nature of happiness, the prevalence of happiness, and factors in happiness.

19. Describe and give examples of adaptation level theory and Solomon's opponent-process theory.

The Neurophysiology of Emotion

20. Describe the roles of the autonomic nervous system, the endocrine system, the brain, and neurochemicals in emotion.

Debate These Myths

MYTH 1: *The experience of emotions is clear-cut—either you feel a certain way or you don't.*

Strategy:

Discuss and give examples of the four major components of an emotion: a feeling state, cognitive processes, physiological changes, and associated behavior:

Explain and give examples of how different individuals can experience the same physiological state, but label their emotions differently (refer to Schachter's work):

Explain how the unconscious can make it difficult to identify an emotion:

Other statements or examples for debating MYTH 1:

Change MYTH 1 into a true statement:

MYTH 2: *People and situations cause our emotions.*

Strategy:

Discuss the components and origins of emotions:

Discuss the roles of perception and interpretation of events in creating and labeling emotions:

Discuss the roles of the autonomic nervous system, the endocrine system, and the brain in emotion:

Other statements and examples for debating MYTH 2:

Change MYTH 2 into a true statement:

Test Yourself: Multiple-Choice Questions

Directions: Circle the best response for each of the following questions.

1.   An example of a feeling state would be:
    a. the label *fear*   c.   increased heart rate
    b. subjective feeling of anger   d.   an attempt to escape

2.   An example of a physiological change would be:
    a. faster breathing   c.   running away
    b. screaming in frustration   d.   hitting a pillow

3.   In developing measures of emotion, the biggest problem faced by psychologists is that emotions:
    a. are fleeting   c.   must be inferred
    b. are behaviorally expressed   d.   are innate

4.   The Manifest Anxiety Scale is an example of a measure of emotion based on:
    a. direct observation   c.   self-report
    b. interview   d.   physiological measures

5.   The Mood Adjective Check List (MACL) is widely used to assess:
    a. changes in mood   c.   the physiological bases of moods
    b. the accuracy of mood labeling   d.   moods in very young children

6.   The self-report method for studying emotion is problematic for all of the following reasons *except:*
    a. people tend to deny negative emotions
    b. there are cultural differences in emotion
    c. emotions are subjectively experienced
    d. only general arousal can be detected

7.   An example of a direct observational measure of emotion is the:
    a. Manifest Anxiety Scale
    b. EEG
    c. MACL
    d. Timed Behavioral Checklist for Performance Anxiety

8.   The EDA measures:
    a. heart rate   c.   firing of the ANS
    b. electrical brain activity   d.   muscle tension

9.   All of the following are physiological measures *except*:
    a. EKG   c.   EM
    b. MACL   d.   EDA

10. A polygraph amplified Bill's biological signals and indicated that his heart rate was 90 beats per minute, as compared to 70 the previous hour, and that his blood pressure had also increased. It can be concluded that over the past hour Bill became more:

    a. aroused
    b. anxious
    c. angry
    d. depressed

11. The book *The Expression of the Emotions in Man and Animals* was written in 1872 by:

    a. Robert Plutchik
    b. Carroll Izard
    c. Charles Darwin
    d. William James

12. The characteristics of having innate neural substrates, universal expression, and unique feeling states belong to:

    a. adaptive reactions
    b. primary emotions
    c. physiologically measurable emotions
    d. all of the above

13. According to Plutchik, emotions can vary in three important dimensions: intensity, similarity, and:

    a. polarity
    b. utility
    c. color
    d. subjectivity

14. Plutchik concluded that eight basic adaptive reactions serve as prototypes for all emotions and that these adaptive reactions can best be viewed as :

    a. eight distinct, exclusive feelings
    b. four pairs of polar opposites
    c. eight types of learned responses
    d. four pairs of unique physiological states

15. Silvan Tomkins would agree with the statement that we:

    a. experience four primary emotions
    b. learn to label what we feel from experience
    c. cry to relieve tension
    d. feel happy when we smile

16. The majority of studies on facial feedback theory support the hypothesis that:

    a. emotions are learned through conditioning of facial expression
    b. there are cultural differences in the facial feedback of emotion
    c. facial expressions generate emotional experience
    d. a person's facial expression is often a pure indication of an emotion

17. The modern-day theorist who followed in Darwin's footsteps by suggesting that the emotions have evolved in parallel with the evolution of the brain is:

    a. Carroll Izard
    b. Robert Plutchik
    c. Silvan Tomkins
    d. Neal Miller

18. That emotions are innate would be supported by all of the following theorists *except*:

    a. Silvan Tomkins
    b. Carroll Izard
    c. Neal Miller
    d. Walter Cannon

19. All of the following emotional expressions are present in newborns *except*:

    a. disgust
    b. smiling
    c. interest
    d. fear

20. The majority of cross-cultural studies of emotions have provided evidence that facial expressions of emotion are:
   a. hard to classify
   b. largely innate
   c. completely impervious to experience
   d. consistent only in literate cultures

21. The evidence for cross-cultural agreement on emotional expression implies that emotion is largely:
   a. culture-specific
   b. innate
   c. learned
   d. cognitively based

22. The view that emotions are a direct expression of the genetic potentials of an individual and that learning simply modifies them in terms of frequency of expression, strength, and stability is associated most closely with:
   a. Robert Plutchik
   b. Jack Panksepp
   c. Stanley Schachter
   d. William James

23. Jill panics when she sees a snake, whereas Margaret panics when she hears the voice of her ex-husband. Jill and Margaret have learned to respond to different:
   a. emotions
   b. genetic cues
   c. labels
   d. activators

24. According to the biological theorists, emotions are inherited and emerge with physiological maturation. However, learning and experience play a role in:
   a. coping responses
   b. frequency of expression
   c. activation of emotion
   d. all of the above

25. Which one of the following statements regarding the learning theory view of emotion is the most accurate?
   a. Research has shown that rats learn to fear the color white more quickly than the color black.
   b. Robert Plutchik is known for his research on the learning of the fear response.
   c. William James was an early proponent of the learning theory view of emotion.
   d. Neal Miller's research demonstrated that fear is learned and can serve as a drive for future learning.

26. Clark Hull and other learning theorists built on Miller's research to explain how:
   a. emotional expression is inherited
   b. emotional expression is influenced by cultural factors
   c. secondary drives and emotions are acquired through learning processes
   d. primary drives and emotions are acquired through learning processes

27. James Averill has suggested that emotions are:
   a. social constructs
   b. cognitive labels
   c. biologically determined
   d. physiological reactions

28. Because it is likely that human beings are genetically prepared to learn to fear some objects more than others, it would be the most difficult to teach someone to fear:
   a. spiders
   b. chairs
   c. garden hoses
   d. kittens

29. The James-Lange theory of emotion is considered to be:
   a. a learning theory
   b. cognitive
   c. physiologically oriented
   d. a modern theory

30. According to the James-Lange theory:

   a. your heart beats faster when you see a feared object

   b. when people around you appear angry, you feel angry too

   c. butterflies in your stomach make you feel anxiety

   d. smiling is an automatic response to pleasure

31. That a stimulus simultaneously leads to both the visceral response and the emotional sensation is the basis of:

   a. the Cannon-Bard theory   c. psychobiological theory

   b. the James-Lange theory   d. facial feedback theory

32. The view that there are four basic emotions, each of which is associated with a command system found in the brain, and that these four basic systems interact to produce other emotions through a neurochemical process is the basis of:

   a. the James-Lange theory   c. psychobiological theory

   b. the Cannon-Bard theory   d. facial feedback theory

33. Criticisms of psychobiological theory include:

   a. inflexibility of hardwired circuits   c. neither a nor b

   b. specificity of locations of emotion circuits d. both a and b

34. Which one of the following statements regarding cognitive labeling theory is the most accurate?

   a. Cognitive labeling theory is based on the premise that the origin of emotional responses is genetic.

   b. Schachter's cognitive labeling theory was an attempt to build on and clarify the James-Lange theory of emotion.

   c. Cognitive labels can be applied only if the individual is fully aware of experiencing a specific emotion on a physiological level.

   d. No valid criticisms have been leveled against Schachter's cognitive labeling theory because the research was well controlled.

35. An interpretation of physiological arousal, based on situational cues and past experience that identifies the emotion associated with the arousal is considered a:

   a. facial expression   c. cognitive label

   b. learned response   d. neural circuit

36. Barbara was feeling slightly nauseous and was beginning to perspire while she was waiting to see the dentist. She interpreted her physiological state as meaning she was nervous about seeing the dentist, when actually she was coming down with the flu. Barabara's interpretation of her physiological state was:

   a. a cognitive label   c. both a and b

   b. a misattribution   d. neither a nor b

37. In Schachter and Singer's study on cognitive learning theory, subjects in the control group:

   a. received an injection of saline solution

   b. were told there would be no side effects

   c. were warned of possible side effects

   d. were warned about false side effects

38. All subjects in Schachter and Singer's study received:

   a. epinephrine   c. a vitamin compound

   b. saline solution   d. an injection

39. Of particular interest in the study performed by Schachter and Singer was the behavior of the:

   a. control group   c. uninformed group

   b. informed group   d. misinformed group

40. The research on cognitive labeling theory demonstrated that:

a. we always need environmental cues to know what we are feeling

b. there exists a body of research that no one criticizes

c. both a and b

d. neither a nor b

41. According to cognitive labeling theory, we use environmental cues the most for labeling our emotions when:

a. we do not know why we are experiencing a certain physiological state

b. we want to change an unpleasant into a pleasant emotion

c. there is an absence of change in physiological state

d. we know what to expect to feel

42. Nancy felt gratitude toward the man who returned her wallet, even though the cash was missing, because she perceived him to be performing an honest action; what she did not know was that he stole her wallet in the first place. In the context of theories of emotion, Nancy:

a. labeled her feeling based on both physiological and environmental cues

b. experienced emotions that are first experienced early in infancy

c. transferred her excitation

d. made a misattribution

43. In the middle of his workout, Justin's wife told him that their son just failed another math test in school. Justin became uncharacteristically angry, most likely due to a:

a. cognitive label   c. misattribution

b. transfer of excitation   d. somatic reaction

44. When Jenny was late to work, her boss lashed out at her in front of the entire office. Jenny evaluated the situation and then evaluated her coping resources for dealing with it. She decided that instead of crying, she would apologize for her tardiness and get down to work. The processes Jenny engaged in are most closely associated with:

a. facial feedback theory   c. cognitive appraisal theory

b. misattribution theory   d. psychoanalytic theory

45. Unlike Schachter, Lazarus proposed that emotions are products of:

a. cognitive activity   c. both a and b

b. specific physiological patterns d. neither a nor b

46. The limbic system is viewed as controlling the outcome of cognitive processes and thereby guiding the person to engage in approach and avoidance behavior, and emotion as the combination of appraisal and action, by:

a. William James   c. Magda Arnold

b. Richard Lazarus   d. Stanley Schachter

47. Happiness has been shown to be the most related to:

a. coping styles   c. use of drugs

b. having a pet   d. having a lot of money

48. Richard Solomon's opponent-process theory suggests that emotions:

a. help us adapt to new, unfamiliar situations

b. are processed in the sympathetic and parasympathetic nervous systems

c. are labeled in spite of underlying physiological processes

d. balance toward a neutral point in both the long run and the short run

49.   The pituitary gland and adrenal glands are part of the:
    a. central nervous system   c. endocrine system
    b. autonomic nervous system   d. limbic system

50.   Although earlier hypotheses suggested that the hippocampus may be the primary limbic structure in emotion, the current work of James LeDoux focuses principally on the:
    a. amygdala   c. thalamus
    b. hypothalamus   d. Papez loop

Test Yourself: Fill in the Blanks

Directions: Fill in the blanks with the correct term or name.

1. _____ involves the measurement and study of a variety of internal body states that reflect the functioning of the autonomic, skeletal, and central nervous systems and typically indicate a person's level or arousal.

2. _____ wrote *The Expression of the Emotions in Man and Animals* in 1872.

3. _____ are basic feeling states that have evolved over the centuries because they are adaptive.

4. The idea that facial expression produces emotion is the basis of _____ theory.

5. _____, a modern-day theorist, suggests that the emotions have evolved in parallel with the evolution of the brain.

6. _____ are stimuli or situations that might, on the basis of learning, cause an emotion to be expressed.

7. The _____ theory of emotion, developed in the nineteenth century, has shaped work on emotion for an entire century.

8. The _____ theory of emotion proposed that internal or external stimuli lead to sensory impulses that are sent to the cortex of the brain.

9. Stanley Schachter developed the _____ theory of emotion, which accounts for the same physiological response pattern being associated with a wide variety of emotions.

10. According to _____ theory, mislabeling an emotion or motive can lead to unnecessary and inappropriate action.

11. Due to a phenomenon known as _____, arousal in one situation can increase a person's arousal to another stimulus.

12. _____ involves evaluating the significance of stimuli in relation to one's well-being and then evaluating coping resources.

13. _____ involve cognitively processing a possible behavior.

14. _____ reactions are physiological responses that accompany and are a part of the overall emotional experience.

15. _____ proposed that each emotion has three major components: cognitive appraisals, action impulses, and patterned somatic reactions.

16. The _____ in Freudian theory is an area of the personality containing emotions, motives, and memories of past experiences of which we are not aware but that nevertheless influence behavior.

17. According to _____ theory, every emotion causes an opposite emotion to occur.

18. The _____ nervous system, Cannon's "emergency" system, acts to facilitate the arousal of major functions by producing a widespread neural discharge that mobilizes the body.

19. A circuit in the brain, known as the _____, mediates emotional responses.

20. The endocrine glands that play the greatest role in emotional arousal are the _____ glands.

Test Yourself: Matching Questions

Directions: For each item in column I, select the item in column II that is most closely associated with it.

I	II
_____ 1. primary emotions	a. dominant during relaxed state
_____ 2. Robert Plutchik	b. produces ACTH
_____ 3. Silvan Tomkins	c. basic, adaptive feeling states
_____ 4. Carroll Izard	d. opponent-process theory
_____ 5. Charles Darwin	e. fear as an acquired drive
_____ 6. activators	f. consists of glands
_____ 7. Neal Miller	g. structure of emotions
_____ 8. psychobiological theory	h. innate facial expressions
_____ 9. Stanley Schachter	i. cognitively processing a possible behavior
_____ 10. action impulse	j. facial feedback theory
_____ 11. Richard Solomon	k. cognitive labeling theory
_____ 12. sympathetic nervous system	l. emotions are related to neural circuits
_____ 13. parasympathetic nervous system	m. trigger emotions through learning
_____ 14. endocrine system	n. Cannon's "emergency" system
_____ 15. pituitary gland	o. cultural universality of emotion

Test Yourself: Answer Key

Multiple Choice

1. b	(460)	11. c	(465)	21. b	(473–74)	31. a	(477)	41. a	(479)
2. a	(460)	12. b	(468)	22. a	(474)	32. c	(477)	42. d	(480)
3. c	(460)	13. a	(468–69)	23. d	(474–75)	33. d	(477)	43. b	(481)
4. c	(461)	14. b	(468–69)	24. d	(475)	34. b	(478)	44. c	(481–82)
5. a	(462)	15. d	(470)	25. d	(475)	35. c	(478–79)	45. b	(482)
6. d	(462–63)	16. c	(471)	26. c	(476)	36. c	(478–80)	46. c	(482)
7. d	(463)	17. a	(471)	27. a	(477)	37. a	(479)	47. a	(486)
8. c	(463)	18. c	(475)	28. b	(475)	38. d	(479)	48. d	(488)
9. b	(463)	19. d	(473)	29. c	(476)	39. c	(479–80)	49. c	(490–91)
10. a	(464)	20. b	(473–74)	30. c	(476–77)	40. d	(480)	50. a	(491)

Fill in the Blanks

1. psychophysiology
2. Charles Darwin
3. primary emotions
4. facial feedback theory
5. Carroll Izard
6. activators
7. James-Lange
8. Cannon-Bard
9. cognitive labeling
10. misattribution
11. transfer of excitation
12. cognitive appraisal
13. action impulses
14. patterned somatic
15. Richard Lazarus
16. unconscious
17. Richard Solomon's or opponent-process
18. sympathetic

19. Papez loop

20. adrenal

Matching Questions

1. c	6. m	11. d
2. g	7. e	12. n
3. j	8. l	13. a
4. h	9. k	14. f
5. o	10. i	15. b

Do These Mini Projects

1. The purpose of this project is to relate your personal experience of emotion to the theories of emotion presented in chapter 13. At some point during the next week, if you experience a clear emotion, like anger, anxiety, or happiness, take the time to examine which theory or theories of emotion best depict your experience and labeling of the emotion. Would the James-Lange theory apply? Did your experience of emotion result from the activation of physiological processes? To what extent? What about the Cannon-Bard theory? Did these processes occur simultaneously and with nervous system processing? To what extent, if any, did cognitive processes and cognitive labeling influence your experience and expression of emotion? Did you make any misattributions? What were the consequences, if any?

2. Ask a family member or friend to participate with you in an exercise to study facial expressions and emotion. Select an emotion (like surprise, joy, anger, fear, sadness, disgust, or any other major one) and try to communicate it to the other person with just facial expression. Then reverse roles so that each of you has the opportunity to communicate an emotion with just facial expression and to guess the emotion being expressed facially. How accurate were you and your partner in recognizing and communicating emotion through facial expression alone? How do you account for this accuracy?

Pull It All Together

1. Chapter 13 on emotion falls between chapter 12 on motivation and chapter 14 on personality. In some ways, you might say that the chapter is well placed because emotion provides a link between motivation and personality. Explain the complex relationships between emotion and motivation and emotion and personality, as you understand these concepts now.

2. Notice how this chapter on emotion draws upon practically everything else studied in the text book thus far—neuroscience, research methods, sensation and perception, nature and nurture, learning and memory, cognitive and linguistic processes, development, and motivation. Either verbally or spatially (e.g., by making a chart or schematic drawing), describe the interrelationships between the study of emotion and the study of these previous topics and themes, and jot down salient points.

CHAPTER 14
PERSONALITY: THEORY, RESEARCH, AND ASSESSMENT

Chapter Outline

Personality Assessment

    Objective Personality Tests

    Projective Personality Tests

Chapter Overview

Chapter 14 covers the topic of personality, including the theory, research, and assessment of this construct. The field of personality is closely related to the study of emotion, covered in chapter 13. Personality is also closely related to the fields of stress, psychopathology, and treatment—the topics of chapters 15, 16 and 17. The field of personality has shed light on important processes in psychopathology, and the study of both personality and abnormal behavior have contributed to clinical treatment.

Chapter 14 contains seven major sections: (1) "The Human Personality," (2) "Psychodynamic Theory," (3) "Cognitive-Behavioral Approaches," (4) "Humanistic Theory," (5) "Traits, Situations, and Their Interactions," (6) "The Neurophysiology of Personality," and (7) "Personality Assessment."

The first section ("The Human Personality") begins with a brief discussion of the early Greeks, who tried to explain emotion in terms of balances among four bodily substances, or humors, and the later development of phrenology. The author of the text points out that the study of personality takes two forms: theory and research. The study of personality is then placed within the context of the issues of nature-nurture and evolution. Most theorists subscribe to an evolutionary view that the genetic component of personality is about 50 percent.

The second section ("Psychodynamic Theory") covers Freud's psychoanalytic theory and includes a discussion of other psychodynamic theorists, including Carl Jung, Alfred Adler, Karen Horney, and Harry Stack Sullivan. The influence of Freud's work on psychoanalytic theory is widespread, and perhaps began with his publication in 1900 of his first book, *The Interpretation of Dreams*. After giving a brief history of psychoanalysis, the text discusses Freud's contributions, including the role of the unconscious, energy dynamics and the structure of personality, the processes of conflict and anxiety, and defense mechanisms. According to Freud, unconscious factors, often revealed in dreams, have far greater influence on our behavior than do conscious ones. Freud's view of the human body as an organic energy system is explained. The role of libido, the pleasure principle, the id, ego, and superego in personality are discussed. According to Freud, the structures of the personality compete for the energy in the system, and this continuing conflict is a major source of anxiety. The defense mechanisms that reside in the unconscious part of the ego force the anxiety-producing impulses into the unconscious. The text then explains how defense mechanisms operate.

Contemporary psychoanalytic theory is based on ego psychology, a modification of psychoanalytic theory in which the ego, rather than the id, becomes the primary basis for human development and functioning. The current dominant approach in psychoanalysis is called object relations theory and focuses on the importance of each person's relationships with a variety of objects. Carl Jung developed an influential analytic theory of conscious and unconscious functioning. The social analysts—Alfred Adler, Karen Horney, and Harry Stack Sullivan—each emphasized the influence of social factors in personality. They differed from Freud by deemphasizing the role of biological factors, giving consciousness a relatively more important role, using the construct of self, and introducing sociocultural factors. Their specific theories and the differences among these theorists is discussed. The section ends with an evaluation of psychodynamic theory.

The third section ("Cognitive-Behavioral Approaches") traces the origins of the cognitive-behavioral school to the behaviorism of John B. Watson and B. F. Skinner. Skinner chose to ignore such constructs as id, ego, and superego because he believed they reduced the objectivity of psychology and made its research less scientific. In Skinner's view, the behavior patterns we often refer to collectively as personality are acquired entirely through reinforcement. The cognitive-behavioral model builds on the behavioral model by adding the unobservable dimension of cognitive processes to the study of personality. The text discusses the pros and cons of the cognitive-behavioral approach to personality.

The fourth section ("Humanistic Theory") describes humanism as offering the alternative view that human beings are unique in the animal kingdom, not merely perched on the highest rung on the ladder of evolution. Unlike other animals, we have a self-concept, a perception of what we are like. Carl Rogers, a great pioneer in the field of personality, started the school of humanism. The two major structural components in Rogerian theory, the organism and the self, are discussed. Rogers believes that just one motivational system, called the actualization tendency, provides the impetus for all behavior. The system of self-actualization causes the individual to strive for self-enhancement and to maintain the consistency of the self-concept with conditions of worth. An evaluation of the humanistic approach to personality is presented.

The fifth section ("Traits, Situations, and Their Interactions") presents theories based on the assumption that behavior is heavily influenced by traits (stable, consistent, internal characteristics); another theory that situations are more influential; and interactionism theories, which combine both trait and situational concepts. Gordon Allport, a trailblazing pioneer in trait theory, believed that every personality is made up of a set of traits and that these traits shape behavior and cause it to be consistent over time and across situations. Raymond B. Cattell, another trait theorist, has applied powerful multivariate statistical techniques, most often factor analysis, to the study of personality. Cattell believes that traits alone cannot predict behavior. He proposed that the behavior you are likely to display at a given moment can best be predicted by knowing both your standing on relevant traits and the nature of the situation in which you find yourself. British theorist Hans Eysenck, who also used factor analysis to search for a set of personality dimensions, developed a typology based on just three dimensions that he believed are strongly influenced by biology. The major current alternative is known as the Big 5. Rather than 3 or 23 factors, some investigators now believe the correct number is 5: extraversion, agreeableness, conscientiousness, neuroticism, and openness.

In sharp contrast to the Big 5 and all the other trait theories is Walter Mischel's situationism. Mischel and his colleagues theorized that behavior is under the control of external situations, not internal traits. An alternative to both trait and situational theories is interactionism, which combines features of both. The text evaluates the various trait and interactional theories.

The sixth section ("The Neurophysiology of Personality") describes the neurophysiological bases of personality as complex, and the location of personality determinants in the brain as yet unknown. More is known about abnormal personality than normal personality. The part of the brain most clearly associated with personality is the frontal cortex. Some studies have shown that a role is played by the temporal and parietal lobes. Neural circuits, which are formed by set of interconnected neurons that may be scattered through various areas of the brain, might play a role in personality.

The final section ("Personality Assessment") covers techniques for systematically gathering information about a person in order to understand and predict behavior. The goal is to obtain reliable, valid measures of individual differences that will permit the accurate prediction of behavior. Personality assessment techniques are divided into objective and projective. Objective personality tests present the test taker with a number of specific items to which the test taker is asked to respond, either on paper or on a computer screen. Examples of objective personality measures are the MMPI (the Minnesota Multiphasic Personality Inventory), the MMPI-2, the 16 PF (Sixteen Personality Factor Questionnaire), and the NEO-PI (NEO Personality Inventory). A projective personality test is one in which the subject is given an ambiguous stimulus and asked to respond spontaneously. All projective tests are based on the hypothesis that the individual's response to an ambiguous stimulus represents a projections of inner, often unconscious, feelings and needs. Projective tests described include the Rorschach Inkblot Test and the Thematic Apperception Test (TAT).

How to Master Chapter 14

Refer to These Learning Objectives

You should be able to achieve the following learning objectives after mastering the material in chapter 14:

The Human Personality

1. Describe the early, nonscientific means for determining personality characteristics.

2. Define personality and place the study of personality within the context of the field of psychology.

3. Explain the roles of evolution, nature, and nurture in personality.

4. Discuss what research has revealed about the genetic and environmental components of personality.

Psychodynamic Theory

5. Discuss Sigmund Freud's psychoanalytic theory of personality.

6. Define and explain the roles of the unconscious, libido, personality structure, anxiety, intrapsychic conflict, and defense mechanisms in Freud's theory.

7. Distinguish between Freud's psychoanalysis and contemporary psychoanalytic theory.

8. Describe the main features of Carl Jung's analytic theory.

9. Describe the nature of conscious and unconscious functioning, attitudes, and functions in Jung's theory.

10. Describe the main features of the theories of the social analysts: Alfred Adler, Karen Horney, and Harry Stack Sullivan.

11. Explain the pros and cons of psychodynamic theory.

Cognitive-Behavioral Approaches

12. Describe the nature of cognitive-behavioral approaches to the study of personality.

13. Explain the views of B. F. Skinner regarding personality.

14. Explain how cognitive-behavioral theories differ from behavioral theory.

15. Describe the main features of Albert Bandura's social learning theory of personality.

16. Explain the pros and cons of cognitive-behavioral theory.

Humanistic Theory

17. Define humanism, and describe the approach of humanistic theories.

18. Discuss the theory and research of Carl Rogers, and describe the main features of his theory of personality.

19. Define and give examples of self-concept, actualization, and self-actualization.

20. Explain the pros and cons of humanistic theories.

Traits, Situations, and Their Interactions

21. Explain the nature of trait theory and distinguish it from situationism.

22. Describe the main features of the theories of Gordon Allport, Raymond B. Cattell, and Hans Eysenck.

23. Explain what is meant by the Big 5 and how this theory differs from other trait theories.

24. Describe the main features of Walter Mischel's situationism.

25. Discuss the nature of interactionism.

26. Explain the pros and cons of trait and interactional theories.

The Neurophysiology of Personality

27. Discuss what is known about the neurophysiology of personality.

Personality Assessment

28.   Define personality assessment and distinguish between objective and projective tests.

29.   Describe the MMPI and MMPI-2 and other objective measures of personality.

30.   Describe the Rorschach Inkblot Test and the Thematic Apperception Test (TAT).

Debate These Myths

MYTH 1: *Personality is such a commonplace concept that it is easy to define.*

Strategy:

Discuss the issues and assumptions in personality theory:

Discuss how personality is defined and examined by psychodynamic theorists, and include in your discussion the areas of agreement and disagreement regarding personality among the psychodynamic theorists:

Discuss how personality is viewed by behavioral and cognitive-behavioral theorists:

Explain how the behavioral theorists differ from the psychodynamic theorists, and how the cognitive-behavioral theorists differ from the behavioral theorists:

Describe how personality is viewed by the humanists:

Describe the differences among trait theorists, situational theorists, and interactionists:

Other statements or examples for debating MYTH 1:

Change MYTH 1 into a true statement:

MYTH 2: *Children's personalities are molded by their parents and environments.*

Strategy:

Discuss the nature-nurture issue with regard to personality:

Discuss the findings of research (e.g., twin and adoption studies) concerning the roles of genetic and environmental factors in the formation of personality.

Other statements or examples for debating MYTH 2:

Change MYTH 2 into a true statement:

Test Yourself: Multiple-Choice Questions

Directions: Circle the best response for each of the following questions.

1. According to the early Greeks, personality could be explained in terms of balances among four substances called:
   a. humors
   b. factors
   c. drives
   d. traits

2. The study of human personality draws upon research in:
   a. perception
   b. neuroscience
   c. emotion
   d. all of the above

3. The study of personality takes two forms:
   a. traits and states
   b. behavioral and psychodynamic
   c. theory and research
   d. learning and cognition

4. Research in personality may be any of the following *except*:

   a. direct
   c. exploratory
   b. informal
   d. empirical

5. Which one of the following statements is the most accurate regarding the role of genetic factors in the determination of personality?

   a. Genetic factors account for about 50 percent of personality.
   b. There is little room for environmental influence on personality.
   c. Twin studies are inconclusive regarding the impact of genetics.
   d. Twins develop similar personalities because they are reared together.

6. The number of twin pairs studied in research on personality is in the:

   a. dozens
   c. thousands
   b. hundreds
   d. tens of thousands

7. Evolutionary and adaptive processes have been used to account for

   a. conscious functioning
   c. unconscious functioning
   b. both a and b
   d. neither a nor b

8. Which one of the following statements regarding the Minnesota Study of Twins Reared Apart is the most accurate?

   a. The identical twins in the study who were reared apart first had contact at age 20 years.
   b. Identical twins reared apart were as similar to each other in personality as identical twins reared together.
   c. Identical twins reared apart were as similar to each other on several dimensions of personality as fraternal twins reared apart.
   d. The identical twins reared apart had been separated, on the average, at 6 months of age.

9. It is a striking observation that a vast majority of individuals have:

   a. early childhood trauma
   c. suffered from clinical depression
   b. severe personality disorders
   d. entirely normal personalities

10. Support for the heritability of personality traits has been provided by:

   a. twin studies
   c. both a and b
   b. adoption studies
   d. neither a nor b

11. The percent of personality accounted for by genetic factors is about:

   a. 10 percent
   c. 50 percent
   b. 30 percent
   d. 80 percent

12. It can be concluded from research focused on the nature-nurture issue as it relates to personality that:

   a. some traits are heavily influenced by heredity, others primarily by environment
   b. all traits are equally influenced by heredity
   c. all traits are equally influenced by the environment
   d. predispositions toward a trait will result in the development of that trait

13. *The Interpretation of Dreams* was written in 1900 by:

   a. Sigmund Freud
   c. Karen Horney
   b. Carl Jung
   d. Alfred Adler

14. If you are asked to remember how you felt yesterday when you woke up in the morning, it is likely you could bring this information into your awareness. According to Freud, this level of information is stored in an accessible place called the:

a. conscious
b. preconscious
c. unconscious
d. ego

15. According to Freud, the most powerful drives that are responsible for most aspects of human behavior are contained in the:

a. superego
b. preconscious
c. ego
d. unconscious

16. The energy Carol used to commute to her job was no longer available that morning for concentrating at a meeting. This example of energy economy is most closely associated with the personality theory of:

a. Carl Rogers
b. Harry Stack Sullivan
c. Alfred Adler
d. Sigmund Freud

17. In Freud's theory, the conflict among the id, ego, and superego is a major source of:

a. depression
b. power
c. anxiety
d. energy

18. When Eve picked up her dress at the dry cleaners and it still had the same stain on it, her first impulse was to call the man behind the counter a "jerk" and cause a scene, but she decided instead to ask politely that he try again to remove the stain. According to Freud, Eve's first impulse originated in her:

a. id
b. ego
c. superego
d. defenses

19. Referring back to question 18, Eve's decision to respond rationally came from her:

a. id
b. ego
c. superego
d. defenses

20. Referring back to question 18, if Eve had called the man a "jerk" and caused a scene, and then felt guilty about her reaction, the part of her personality that would make her feel guilty is the:

a. id
b. ego
c. superego
d. defenses

21. Referring back to question 18, if Eve's personality structures had engaged in an intense conflict, thereby creating a level of intrapsychic conflict and anxiety that was more than Eve could tolerate, she might protect herself from the anxiety by forgetting through the defense mechanism known as:

a. repression
b. rationalization
c. displacement
d. projection

22. Referring back to question 18, if Eve had made the choice to call the man a "jerk", she might have justified her actions to herself by explaining away the value of good manners through the defense mechanism of:

a. repression
b. rationalization
c. displacement
d. projection

23. Referring back to question 18, if Eve had left the cleaners without saying anything about the stain, and upon arrival at home had picked a fight with her teenage son, she would be demonstrating the use of the defense mechanism known as:

a. repression
b. rationalization
c. displacement
d. projection

24. Unlike traditional psychoanalytic theory, contemporary psychoanalytic theory focuses more on the:

a. id
b. ego
c. superego
d. childhood

25. Object relations theory, which focuses on the importance of each person's relationships with a variety of objects, is currently the dominant approach in:

    a. humanism
    c. interactionism
    b. trait theory
    d. contemporary psychoanalysis

26. According to Jung, self-perception and personal identity are controlled by the:

    a. ego
    c. self-concept
    b. archetype
    d. persona

27. According to Jung, the father, the mother, and the child would be considered:

    a. personas
    c. archetypes
    b. a collective unconscious
    d. social units

28. The concepts of introversion and extraversion were first introduced to the field of psychology by:

    a. Sigmund Freud
    c. Alfred Adler
    b. Gordon Allport
    d. Carl Jung

29. All of the following are true about the social analysts *except* that they:

    a. introduced the self as a construct in their theories
    b. emphasized the role of biological factors
    c. introduced sociocultural factors into psychodynamic theory
    d. gave consciousness a more important role

30. When Peter was age four, his baby brother was born, which made Peter feel insecure and jealous at first. As Peter grew up, he resolved his feelings by becoming a high achiever. This type of birth-order dynamic was emphasized by the theory of:

    a. Sigmund Freud
    c. Alfred Adler
    b. Karen Horney
    d. Carl Jung

31. Beth's therapist reasoned that Beth suffered from basic anxiety due to a lack of parental love, and that this basic anxiety led to her feeling hopeless and isolated in a hostile world. Beth's therapy was based on the theory proposed by:

    a. Karen Horney
    c. Sigmund Freud
    b. Harry Stack Sullivan
    d. Alfred Adler

32. The social analyst who emphasized the importance of interpersonal relationships and proposed the existence of specialized mechanisms called dynamisms (habits or patterns of behavior that have previously been associated with the satisfaction of a particular need) is:

    a. Sigmund Freud
    c. Alfred Adler
    b. Karen Horney
    d. Harry Stack Sullivan

33. A major criticism that has been leveled against psychodynamic theory is that the theory:

    a. ignores genetic factors
    c. lacks scientific precision
    b. focuses on female sexuality
    d. ignores the impact of early experience

34. Kevin, age 33, would prefer to stay at home and read than go to a party. He also prefers long walks on the beach and exercising in his basement gym than playing team sports. B. F. Skinner would most likely describe Kevin as:

    a. an introvert who was traumatized early in life during a social event
    b. exhibiting solitary behaviors for which he had been reinforced in the past
    c. depressed and in need of medication
    d. not recognizing the pleasure he would derive from social experiences

35. According to B. F. Skinner, the behavior patterns we refer to collectively as personality are entirely acquired through:
   a. social learning
   b. reinforcement
   c. cognitive processes
   d. genetics

36. Every time Lorna makes a small mistake, she jumps to the conclusion that she is stupid and expects to fail. This thought pattern that has made her depressed would be of particular interest to a:
   a. strict behaviorist
   b. cognitive-behavioral theorist
   c. social learning theorist
   d. psychoanalyst

37. The concept of self-efficacy, an evaluation of one's own effectiveness in dealing with situations, is central to:
   a. psychodynamic approaches
   b. trait theory
   c. humanistic approaches
   d. social learning theory

38. The view that human beings are unique in the animal kingdom, not merely perched on the highest rung on the ladder of evolution, is most closely associated with:
   a. cognitive-behavioral theory
   b. trait theory
   c. humanism
   d. psychodynamic theory

39. The self-concept, an organized pattern of perceptions and evaluations of one's own characteristics, is a central concept in the theory of personality proposed by:
   a. Sigmund Freud
   b. B. F. Skinner
   c. Carl Rogers
   d. Albert Bandura

40. When an individual is striving toward self-actualization, experience is evaluated to determine whether it will enhance:
   a. the self
   b. fulfillment of needs
   c. social learning
   d. the persona

41. Research on Rogerian theory has shown that:
   a. self-concept has proved to be a very useful construct
   b. self-concept is too vague to measure
   c. studies on the self-concept are difficult to replicate
   d. the basis of the self-concept is unconscious

42. Gordon Allport would classify shyness, warmth, and aggressiveness as:
   a. secondary traits
   b. central traits
   c. cardinal traits
   d. unique traits

43. The use of factor-analytic techniques for the study of personality is most closely associated with:
   a. Allport and Mischel
   b. Cattell and Eysenck
   c. Cattell and Mischel
   d. Eysenck and Allport

44. "The Big 5" refers to the:
   a. five unique factors that demonstrate individual differences
   b. five factors that underlie personality development
   c. five central and universal factors in personality
   d. five genetic components of personality

45. In personality theory, interactionism is the view that behavior is influenced by:
   a. genetics, environment, and their interaction
   b. stimulus, response, and their interaction
   c. self-concept, the unconscious, and their interaction
   d. traits, situations, and their interaction

46. The most clearly implicated part of the brain in terms of involvement with personality is the:
   a. thalamus
   c. hypothalamus
   b. frontal cortex
   d. occipital lobe

47. The goal of personality assessment is to measure personality by using methods that are:
   a. systematic
   c. reliable
   b. valid
   d. all of the above

48. The method of criterion keying has been applied to:
   a. the MMPI
   c. the TAT
   b. the Rorschach
   d. all of the above

49. All of the following are objective personality tests *except*:
   a. the MMPI
   c. the TAT
   b. the MMPI-2
   d. the NEO-PI

50. Jack was shown a series of pictures, each one showing one or more people engaged in a vague activity. He was asked to tell a story about each picture. The test Jack was taking is:
   a. the Thematic Apperception Test
   c. both a and b
   b. a projective test
   d. neither a nor b

Test Yourself: Fill in the Blanks

Directions: Fill in the blanks with the correct term or name.

1. The early Greeks explained personality in terms of bodily substances they called _____.

2. _____ is defined as an individually unique, consistent pattern of behavioral and psychological attributes that endure over time and across situations.

3. Psychoanalytic theory is now part of a broader school of thought called _____ theory.

4. _____ is an unpleasant emotional state characterized by nervousness and apprehension.

5. According to Freud, the _____ operates on the reality principle.

6. Freud postulated the existence of _____, processes that reside in the unconscious portion of the ego and act to reduce anxiety.

7. According to Freud, the major defense mechanism is _____, in which the ego uses its energy to force anxiety-producing impulses into the unconscious.

8. Skinner viewed personality as behavior patterns acquired through _____, anything that increases the probability of a response.

9. According to Rogers, _____ is an organized pattern of perceptions and evaluations of one's own characteristics.

10. _____ is an inborn tendency of the total organism to realize all its potentials, to grow and improve, and to maintain and enhance itself.

11. Eysenck's theory is a _____, an approach that focuses on a small number of very broad dimensions.

12. _____ personality tests present the test taker with a wide number of specific items to which the test taker is asked to respond either on paper or on a computer screen.

13. The _____ is the best known and most widely employed of all objective personality tests.

14. _____ is a method in which a group of people diagnosed as having a specific psychological disorder is identified and their responses compared with those of normal control participants.

15. The _____ is a personality inventory developed by Raymond Cattell.

16. The Big 5 factor theorists Costa and McCrae developed the personality tool known as the _____.

17. A _____ test is one in which the individual is given an ambiguous stimulus and is asked to respond spontaneously.

18. The _____ hypothesis states that the individual's response to an ambiguous stimulus represents a projection of his own inner—often unconscious—feelings and needs.

19. The first formal projective assessment device was the _____ test, in which the individual is asked to respond to inkblots.

20. A projective assessment device called the _____ asks the participant to respond to a series of ambiguous pictures that show one or more people engaging in a vague activity.

Test Yourself: Matching Questions

Directions: For each item in column I, select the item in column II that is most closely associated with it.

I	II
_____1. Sigmund Freud	a. views human beings as unique
_____2. libido	b. pioneer in trait theory
_____3. defense mechanisms	c. projective assessment device
_____4. repression	d. developed psychoanalytic theory
_____5. persona	e. started school of humanism
_____6. Carl Jung	f. psychic energy
_____7. Alfred Adler	g. objective personality test
_____8. Harry Stack Sullivan	h. act to reduce anxiety
_____9. Karen Horney	i. used functional analysis of behavior
_____10. B. F. Skinner	j. selective forgetting
_____11. humanism	k. hypothesized basic anxiety
_____12. Carl Rogers	l. hypothesized collective unconscious
_____13. Gordon Allport	m. social facade
_____14. MMPI	n. emphasized interpersonal relationships
_____15. Rorschach test	o. emphasized innate social interest

Test Yourself: Answer Key

Multiple Choice

1. a	(497)	11. c	(498)	21. a	(503)	31. a	(506)	41. a	(512)
2. d	(496)	12. a	(498)	22. b	(503)	32. d	(5067)	42. b	(514)
3. c	(497)	13. a	(500)	23. c	(503)	33. c	(507)	43. b	(515)
4. b	(497)	14. b	(501)	24. b	(504)	34. a	(508)	44. c	(516)
5. a	(498)	15. d	(501)	25. d	(504)	35. b	(508)	45. d	(517)
6. d	(498)	16. d	(501)	26. a	(504)	36. b	(508)	46. b	(520)
7. c	(498)	17. c	(502)	27. c	(5045)	37. d	(509)	47. d	(522)
8. b	(498)	18. a	(502)	28. d	(505)	38. c	(510)	48. a	(522)
9. d	(497)	19. b	(502)	29. b	(506)	39. c	(510)	49. c	(525)
10. c	(498)	20. c	(502)	30. c	(506)	40. a	(512)	50. c	(525)

Fill in the Blank

1. humors
2. personality
3. psychodynamic
4. anxiety
5. ego
6. defense mechanisms
7. repression
8. reinforcement
9. self-concept
10. actualization
11. typology
12. objective
13. MMPI or Minnesota Multiphasic Personality Inventory
14. criterion keying
15. Sixteen Personality Factor Questionnaire (16 PF)
16. NEO Personality Inventory (NEO-PI)
17. projective
18. projective

19. Rorschach

20. TAT or Thematic Apperception Test

Matching Questions

1. d	6. l	11. a
2. f	7. o	12. e
3. h	8. n	13. b
4. j	9. k	14. g
5. m	10. i	15. c

Do These Mini Projects

1. This project is designed to help you distinguish the personality theories from each other based the issues and assumption discussed early in the chapter. Across the top of a page, write the names of the theories: *Psychodynamic; Behavioral; Cognitive-Behavioral;Humanistic; Trait.* Along the side of the page, list the issues and assumptions: *Determinism versus Free Will; The Origins of Personality; Motivation; Holism versus Elementalism; and The Continuity of Personality.* Having done this, you have formed a grid. In each of the boxes of the grid, write down the stand each theory takes on each of the listed issues and assumptions.

2. Write down the names of the five traits that are considered the Big 5: (1) *Extraversion;* (2) *Agreeableness;* (3) *Conscientiousness;* (4) *Neuroticism;* and (5) *Openness to Experience.* How would you define the characteristics of these traits? Do you agree that these traits represent the 5 most central and universal factors in personality? Why or why not? Why would a researcher (in this case, Lawrence Pervin) consider the growing consensus concerning the Big 5 "dangerous"?

Pull It All Together

1. The chapter on personality is closely related to the chapter on emotion that preceded it and helps form the foundation of the chapters to come on stress, psychopathology, and treatment. Notice how the chapter material draws upon previously covered material in development, neuroscience, motivation, emotion, learning, and cognition. Notice that the nature-nurture issue is still being carried through as an important theme.

2. Personality is a familiar, yet complex, topic. How do the concepts presented in this chapter support what you already knew about personality? What did you gain from this chapter that either challenged or added to your knowledge?

CHAPTER 15
HEALTH AND STRESS

Chapter Outline

Chapter Overview

Chapter 15 covers the topic of health psychology, which examines the relationship between health and stress. We all have problems and pressures in our lives, but not everyone copes with stress in the same way. Exactly what stress is, where it comes from, how it affects us physically and emotionally, and what we can do to reduce stress and its effects are explained in this chapter. Health and stress are closely related to emotion (chapter 13) and personality (chapter 14) as well as abnormal behavior (chapter 16) and psychotherapy (chapter 17). Stress can be a factor in the development of emotional reactions and personality, and these aspects of human functioning can, in turn, affect how we handle stress. Stress can also play a role in the development of abnormal behavior patterns that can result in people seeking treatment or therapy.

Chapter 15 contains five major sections: (1) "Health Psychology," (2) "The Psychology of Stress," (3) "The Neurophysiology of Stress," (4) "Stress and Physical Illness: Nature and Nurture," and (5) "Reducing Stress and Its Effects."

The first section ("Health Psychology") defines the task of health psychology as understanding and promoting the patterns of behavior that are associated with good health. The field of health psychology is part of the larger field of behavioral medicine. The goal of behavioral medicine is to integrate the psychologist's knowledge of behavioral principles with bodies of knowledge based in other fields, which include medicine, health education, medical sociology, physical education, and medical anthropology. Behavioral medicine and health psychology are relatively new disciplines that have developed largely because the pattern of physical diseases has gradually changed. Infectious diseases that used to be out of our control can now be controlled through medication. Now with infectious diseases under control and people living longer, the primary killers are heart disease, cancer, and stroke. These diseases develop over a long period of time and are, to a large extent, preventable. Health behaviors can either shorten or prolong life.

The text discusses destructive health behaviors and their consequences (including unhealthy patterns of alcohol consumption). Health belief models are cognitive theories of health behavior and include descriptions of perceptions that will maintain healthy and unhealthy behaviors. Many people rationalize their behavior in order to maintain unhealthy habits. This section concludes with a discussion of the psychology of illness.

The second section ("The Psychology of Stress") defines stress as the nonspecific biological, emotion, and behavioral process that occurs when physical or psychological well-being is disrupted or threatened. It usually involves heightened physiological arousal, accompanied by negative emotions, including anxiety. The stress response is a combination of negative physiological and emotional reactions to the stressor. Various sources of stress are considered. Reactions to stress vary from mild to severe, depending on the circumstances and the way the individual deals with the stressor. The most common reaction to stress is anxiety—a vague, uncomfortable feeling state involving a sense that something unpleasant is occurring or is about to occur. Prolonged stress can lead to burnout. Severely stressful experiences can trigger traumatic reactions that can include panic attacks or even suicidal reactions. Post-traumatic stress disorder (PTSD) is the most prolonged and, apart from suicide, the most serious of all reactions to severe stress.

The third section ("The Neurophysiology of Stress") examines the relationship between the mind and the body with regard to stress. The section begins with a brief historical overview, then presents Selye's general adaptation syndrome (GAS). GAS occurs in three stages: the alarm reaction; a stage of resistance; and exhaustion. The cortex of the brain is central to the stress response, primarily because it is involved in the perception and interpretation of stimuli as being stressful or nonstressful. Areas of the limbic system are involved in the stress response, and the hypothalamus is active in cases where stressful stimulation produces an emotional response. Specific nuclei of the hypothalamus control the sympathetic and parasympathetic branches of the ANS, which serves as the principal peripheral mediator of the stress response. The principal neurotransmitter for the sympathetic system is norepinephrine, though acetylcholine is also released at some sites.

Continuation of the stress response described by Selye requires endocrine involvement to maintain the physiological reactions to stress at heightened levels. The hypothalamus, ANS, and endocrine system work together, and this overall system is referred to as the hypothalamic-pituitary-adrenal (HPA) axis. A final physiological component of the response to stress is the immune system. The section describes three components of the immune system that are particularly important in fighting disease, and then discusses factors that affect the immune system, the relationship between the endocrine and immune systems, and the relationship between stress and immunity.

The fourth section ("Stress and Physical Illness: Nature and Nurture") explains the relationship between stress and physical illness. That a wide variety of illnesses may be caused or aggravated by stress is convincingly supported by research. The section discusses factors that contribute to stress and are related to subsequent illness, and research on the impact of stress on developing ulcers in monkeys. The particular disease processes for which stress is thought to be a major contributing factor are termed psychosomatic (mind-body) disorders or psychophysiologic disorders (physical ailments in which emotional distress, such as that associated with stress, can be a contributing or exacerbating factor). Included among the psychosomatic disorders are hypertension (high blood pressure), coronary heart disease, diabetes, ulcers, multiple sclerosis, and cancer. Evidence concerning the role of stress in cancer is preliminary and mixed, so no conclusions can be drawn yet. The section mentions other disorders that might be partially caused, aggravated, or precipitated by stress.

The final section ("Reducing Stress and Its Effects") begins with a discussion of the striking effect of social support on stress and health. The author of the text states that we can better predict the probability of death by knowing the amount of social support a person has than by knowing her or his history of smoking, drinking, overeating, and other poor health habits. Coping is an active effort to reduce stress by solving the problems that elicit it. Coping involves both cognitive and behavioral efforts to manage environmental and internal demands and stresses. The section describes effective coping strategies. An alternative to coping is the use of defense mechanisms. The section ends with a description of techniques designed to prevent and reduce stress and disease. The methods include stress management, relaxation techniques, meditation, biofeedback, and antianxiety agents or minor tranquilizers.

How to Master Chapter 15

Refer to These Learning Objectives

You should be able to achieve the following learning objectives after mastering the material in chapter 15:

Health Psychology

1. Define health psychology and explain its relationship to behavioral medicine.

2. Discuss health and stress from an evolutionary perspective.

3. Describe and give examples of destructive health patterns, including risky sexual behavior and alcohol consumption.

4. Discuss the pandemic of acquired immune deficiency syndrome (AIDS), which destroys the immune system.

5. Describe health belief models and their relationship to cognitive theory.

6. Give examples of types of beliefs that would have a negative impact on behavior and health and examples of those that would have a positive impact on behavior and health.

7. Discuss the factors that influence decisions to go to a doctor and the factors that contribute to disregarding medical advice.

8. Define secondary gains and give examples of secondary gains people can achieve by playing the sick role.

The Psychology of Stress

9. Define and distinguish between stress and stressor.

10. Describe the impacts of life change, hassles, job stress, stress in the home, and acculturation in our lives.

11. Define and give examples of the following psychological reactions to stress: anxiety; burnout; traumatic reactions; post-traumatic stress disorder (PTSD).

The Neurophysiology of Stress

12. Discuss Selye's general adaptation syndrome (GAS) and describe its stages.

13. Describe the roles of cortical and subcortical structures in the neurophysiology of stress.

14. Describe the roles of the autonomic and endocrine systems in the neurophysiology of stress and how these systems work together.

15. Explain what is meant by the hypothalamic-pituitary-adrenal (HPA) axis and its relationship to stress.

16. List and describe three components of the immune system.

17. Explain and give examples of the relationship between stress and the immune system.

Stress and Physical Illness: Nature and Nurture

18. Discuss the nature-nurture issue with regard to stress and physical health.

19. Describe and give examples of the situational factors that can trigger stress.

20. Explain the impact of genetic predisposition on stress.

21. Describe Brady's research on stress in executive monkeys and the conclusions drawn from this research.

22. Describe research findings that contradict Brady's findings on the roles of prediction and control in stress.

23. Explain the roles of prediction and control in stress in humans.

24. Explain and give examples of multifactorial causation with regard to stress and health.

25. Explain what is meant by psychosomatic disorders or psychophysiologic disorders.

26. Discuss the research findings on the relationship between stress and coronary heart disease (CHD), ulcers, cancer, headache, hypertension, asthma, rheumatoid arthritis, and skin disorders.

Reducing Stress and Its Effects

27. Discuss the relationship between social support and stress.

28. Define coping and give examples of coping strategies.

29. Discuss how using defense mechanisms differs from coping.

30. Discuss research findings on the health effects of coping.

31. Describe the following techniques for preventing and reducing stress and disease: stress management; relaxation techniques; meditation; biofeedback; stress-reducing drugs.

Debate These Myths

MYTH 1: *Psychosomatic illnesses are imaginary illnesses.*

Strategy:

Define psychosomatic illness:

Define psychophysiologic disorder:

Give examples of psychosomatic or psychophysiologic disorders and their relationships to stress:

Explain the nature of these psychosomatic/psychophysiologic disorders:

coronary heart disease:

ulcers:

cancer:

other disorders:

Other statements or examples for debating MYTH 1:

Change MYTH 1 into a true statement:

MYTH 2: *Everyone feels stressed out by everyday hassles.*

Strategy:

Define stress and stressor and distinguish between them:

Give examples of how we can *increase* the stress we feel from everyday hassles:

Give examples of techniques we could use to *decrease* the stress experienced from everyday hassles:

Discuss the extent of our control over handling stressors:

Discuss how individual differences in dealing with stress express themselves:

Other statements and examples for debating MYTH 2:

Change MYTH 2 into a true statement:

Test Yourself: Multiple-Choice Questions

Directions: Circle the best response for each of the following questions.

1. Health psychology is part of the larger interdisciplinary field of:
    a. behavior genetics
    c. behavioral medicine
    b. neuroscience
    d. personality

2. Which one of the following statements regarding the primary causes of death in younger age groups is the most accurate?
    a. The primary causes of death among adolescents are smoking and physical abuse.
    b. Mortality in the younger age groups is higher than it was a century ago
    c. Younger people have more adaptive skills than older people to avoid the primary causes of death in our society.
    d. Young people have the power to prevent the current primary causes of death in their age group.

3. The disciplines of medical sociology, physical education, and health education are part of:

   a. health psychology   c. stress management

   b. behavioral medicine   d. neuroscience

4. From an evolutionary perspective, it can be safely said that alcohol:

   a. has no adaptive value   c. is always a dangerous substance

   b. can be of value in small amounts   d. is necessary for survival

5. "Death by inches" is a phrase that was coined by:

   a. Shakespeare   c. James

   b. Selye   d. Lazarus

6. A pandemic is an extreme epidemic that is:

   a. widespread and growing rapidly   c. currently subsiding

   b. at least 100 years old   d. curable

7. The first cases of AIDS were diagnosed in the United States in:

   a. 1961   c. 1981

   b. 1971   d. 1991

8. The number of cases worldwide of AIDS reported by the World Health Organization in 1995 was:

   a. 500,000   c. 2 million

   b. 1 million   d. 4.5 million

9. All of the following are true regarding HIV and AIDS *except*:

   a. transmission from a man to a woman is more likely than transmission from a woman to a man

   b. a maximum of 10 million people are currently infected with HIV

   c. many people lack knowledge about AIDS prevention

   d. excessive fatigue and weight loss are early symptoms

10. Once AIDS is diagnosed, death usually occurs within:

   a. 1 year   c. 3 years

   b. 2 years   d. 5 years

11. The symptoms of excessive fatigue, night sweats, and skin discoloration are most closely associated with:

   a. coronary heart disease   c. HIV infection

   b. asthma   d. ulcers

12. HIV transmission can occur through sexual activity such as:

   a. heterosexual intercourse   c. oral intercourse

   b. anal intercourse   d. any of the above

13. The Natural AIDS Survey of Heterosexual Adults showed that the percentage of heterosexual adults who still do not use condoms with new sex partners and do not practice safe sex is:

   a. 25 percent   c. 50 percent

   b. 35 percent   d. 65 percent

14. Statistical data shows that, compared to nonalcoholics, alcoholics live, on the average:

   a. 5 years less   c. 19 years less

   b. 12 years less   d. the same number of years

15.   Which of the following is an example of a health belief?

   a.   jogging every day, rain or shine

   b.   thinking that exercise is a waste of time

   c.   feeling tired after an aerobics class

   d.   all of the above are health beliefs

16.   Jack says to himself about his excessive consumption of alcohol, "Even though my father was an alcoholic who died of liver disease, he drank more than I did and he never exercised. Besides, I can stop drinking any time I want to. I just see no need to." Jack's thought process regarding his excessive drinking demonstrates that Jack:

   a.   is not a well-educated person

   b.   exercises on a regular basis

   c.   is rationalizing his drinking behavior

   d.   will die of liver disease

17.   Marion perceived her decision to stop smoking as based on weighing the possibility of poor health in the future against enjoyment of smoking. In the context of a health belief model, Marion's perceived the situation in terms of:

   a.   will power   c.   a cost-benefit balance

   b.   a remote possibility   d.   panic

18.   Steve told himself that smoking would never hurt him because his father was a smoker and lived to be 80. This form of reasoning is considered:

   a.   rationalization   c.   both a and b

   b.   a defense mechanism   d.   neither a nor b

19.   Referring back to question 18, if Steve were to reexamine and challenge his beliefs, do a cost-benefit balance, he would be:

   a.   coping   c.   both a and b

   b.   adaptive   d.   neither a nor b

20.   Concern about imposing, reluctance to interrupt prior plans, and fear of seeming foolish are just some of the reasons that people:

   a.   avoid going to the doctor   c.   disregard medical advice

   b.   play the sick role   d.   receive secondary gains

21.   Connie at age 6 began to notice that the only time she could stay home from school to be with her mother was when she was sick. Connie became sick almost every week. For Connie, staying home with her mother while sick became a:

   a.   stressor   c.   defense mechanism

   b.   secondary gain   d.   traumatic experience

22.   Of the following, the one that secondary gains reinforce the most is:

   a.   illness   c.   stress

   b.   LCUs   d.   medical advice

23.   The stress response combines physiological reactions with :

   a.   biofeedback   c.   emotional reactions

   b.   reinforcement   d.   all of the above

24.   The Social Readjustment Rating Scale (SRRS) measures:

   a.   units of life change   c.   physiological reactions to stress

   b.   levels of frustration   d.   the mind-body relationship

25. Which one of the following is the best example of a stressor?

a. a panic attack
b. low self-esteem
c. traffic when late to work
d. feeling depressed

26. Stressor is to stress as:

a. internal is to external
b. situation is to process
c. cortical is to subcortical
d. hassle is to life change unit

27. When Susan spotted her boss, her stomach started churning, her heart beat faster, and she wanted to run. In this scene, the stressor is:

a. Susan's stomach churning
b. Susan's wanting to run
c. Susan's heart beating faster
d. Susan's boss

28. Getting into your car to head for work in the morning and finding that it won't start is considered a:

a. stressor
b. a hassle
c. both a and b
d. neither a nor b

29. The current divorce rate is closest to:

a. 25 percent
b. 40 percent
c. 50 percent
d. 75 percent

30. The most common and obvious reaction to stress is:

a. anxiety
b. headache
c. trauma
d. depression

31. Mildred was taking her care of her 96-year-old incapacitated mother, day and night, on top of trying to maintain a job and marriage. She was becoming anxious, irritable, depressed, even withdrawn and suspicious, and she was exhausted. Margaret was demonstrating the major symptoms of:

a. a panic reaction
b. burnout
c. a traumatic reaction
d. PTSD

32. The denial state of a traumatic reaction is characterized by:

a. sleep disturbances
b. startle reactions
c. extreme vigilance
d. diarrhea

33. *Shell shock* and *battle fatigue* are now referred to as:

a. post-traumatic stress disorder
b. PTSD
c. both a and b
d. neither a nor b

34. Research has shown that all of the following reaction are common experiences for many Vietnam veterans *except*:

a. nightmares
b. underachievement
c. bad marriages
d. high self-esteem

35. Broken connections with positive images, difficulties in relationships, major alterations of life course, depression, nightmares, psychophysiologic disorders, and addiction were identified by Blank as symptoms of:

a. anxiety
b. PTSD
c. burnout
d. immune system failure

36. The general adaptation syndrome (GAS) is best described as:

a. the predictable response of the body in reaction to stress
b. occurring primarily in the limbic system
c. an unhealthy overreaction to a stressor
d. a system that was once adaptive but is now harmful

37. The part of the brain that is central to the stress response because it is involved in the perception and interpretation of stimuli as being stressful or nonstressful is the:

    a. hypothalamus   c. cortex

    b. pituitary   d. adrenal medulla

38. Norepinephrine is the principal neurotransmitter for the

    a. endocrine system   c. central nervous system

    b. sympathetic system   d. T-cell lymphocytes

39. The most immediate neuroendocrine response to stress occurs when sympathetic nerved impulses from the hypothalamus stimulate the:

    a. cerebral cortex   c. adrenal medulla

    b. HPA axis   d. pituitary gland

40. Antibodies are produced in the immune system by the:

    a. B-cell lymphocytes   c. natural killer (NK) cells

    b. T-cell lymphocytes   d. all of the above

41. With reduced immunity, we would expect to see, occurring along with it:

    a. a decrease in infectious diseases

    b. an increase in infectious diseases

    c. an abundance of NK cells

    d. an abundance of lymphocytes

42. Hypertension, coronary heart disease, asthma, and migraine headaches are all associated with:

    a. women more than men   c. alcoholism

    b. poor childhoods   d. genetic predispositions

43. The research on executive monkeys is important because it sheds light on stress factors that include:

    a. genetic predispositions   c. intelligence

    b. prediction and control   d. sexual confusion

44. Evidence suggests that human beings deal with stress more effectively when they can:

    a. predict or control aversive events

    b. understand the meaning of their genetic predispositions

    c. repress their stress-produced anxiety

    d. obtain medical advice

45. The main feature of a psychophysiologic disorder is that it is a physical ailment that is made worse by:

    a. emotional distress   c. both a and b

    b. poor health habits   d. neither a nor b

46. Research has demonstrated that a risk factor for CHD (coronary heart disease) is:

    a. hostility   c. an eating disorder

    b. an "I don't care" attitude   d. air travel

47. All of the following disorders have been associated with stress *except*:

    a. headache   c. spina bifida

    b. cancer   d. rheumatoid arthritis

48. Of the following, the best way to help reduce most people's stress is to:

    a. improve their financial situation

    b. increase their social support

    c. teach them how to avoid stressful situations

    d. give them more personal space

49. When Dan was told he would have to make another long business trip, he first judged the situation to be highly stressful on his marriage, and then he decided to postpone telling his wife about the trip. This is an example of:

    a. cognitive appraisal   c. stress inoculation

    b. social readjustment   d. stress management

50. The effects of meditation are most closely like the effects of:

    a. biofeedback   c. progressive relaxation

    b. antianxiety agents   d. stress inoculation

Test Yourself: Fill in the Blanks

Directions: Fill in the blanks with the correct term or name.

1. _____ is a fatal disease in which the _____ gradually destroys the ability of the immune system to fight off a wide range of infectious agents.

2. _____ models are cognitive theories of health behavior.

3. _____ gains are rewards for being ill.

4. _____ is the nonspecific biological, emotional, and behavioral process that occurs when physical or psychological well-being is disrupted or threatened.

5. In order to determine which events in life are the most stressful, Thomas Holmes and his colleagues developed the _____ Scale, which is still widely used.

6. _____ is the process of adapting to and becoming integrated with a new cultural environment.

7. _____ is a vague, uncomfortable feeling state involving a sense that something unpleasant is occurring or is about to occur.

8. When stress is prolonged, it can lead to _____, which is marked by a gradual increase in psychological, behavioral, and physical symptoms until the person can no longer function effectively.

9. A reaction that is much stronger than anxiety and occurs as a psychological reaction to a severely stressful experience, called a _____, is constituted by two major psychological states: intrusion and denial.

10. _____ is the most prolonged and apart from suicide, the most serious of all reactions to severe stress.

11. Based on his extensive research, Selye proposed that the body reacts to stress in a predictable response called the _____ syndrome (GAS).

12. The principal, overall neurophysiological system described in the chapter as involved in the stress response is often called the _____-_____-_____ (HPA) axis.

13. Three components of the immune system that are particularly active in fighting disease are the _____lymphocytes, the T-cell _____, and the _____ (NK) cell.

14. The case for the _____ causation model of stress is supported by a large body of research.

15. _____ is an active effort to reduce stress by solving the problems that elicit it.

16. Richard Lazarus argued that individual differences in the responses to stress are a function of _____, the person's evaluation through thought processes of a potentially stressful event or situation.

17. A four-stage approach to verbal _____ has been recommended by Donald Meichenbaum: preparation, confrontation, coping with anxiety-producing thoughts and feelings, and self-reinforcement.

18. Teaching multiple techniques for preventing and reducing stress is known as _____.

19. Edmund Jacobson demonstrated that relaxation reverses the physiological effects of stress and pioneered an approach to reducing muscle tension called _____, which teaches how to relax one muscle group at a time.

20. The primary drugs used for stress reduction are the _____ or minor tranquilizers.

Test Yourself: Matching Questions

Directions: For each item in column I, select the item in column II that is most closely associated with it.

I	II
_____1. health belief models	a. releases cortisol
_____2. secondary gains	b. minor tranquilizers
_____3. burnout	c. personality factor in CHD
_____4. traumatic reaction	d. cognitive theories
_____5. PTSD	e. physical
_____6. GAS	f. rewards for being ill
_____7. adrenal cortex	g. reduction in muscle tension
_____8. somatic	h. alarm, resistance, exhaustion
_____9. ischemia	i. caused by prolonged stress
_____10. B-cell lymphocyte	j. executive monkey research
_____11. Joseph Brady	k. stronger than simple anxiety
_____12. Richard Lazarus	l. insufficient blood supply to heart
_____13. Type A personality	m. produces antibodies
_____14. relaxation response	n. most prolonged, serious reaction to stress
_____15. antianxiety agents	o. cognitive appraisal research

Test Yourself: Answer Key

Multiple Choice

1. c	(530)	11. c	(536)	21. b	(539)	31. b	(542)	41. b	(547)
2. d	(531)	12. d	(536)	22. a	(539)	32. a	(542)	42. d	(549)
3. b	(530)	13. d	(536)	23. c	(540)	33. c	(542)	43. b	(549)
4. b	(531)	14. c	(537)	24. a	(540)	34. d	(542–43)	44. a	(549)
5. a	(531)	15. b	(537)	25. c	(540)	35. b	(543)	45. c	(551)
6. a	(531)	16. c	(538)	26. b	(540)	36. a	(544)	46. a	(551)
7. c	(531)	17. c	(538)	27. d	(540)	37. c	(546)	47. c	(553–54)
8. d	(533)	18. c	(538)	28. c	(540)	38. b	(546)	48. b	(556)
9. b	(536)	19. c	(538)	29. c	(541)	39. c	(546)	49. a	(556)
10. b	(536)	20. a	(539)	30. a	(542)	40. a	(547)	50. c	(558)

Fill in the Blanks

1. acquired immune deficiency syndrome (AIDS), human immunodeficiency virus (HIV)
2. health belief
3. secondary
4. stress
5. Social Readjustment Rating
6. acculturation
7. anxiety
8. burnout
9. traumatic reaction
10. post-traumatic stress disorder or PTSD
11. general adaptation
12. hypothalamic-pituitary-adrenal
13. B-cell, lymphocytes, natural killer
14. multifactorial
15. coping
16. cognitive appraisal
17. self-instruction
18. stress management

19. progressive relaxation

20. antianxiety agents

Matching Questions

1. d	6. h	11. j
2. f	7. a	12. o
3. i	8. e	13. c
4. k	9. l	14. g
5. n	10. m	15. b

Do These Mini Projects

1. Make a list of five stressors—disruptive events or situations—that could easily trigger the stress response. Under each stressor, make two columns. In the first column, list perceptions or beliefs that would *increase* the stress response. In the second column, list perceptions or beliefs that would *reduce* the stress response. How powerful are perceptions in increasing and reducing stress? Bring your information to class for sharing.

2. Observe your stress response the next time you are faced with a stressor. Using Selye's model of the general adaptation syndrome, observe yourself in the three stages of the GAS: alarm, resistance, and exhaustion. Record on either paper or audiotape the nature of your stress response as you progress through the three stages. Now take a step back and evaluate whether the situation was as threatening as you perceived it to be, or if you put yourself through the ups and downs of the GAS unnecessarily. What could you have done to cut down the stress reaction?

3. Select newspaper and magazine articles about people who were exposed to traumatic experiences. What was the trauma? How did the people react? Would you anticipate a PTSD reaction? What form might it take? Bring the articles and your notes to class for sharing.

Pull It All Together

1. The topic of health and stress is one with which we can all identify. As you review the material, relate the information on stress, anxiety, coping, and physical health to examples from your own life and the lives of friends and family members. Consider how your health belief system and the method of cognitive appraisal can help give you more control over stress and illness.

2. Notice how the information in chapter 15 is related to material presented in the text up to this point. Health and stress are related to cognitive processes, neuroscience, motivation, emotion, and personality. The evolutionary theme that has been reiterated throughout the text is again considered in the context of health and stress. How is the GAS an adaptive response? What would happen if we did not have such a mechanism to respond to danger? On the other hand, what happens to people who consider everything dangerous? The next chapter (chapter 16) will consider abnormal behavior and reactions, or psychopathology.

Chapter Outline

Chapter Overview

Chapter 16 covers the topic of abnormal behavior. Everyone feels anxious or depressed occasionally. However, some individuals experience symptoms so severe that they become unable to function effectively in their daily lives. Many seek help for their problems from mental health professionals, who can examine their symptoms in detail, diagnose the problems, and plan treatment. Knowledge of abnormal behavior is essential for assessment, diagnosis, and treatment. The study of abnormal behavior is closely related to topics previously covered, including emotion (chapter 13), personality (chapter 14), and stress (chapter 15). Chapter 17 will cover treatment methods.

Chapter 16 contains six major sections: (1) "Abnormal Behavior: Perspectives and Models," (2) "Anxiety, Somatoform, and Dissociative Disorders," (3) "Schizophrenia," (4) "Delusional and Personality Disorders," (5) "Mood Disorders," and (6) "The Neurophysiology of Abnormal Behavior."

The first section ("Abnormal Behavior: Perspectives and Models") begins with a discussion of the complex issue of defining abnormal behavior or psychopathology. Defining abnormal behavior is difficult for three reasons: (1) Abnormality is a construct, an abstraction, and therefore subject to varied definitions; (2) psychologists often disagree as to what constitutes a specific instance of abnormal behavior; and (3) there are cultural differences in what can reasonably be considered abnormal. Three approaches used in defining abnormality—maladaptation, social deviance, and statistical variation. Regardless of definition, abnormal behavior is a problem of major proportions. Statistics show how widespread the problem is. In ancient time, people believed in demonology. Modern mental health professionals consider abnormal behavior to be the result of a combination of physiological and psychological factors that can be determined through research.

Freud hypothesized, as do most psychologists and psychiatrists today, that abnormal behavior is caused by interactive combinations of environmental and biological factors. After a brief discussion of evolution and neuroscience, this section describes major causal models of abnormality, including the medical model, psychological models, and the diathesis-stress model. The classification of mental disorders is virtually as old as civilization itself. In the nineteenth century, the German scientist Emil Kraeplin formulated a diagnostic system that contained an orderly set of categories and subcategories. His system, with revisions, has served as the model for all diagnostic and classification manuals since. The current system is the DSM-IV Multi-Axial Diagnostic System, the fourth revision of the *Diagnostic and Statistical Manual* published by the American Psychiatric Association. The text describes the five axes of the DSM-IV and how they are used. The section discusses problems with psychiatric diagnosis, including reliability, validity, labeling, and medical students' disease, and ends with a brief discussion of the values of classification and diagnosis.

The second section ("Anxiety, Somatoform, and Dissociative Disorders") covers three main types of disorder. Anxiety is a vague feeling of dread, a fear with no specific object, an emotion that everyone experiences at times. Anxiety disorders are characterized by high levels of anxiety accompanied by patterns of ineffective, maladaptive behavior. A generalized anxiety disorder is one in which the person feels anxious and apprehensive, has a sense of impending disaster, and believes he is falling apart or losing control. Much of the anxiety is free-floating, anxiety that cannot be attributed to any specific current event. Panic disorder is marked by the occurrence of panic attacks—sudden, severe states of anxiety so extreme that the individual is unable to function effectively for a time period that can range from minutes to hours. Obsessive-compulsive disorder (OCD) is characterized by persistent, uncontrollable thoughts (obsessions) and repetitive, unavoidable, ritualistic acts (compulsions) that accomplish no practical end. Phobic disorders include simple and complex phobias. A phobia is an irrational fear of some object or situation that is accompanied by avoidance behavior.

Somatoform disorders involve physical complaints and symptoms that are similar to those of medical conditions but have no underlying organic cause. Dissociative disorders involve an alteration of consciousness, usually in the form of fragmentation or splitting, that interferes with the sense of personal identity. The subcategories described include dissociative amnesia, dissociative fugue, and dissociative identity disorder (formerly called multiple personality disorder).

The third section ("Schizophrenia") defines schizophrenia as a disorder in which the person displays reduced contact with reality, accompanied by thought disturbances that result in abnormal perceptual, motor, emotional, and social functioning. The primary symptoms of schizophrenia include disturbances of thought and language, disturbances of perception, disturbances in motor behavior, and disturbance of affect. Because symptoms vary greatly from one patient to another, it is often difficult to diagnose schizophrenia. The DSM-IV identifies five major subcategories of the disorder: (1) disorganized, (2) catatonic, (3) paranoid, (4) undifferentiated, and (5) residual. Distinctions are made between process and reactive schizophrenia. The text discusses psychological causes, including the psychodynamic concept of regression and the schizophrenogenic mother, the double-bind hypothesis, the social learning approach, and the sociogenic hypothesis.

The fourth section ("Delusional and Personality Disorders") explains that delusional disorders affect cognitive processes and impair the ability to think clearly and rationally. Personality disorders do not center around cognitive processes; rather, they are long-standing patterns of maladaptive social and emotional functioning. Delusional disorders are psychotic disorders characterized most often by delusions of persecution or grandeur. Personality disorder is diagnosed when the patient exhibits rigid, extreme, dominant personality characteristics that are maladaptive and impair social functioning. Unlike other categories of disorder, the personality disorders do not involve high levels of anxiety, physical problems, reduced contact with reality, or bizarre patterns of behavior. Rather, they are pervasive, long-term behavior patterns that influence most areas of life. The major subcategories are the dependent personality, histrionic personality, borderline personality, and antisocial personality. The text describes the antisocial personality in greater depth than the others.

The fifth section ("Mood Disorders") covers severe mood disturbances. Major depressive disorder, also called unipolar disorder, is diagnosed when there is a persistent, negative mood state that includes profound sadness accompanied by feelings of hopelessness, dejection, despair, loneliness, and boredom. Crying spells are common, and the person reports feeling demoralized. Major depression can occur as a single episode, but this disorder is more likely to be chronic with multiple episodes. Bipolar disorder involves both depressive and manic episodes. A manic episode is a distinct period of time during which the individual's mood becomes elevated and expansive and the person displays hyperactivity, excessive cheerfulness, and heightened irritability. The section discusses suicide, including statistical information and ends with a discussion of causes of mood disorder, including stressful life events, behavioral approaches, and cognitive views, including learned helplessness.

The final section ("The Neurophysiology of Abnormal Behavior") focuses on schizophrenia, mood disorders, and cognitive disorders. Biological factors in schizophrenia include heredity, neurochemistry, and neuroanatomy. Regarding heredity, studies have shown definitively that genetic factors are involved in schizophrenia. Overall, studies suggest that heritability for schizophrenia is about 70 percent, while environmental factors account for about 20 percent of the risk. Many experts believe that the genetic factor in schizophrenia might be expressed as abnormalities in brain chemistry. One hypothesis is that schizophrenia is the result of excessive levels of the neurotransmitter dopamine. Genetic and biochemical factors also play major roles in mood disorders. Studies are exploring the involvement of norepinephrine and serotonin in mood disorders. Cognitive disorders (including delirium, dementia, and anmestic syndrome) result from structural damage to the brain or from neurochemical imbalances and involve impairment of such processes as memory, language, thinking, and perception.

How to Master Chapter 16

Refer to These Learning Objectives

You should be able to achieve the following learning objectives after mastering the material in chapter 16:

Abnormal Behavior: Perspectives and Models

1. Define abnormal behavior.

2. List statistics regarding the prevalence of abnormal behavior .

3. Discuss historical views of mental illness and compare them to modern views.

4. Explain the evolution and neuroscience views of abnormal behavior.

5. Describe these major causal models: the medical model; the psychological models; the diathesis-stress model.

6. Discuss the contributions of Pinel and Kraepelin in the classification of abnormal behavior.

7. Describe the modern system of classification and diagnosis—the DSM-IV Multi-Axial Diagnostic System.

8. Discuss problems with and the value of diagnosis.

Anxiety, Somatoform, and Dissociative Disorders

9. Describe the major characteristics and causes of anxiety, generalized anxiety disorder, panic disorder, obsessive-compulsive disorder, and phobic disorders.

10. Describe the major characteristics and causes of somatoform disorders and the subcategories somatization disorder, conversion disorder, hypochondriasis, and pain disorder.

11. Describe the major characteristics and causes of dissociative disorders, including dissociative amnesia and fugue states.

Schizophrenia

12. Define schizophrenia and describe its primary symptoms and causes.

13. List and describe the principal types of schizophrenia.

Delusional and Personality Disorders

14. Define and distinguish between delusional and personality disorders.

15. Describe the major characteristics and causes of antisocial personality.

Mood Disorders

16. Define and distinguish between major depressive disorder and bipolar disorder.

17. Discuss types of depression, the nature of suicide, and causes of mood disorders.

The Neurophysiology of Abnormal Behavior

18. Discuss the roles of genetic factors, brain biochemistry, and brain anatomy in schizophrenia.

19. Discuss the neurophysiology of mood disorders and cognitive disorders.

Debate These Myths

MYTH 1: Abnormal behavior is easily defined and diagnosed.

Strategy:

Discuss the various definitions, and the scope, of abnormal behavior:

Discuss the different approaches to abnormal behavior as specified by the major causal models:

Describe the complex system used for classifying and diagnosing abnormal behavior:

Look carefully at the characteristics of the various disorders described in the text, and comment on the overlapping features some of them share and how these commonalities could lead to conflicting opinions in terms of diagnosis:

Other statements and examples for debating MYTH 1:

Change MYTH 1 into a true statement:

MYTH 2: *Although everyone gets depressed from time to time, serious depression and suicide are rare.*

Strategy:

Discuss the statistics on the lifetime risk for major depression:

Discuss the figures provided by the World Health Organization on suicide:

Discuss the gender and age groups that are most at risk for major depression and suicide:

Other statements or examples for debating MYTH 2:

Change MYTH 2 into a true statement:

Test Yourself: Multiple-Choice Questions

Directions: Circle the best response for each of the following questions.

1. Another term for abnormal behavior is:

   a. psychoanalysis

   b. hypochondriasis

   c. psychopathy

   d. psychopathology

2. A woman who will not leave her house to go to work in the morning unless all the cans in the pantry are arranged in alphabetical order is engaging in behavior that would be considered:

   a. maladaptive

   b. inefficient

   c. neither a nor b

   d. both a and b

3. Without including alcohol and drug abuse, the annual overall cost of mental illness in the U.S. is at least:

   a. $100 million

   b. $1 billion

   c. $10 billion

   d. $100 billion

4. Including alcohol and drug abuse, the annual overall cost of mental illness in the U.S. is rising to:

   a. $273 billion

   b. $173 billion

   c. $73 billion

   d. $7 billion

5. The idea that abnormal behavior is caused by evil spirits inhabiting the person's body is known as:

   a. bipolar disorder

   b. schizophrenia

   c. demonology

   d. phrenology

6. From an evolutionary perspective, abnormal behavior:

   a. is adaptive today

   b. used to be more adaptive

   c. has adapted out

   d. will eventually disappear

7. Theory and research dealing with biological factors in psychopathology have focused on:

   a. genetics

   b. neuroanatomy

   c. neurochemistry

   d. all of the above

8. Thomas Szasz believes that the medical model:

   a. should be applied to the study of schizophrenia

   b. is not adequate for psychological disorders

   c. should be considered equivalent to the psychodynamic model

   d. delineates specific treatments for mental disorders

9. Behavioral model is to humanistic model as:

   a. potential is to observation

   b. abnormal is to normal

   c. learning is to self-concept

   d. reinforcement is to conflict

10. In the diathesis-stress model, diathesis refers to a:

    a. predisposing influence

    b. current environmental factor

    c. tendency toward homeostasis

    d. disorder of unknown origin

11. Victor's father and paternal grandfather were alcoholics. When his stress level is high, Victor turns to alcohol and sometimes tranquilizers. He has poor coping skills. In this example, the diathesis is:

    a. the history of alcoholism is Victor's family

    b. Victor's stress level

    c. Victor's coping skills

    d. Victor's abuse of chemicals

12.   The current version of the *Diagnostic and Statistical Manual,* the DSM-IV, was published in 1994 by the:

a.   American Psychological Association

b.   American Psychological Society

c.   American Psychiatric Association

d.   American Medical Association

13.   Under the DSM-IV system, the number of diagnostic axes is:

a.   2   c.   4

b.   3   d.   5

14.   Angela suffers from diabetes and high blood pressure. In the DSM-IV system, these conditions would be included under which which axis?

a.   I   c.   III

b.   II   d.   IV

15.   Margaret's highest level of functioning during the past year was rated at 60 by her therapist. Under the DSM-IV system, this information would be recorded for axis:

a.   I   c.   IV

b.   III   d.   V

16.   The main value of diagnosis and classification is:

a.   the use of labels   c.   communication among professionals

b.   creating expectations   d.   identifying impostors

17.   A glance or stray remark triggers insecurity in Martha. Even though on an intellectual level Martha knows she is a competent secretary, she lives in constant fear of losing her job. She feels her heart beating faster every time her supervisor walks by her desk, even if he is smiling. Of the following, it is most likely that Martha suffers from:

a.   anxiety disorder   c.   OCD

b.   a simple phobia   d.   dissociative amnesia

18.   Men with anxiety disorders are at significantly increased risk for:

a.   somatization disorder   c.   disturbances of thought

b.   fatal heart attacks   d.   HIV

19.   Panic disorder, obsessive-compulsive disorder, and phobic disorders are categorized as:

a.   dissociative disorders   c.   somatoform disorders

b.   mood disorders   d.   anxiety disorders

20.   Panic disorder is found with the greatest frequency in:

a.   women   c.   men

b.   children   d.   senior citizens

21.   Dennis could not stop thinking about the germs he had on his hands from all the things he had touched that day. His persistent, uncontrollable thoughts would be considered:

a.   compulsions   c.   obsessions

b.   panic attacks   d.   fugue states

22.   Lorraine could not leave the house until she checked every window and door lock three times and alphabetized the cans in the pantry. Lorraine's behavior would be considered:

a.   compulsive   c.   phobic

b.   obsessive   d.   logical

23.   Obsessive-compulsive disorder is seen in:

    a.   1 percent of the population   c.   10 percent of the population

    b.   5 percent of the population   d.   20 percent of the population

24.   Of the following phobias, the complex phobia is:

    a.   hydrophobia   c.   claustrophobia

    b.   agoraphobia   d.   hematophobia

25.   Ellen refuses to leave her house. She has an overwhelming fear of being in a public place with no access to help. She begins to panic as she approaches the front door of her house when encouraged by family members to try to go out. It is likely that Ellen is suffering from:

    a.   a simple phobia   c.   schizophrenia

    b.   hypochondriasis   d.   agoraphobia

26.   All of the following are somatoform disorders *except*:

    a.   Briquet's syndrome   c. pain disorder

    b.   ulcers   d.   conversion disorder

27.   David frequently suffers from chest pains and light-headedness. His symptoms have increased ever since he lost his job. When he has gone to the emergency room thinking he is having a heart attack, no physical basis for his symptoms could be found. Of the following, it is most likely that David is suffering from:

    a.   a phobic disorder   c.   bipolar disorder

    b.   obsessive-compulsive disorder   d.   a somatoform disorder

28.   The origin of psychogenic pain is:

    a.   genetic   c.   psychological

    b.   environmental   d.   organic

29.   Multiple personality is now called:

    a.   dissociative identity disorder   c.   dissociative amnesia

    b.   dissociative fugue   d.   schizophrenia

30.   Schizophrenia is characterized by:

    a.   reduced contact with reality   c.   hallucinations

    b.   thought disturbances   d.   all of the above

31.   Alicia, an elementary school teacher, maintained the false belief that she was Joan of Arc and had a great mission to fulfill. Alicia was suffering with:

    a.   panic disorder   c.   a delusion

    b.   hallunications   d.   a fugue state

32.   Marlene attacked her sister with a kitchen knife when she heard her deceased father's voice command her to do so because her sister is an evil force on the earth. Marlene, who suffers from schizophrenia, was responding to:

    a.   a delusion   c.   an anxiety attack

    b.   an auditory halluncination   d.   a catatonic episode

33.   The experience of attention deficit and the consciousness flooded with incoming sensory information are most characteristic of people suffering with:

    a.   panic disorder   c.   personality disorder

    b.   schizophrenia   d.   bipolar disorder

34.   Norman, who is diagnosed as schizophrenic, talked without any apparent emotion about discovering his father's dead body on the front lawn. Norman's behavior demonstrates:

    a.   flat affect   c.   both a and b

    b.   blunting of emotions   d.   neither a nor b

35. A person who previously experienced at least one episode of schizophrenia but is presently showing no clear signs of the disorder would now be categorized as:

   a. catatonic
   c. undifferentiated
   b. disorganized
   d. residual

36. The type of schizophrenia characterized by either extreme excitement and hyperactivity or extreme withdrawal and slowing of motor movement and "waxy flexibility" is:

   a. catatonic
   c. disorganized
   b. bipolar
   d. paranoid

37. Process schizophrenia is to reactive schizophrenia as

   a. deep is to superficial
   c. acute is to chronic
   b. manic is to depressive
   d. gradual onset is to rapid onset

38. Katie was given conflicting messages by her father, who said "I love you" but later smacked her across the face when she couldn't finish her dinner. Katie's father's behavior is an example of:

   a. a panic attack
   c. schizophrenic behavior
   b. a double bind
   d. obsessive-compulsive behavior

39. Referring back to question 38, Gregory Bateson would suggest that Katie's father could cause Katie to develop:

   a. schizophrenia
   c. panic disorder
   b. bipolar disorder
   d. a personality disorder

40. The personality disorder associated with instability, unpredictability, moodiness, and having intense, stormy interpersonal relationships is known as:

   a. antisocial personality
   c. dependent personality
   b. histrionic personality
   d. borderline personality

41. Antisocial personality disorder has all of the following characteristics *except*:

   a. irresponsible behavior
   c. a strong sense of remorse
   b. impulsivity
   d. disregard for the truth

42. All of the following are characteristic of major depressive disorder *except*:

   a. negative mood
   c. poor concentration
   b. crying
   d. hallucinations

43. A less severe version of bipolar disorder is known as:

   a. manic disorder
   c. panic disorder
   b. cyclothymic disorder
   d. fugue disorder

44. When there is no obvious precipitating event, the depression is said to be:

   a. endogenous
   c. chronic
   b. reactive
   d. cyclothymic

45. According to the World Health Organization, the number of people who commit suicide each year is nearly:

   a. 20,000
   c. 100,000
   b. 50,000
   d. 500,000

46. According to Freud, depression is the result of:

   a. genetic factors
   c. ego loss
   b. low self-esteem
   d. deprivation of positive reinforcement

47. Learned helplessness, a perceived lack of control over life events, is most closely associated with:
    a. depression
    c. free-floating anxiety
    b. paranoia
    d. delusional thinking

48. Research suggests that heritability for schizophrenia is about:
    a. 20 percent
    c. 70 percent
    b. 50 percent
    d. 100 percent

49. Research has shown that drugs that act by blocking dopamine receptors in the brain have proven highly effective in controlling the symptoms of:
    a. panic disorder
    c. bipolar disorder
    b. schizophrenia
    d. depression

50. Research has shown that depression can be successfully treated with antidepressant drugs that increase levels of:
    a. serotonin
    c. acetylcholine
    b. dopamine
    d. RNA

Test Yourself: Fill in the Blanks

Directions: Fill in the blanks with the correct term or name.

1. According to the _____ model, abnormal behavior results from unconscious conflicts that originate in childhood.

2. According to the _____ model, abnormal behaviors are learned.

3. According to the _____ model, abnormal behavior results from a failure to realize potentials and difficulties maintaining an accurate self-concept.

4. In the _____ model, a predisposing influence combines with a current environmental factor to produce a disorder.

5. The _____ is the current diagnostic manual published in 1994.

6. _____ disorders are characterized by high levels of anxiety accompanied by patterns of ineffective, maladaptive behavior.

7. _____ is characterized by persistent, uncontrollable thoughts and repetitive, ritualistic acts.

8. _____ disorders involve physical complaints and symptoms that are similar to those of medical conditions but have no underlying organic cause.

9. People with a _____ disorder exhibit a loss or impairment of physical functions involving the sensory or motor system.

10. The best known somatoform disorder is _____, in which the person has excessive concerns about health and worries constantly about having a major physical disease.

11. _____ disorders involve an alteration of consciousness, usually in the form of fragmentation or splitting, which interferes with the sense of personal identity.

12. _____ is a disorder in which the person displays reduced contact with reality, accompanied by thought disturbances that result in abnormal perceptual, motor, emotional, and social functioning.

13. The most dramatic form of perceptual disturbance is the _____, a perception that occurs when there is no actual stimulus.

14. _____ disorder is diagnosed when the patient exhibits rigid, extreme, dominant personality characteristics that are maladaptive and impair social functioning.

15. Also called unipolar disorder, _____ disorder is diagnosed when there is a persistent, negative mood state that includes profound sadness accompanied by feelings of hopelessness, dejection, despair, loneliness, and boredom.

16. _____ disorder involves both depressive and manic episodes.

17. _____ is a perceived lack of control over life events.

18. The neurochemical currently receiving the most attention in research on schizophrenia is _____.

19. _____ disorders result from structural damage to the brain or from neurochemical imbalances. They involve impairment of memory, language, thinking, and perception.

20. _____ is a chronic, progressive deterioration of brain functions.

Test Yourself: Matching Questions

Directions: For each item in column I, select the item in column II that is most closely associated with it.

I	II
_____1. Emil Kraeplin	a. perception with no physical stimulus
_____2. medical model	b. psychopath
_____3. psychodynamic model	c. physical symptoms with no organic cause
_____4. humanistic model	d. classified mental disorders
_____5. DSM-IV	e. neurotransmitter
_____6. generalized anxiety disorder	f. disease view of abnormal behavior
_____7. somatoform disorder	g. splitting of consciousness
_____8. hypochondriasis	h. involves unconscious conflicts
_____9. dissociative disorder	i. unipolar disorder
_____10. hallucination	j. free-floating anxiety
_____11. bipolar disorder	k. based on self-concept
_____12. learned helplessness	l. involves depressive and manic episodes
_____13. major depressive disorder	m. diagnostic system
_____14. dopamine	n. perceived lack of control
_____15. antisocial personality disorder	o. excessive health concerns

Test Yourself: Answer Key

Multiple Choice

1. d	(564)	11. a	(567)	21. c	(571)	31. c	(578)	41. c	(582–83)
2. d	(564)	12. c	(567)	22. a	(571)	32. b	(579)	42. d	(584)
3. d	(565)	13. d	(568)	23. a	(571)	33. b	(579)	43. b	(585)
4. a	(565)	14. c	(568)	24. b	(572)	34. c	(579)	44. a	(586)
5. c	(565)	15. d	(568)	25. d	(572)	35. d	(579)	45. d	(586)
6. d	(566)	16. c	(570)	26. b	(574)	36. a	(579)	46. c	(588)
7. d	(566)	17. a	(570)	27. d	(574)	37. d	(579)	47. a	(589)
8. b	(567)	18. b	(570)	28. c	(574)	38. b	(580)	48. c	(591)
9. c	(567)	19. d	(570)	29. a	(575)	39. a	(580)	49. b	(591)
10. a	(567)	20. a	(571)	30. d	(578)	40. d	(581)	50. a	(593)

Fill in the Blanks

1. psychodynamic
2. behavioral
3. humanistic
4. diathesis-stress
5. DSM-IV
6. anxiety
7. obsessive-compulsive disorder or OCD
8. somatoform
9. conversion
10. hypochondriasis
11. dissociative
12. schizophrenia
13. hallucination
14. personality
15. major depressive
16. bipolar
17. learned helplessness
18. dopamine
19. cognitive

20. dementia

Matching Questions

1. d	6. j	11. l
2. f	7. c	12. n
3. h	8. o	13. i
4. k	9. g	14. e
5. m	10. a	15. b

Do These Mini Projects

1. The purpose of this mini project is to help you distinguish between having a normal passing feeling of anxiety or depression versus having a disorder. On a sheet of paper make two columns. Label the first column *Normal Anxiety* and the second column *Anxiety Disorder*. In the first column, make a list of the characteristics of normal anxiety— that is, anxiety that is moderate rather than extreme, that passes relatively quickly, is not recurrent, and does not interfere with daily functioning. In the second column, make a list of the characteristics of an anxiety disorder. Compare your lists and distinguish between normal anxiety and an anxiety disorder. Do the same for *Normal Depression* and *Major Depressive Disorder*. Bring your notes to class for sharing.

2. Call or write to your local community mental health center or facility and obtain material that describes the signs of potential suicide, symptoms of major depressive disorder, and symptoms of bipolar disorder. Bring the information you gather to class for sharing.

Pull It All Together

1. Go back to chapter 1 and find the discussion of the models of psychology. Compare the information you read at the start of the introduction to this psychology course with the discussion of the major causal models in the current chapter on abnormal behavior. What do you know now that you did not know when you started the course regarding these models and their function in the study of psychology?

2. The study of abnormal behavior is closely related to the study of emotions, personality, and stress, topics covered in the chapters that preceded this one. How was it helpful to master the material on emotions, personality, and stress before learning about abnormal behavior? How does understanding normal behavior and processes facilitate understanding of abnormal behavior and processes?

CHAPTER 17
PSYCHOLOGICAL AND BIOMEDICAL THERAPIES

Chapter Outline

Chapter Overview

Chapter 17 covers psychotherapy and biomedical therapy. The chapter begins by defining, in broad terms, psychological and biomedical therapies, and then listing the various subtypes of psychotherapy and biomedical therapy. The author of the text makes the point that many people who suffer from the disorders described in chapter 16 and receive treatment are faced with a large array of psychological and biological treatments. After giving a historical overview, the text describes these various forms of treatment.

Chapter 17 contains six major sections: (1) "Mental Health Care: Perspectives and Practices," (2) "Insight Therapies," (3) "Behavioral and Cognitive-Behavioral Therapies," (4) "Group and Family Therapies," (5) "Issues in Psychotherapy," and (6) "Neurophysiology: The Biomedical Therapies."

The first section ("Mental Health Care: Perspectives and Practices") begins with a historical perspective, tracing the roots of humane treatment of the mentally ill, which culminated in the modern community mental health movement, with its focus on deinstitutionalization. This section also places therapy in the context of treating failures of evolutionary adaptation. The section ends with distinctions made among the various types of mental health professionals.

The second section ("Insight Therapies") covers two major categories of insight therapy: the psychodynamic approaches and the humanistic approaches. The psychodynamic therapies are those based on Freud's psychoanalytic theory and the theories that derived from it. The first psychodynamic approach discussed is psychoanalysis or orthodox psychoanalysis. Its basic techniques are free association, dream analysis, and the analysis of transference. The other types of psychoanalytic approaches, known as modern psychodynamic therapy, include ego psychology and object relations theory.

Humanistic therapies developed in reaction to the psychoanalytic approach. Humanistic approaches view individuals as unique and as having great potential for psychological growth and development. The two humanistic approaches discussed are Carl Rogers's client-centered therapy and Fritz Perls's Gestalt therapy. Client-centered therapy provides a safe therapeutic climate involving reflection and clarification of what the client says. Gestalt therapy emphasizes the importance of increasing the accuracy of the client's perception of reality.

The third section ("Behavioral and Cognitive-Behavioral Therapies") distinguishes these action-oriented approaches from the previously described insight therapies. All behavior therapies are based on the fundamental principles that normal and abnormal behaviors are learned, and therefore treatment is based on processes designed to change behavior. The section describes classical conditioning approaches (including systematic desensitization and aversion therapy) and operant conditioning approaches (token economies and stimulus control).

The cognitive behavioral approaches focus on the thought processes or cognitions that underlie and maintain behavior. The cognitive therapy of Aaron Beck, the rational-emotive therapy of Albert Ellis, and Albert Bandura's modeling are forms of treatment that target the thought processes underlying behavior.

The fourth section ("Group and Family Therapies") defines group psychotherapy as a systematic, therapeutic interaction among several people with a trained therapist as the group leader, and family therapy as dealing with problems involving family structure and family interaction patterns. The text briefly describes Virginia Satir's conjoint family therapy and Salvador Minuchin's structured family therapy.

The fifth section ("Issues in Psychotherapy") begins with an analysis of the effectiveness of psychotherapy. Research has shown that although there is some spontaneous remission (improvement over time with no therapy), therapy is clearly more beneficial than no therapy for individuals with emotional and behavioral problems. Therapy has been shown to be effective for anxiety disorders and depression, but much less effective for schizophrenia. There are no overall differences in effectiveness among the major therapies, but some forms of treatment might be better for some problems than others. Most psychologists are eclectic, practicing more than one form of therapy. Cultural considerations are discussed. The section ends with a discussion of ethical and legal issues in therapy.

The final section ("Neurophysiology: The Biomedical Therapies") examines neurological interventions, psychopharmacology, and the pros and cons of biomedical treatments. The neurological interventions include electroconvulsive therapy (ECT), an effective but controversial treatment for depression and mania, and psychosurgery, the most drastic of biological treatments. The advent of psychopharmacology, the use of psychiatric drugs, in the 1950s brought about a revolution in the treatment of the mentally ill. The text discusses a variety of antianxiety drugs, antipsychotic drugs, antidepressants, and antimanic drugs.

How to Master Chapter 17

Refer to These Learning Objectives

You should be able to achieve the following learning objectives after mastering the material in chapter 17:

Mental Health Care: Perspectives and Practices

1. Discuss how mental health care had been handled historically.

2. Explain what is meant by deinstitutionalization and the community mental health movement, including crisis intervention and prevention.

3. Discuss the concept of therapy from an evolutionary, adaptation perspective.

4. List the types of mental health professionals who are qualified to provide therapy.

Insight Therapies

5. Explain what is meant by insight therapy.

6. Describe the techniques of psychoanalysis and modern psychodynamic theory.

7. Describe the nature and techniques of the humanistic approaches, including client-centered therapy and Gestalt therapy.

Behavioral and Cognitive-Behavioral Therapies

8. Explain what is meant by action therapies.

9. Describe how behavior therapies differ from psychodynamic and humanistic approaches.

10. Describe classical conditioning and operant conditioning techniques.

11. Describe the characteristics and techniques of cognitive therapy, rational-emotive therapy, and modeling.

Group and Family Therapies

12. Describe the nature of group and family therapy.

Issues in Psychotherapy

13. Discuss the research studies on the effectiveness of therapy.

14. Discuss the common denominators of therapy.

15. Discuss cultural, ethical, and legal issues in treatment.

Neurophysiology: The Biomedical Therapies

16. Describe the biomedical therapies, including electroconvulsive therapy, psychosurgery, and psychopharmacology.

17. Explain the neurophysiological mechanisms underlying antianxiety drugs, antipsychotic drugs, antidepressants, and antimanic drugs.

18. Discuss the pros and cons of the biomedical treatments.

Debate These Myths

MYTH 1: *Psychotherapy is ineffective because people cannot really change.*

Strategy:

Discuss the research findings (Sloane, NIMH, meta-analytic studies) on the effectiveness of psychotherapy:

Discuss and give examples of the ôingredientsöö of an effective psychotherapy process:

From your own observations, discuss the stigma that is sometimes still attached to seeking help for emotional problems:

Give examples of behaviors and thought processes that are subject to change:

Other statements or examples for debating MYTH 1:

Change MYTH 1 into a true statement:

MYTH 2: *Psychoanalysis and psychotherapy are the same thing.*

Strategy:

Describe the basis and techniques of psychoanalysis:

233

Explain how psychoanalysis differs from modern psychodynamic approaches:

Explain how psychoanalysis differs from client-centered therapy and Gestalt therapy:

Explain how psychoanalysis differs from other forms of psychotherapy, including behavior therapy and cognitive-behavior therapies:

Other statements or examples for debating MYTH 2:

Change MYTH 2 into a true statement:

Test Yourself: Multiple-Choice Questions

Directions: Circle the best response for each of the following questions.

1.   Which one of the following statements concerning early mental health care is the most accurate?
      a.   Trephining was a practice involving prayer and starvation to drive out evil spirits.
      b.   Exorcism involved boring holes in the skulls of individuals considered mentally ill.
      c.   Dorothea Dix established humane mental health hospitals in Paris in the eighteenth century.
      d.   Benjamin Rush, the founder of American psychiatry, established humanitarian treatment at Pennsylvania Hospital.

2.   Establishing 32 mental hospitals and later organizing the nursing corps for the Northern armies during the Civil War is credited to:
      a.   Dorothea Dix   c.   William Tuke
      b.   Virginia Satir   d.   Benjamin Rush

3.   Phillipe Pinel's treatment of patients would be best described as:
      a.   educational   c.   threatening
      b.   kind   d.   practical

4. The Roman physician whose work on anatomy and physiology dominated medicine for thirteen centuries was named:
   a. Galen
   b. Tuke
   c. Pinel
   d. Hippocrates

5. Partial care and partial isolation from the community are provided by:
   a. mental institutions
   b. community mental health centers
   c. halfway houses
   d. emergency rooms

6. The Community Mental Health Centers Act was passed by Congress at the request of President:
   a. Carter
   b. Clinton
   c. Reagan
   d. Kennedy

7. Of the following environments, the *least* restrictive would be:
   a. community mental health center
   b. halfway house
   c. mental hospital
   d. psychiatric unit of a hospital

8. Of the following, a halfway house would be most suited to the needs of a:
   a. woman suffering from panic disorder who refuses to take appropriate medication
   b. suicidal teenager
   c. drug-addicted woman who is not fully rehabilitated
   d. compulsive male sex offender

9. Of the following, the most common psychiatric emergency is:
   a. intoxication or delirium
   b. psychotic behavior
   c. homicidal behavior
   d. attempted or threatened suicide

10. A psychologist worked with the Collins family to help them function more effectively before Mr. Collins's alcoholism and angry outbursts and Mrs. Collins's enabling behavior put their 5-year-old at risk for emotional problems. This family's working with a mental health professional before problems were out of control would be considered a form of:
    a. crisis intervention
    b. prevention
    c. deinstitutionalization
    d. psychiatric emergency

11. Which of the following professionals would be permitted to engage in biomedical therapy?
    a. psychiatrists
    b. psychiatric nurses
    c. psychologists
    d. all of the above

12. A mental health professional made sure when Mr. Johnson left the nursing home to live with his niece that her home was suitable to Mr. Johnson's needs and that Mr. Johnson and his niece had a stable relationship. It is most likely that this mental health professional is a:
    a. psychiatrist
    b. social worker
    c. psychologist
    d. school psychologist

13. Psychodynamic and humanistic approaches are considered:
    a. biomedical therapies
    b. action-oriented approaches
    c. branches of psychoanalysis
    d. insight therapies

14. A therapist noticed that his patient, John, was expressing strong resentment toward and engaging in power struggles with the therapist as John had done with his father as an adolescent. A psychoanalyst would interpret John's feelings as:
    a. free association
    b. countertransference
    c. a transference
    d. irrational

15. Free association, dream analysis, and the process of transference are most closely associated with:
    a. ego psychology
    b. psychoanalysis
    c. object relations theory
    d. Gestalt therapy

16. Object relations theory is built around the concept that people are:
    a. influenced by powerful drives such as sex and aggression
    b. resistant to change their behavior patterns
    c. innately motivated to strive for actualization
    d. finding it increasingly difficult to bond with each other

17. As part of helping Andrea develop a better self-concept, Andrea's therapist let her know that she accepted her and valued her as a person even though Andrea had made poor judgments in her life. This therapeutic approach is most closely associated with:
    a. psychoanalysis
    b. Gestalt therapy
    c. client-centered therapy
    d. object relations theory

18. All of the following statements regarding client-centered therapy are true *except*:
    a. Human beings are regarded as unique individuals with potential for psychological growth.
    b. It is important that the therapist experience accurate empathy.
    c. Client-centered therapy developed in reaction to the inadequacies of the psychoanalytic approach
    d. This approach emphasizes changing abnormal perceptions of reality into more accurate perceptions.

19. The interpretation of dreams is most closely associated with:
    a. client-centered therapy
    b. Gestalt therapy
    c. psychoanalysis
    d. rational-emotive therapy

20. Gestalt therapy was developed by:
    a. Carl Rogers
    b. Fritz Perls
    c. Otto Kernberg
    d. Albert Bandura

21. Behavior therapy is to client-centered therapy as:
    a. unconconscious is to conscious
    b. action is to insight
    c. Fritz Perls is to Carl Rogers
    d. innate is to learned

22. Behavior therapy is *never* focused on:
    a. cognitive processes
    b. weight reduction
    c. gaining insight
    d. moderate depression

23. When Bill was in treatment for his fear of snakes, the therapist asked Bill to make a list of the most feared stimulus to the least feared stimulus. The least feared was a garden hose. The therapist taught Bill to think about a garden hose while doing breathing exercises, and then to move progressively up the list of feared stimuli, pairing the images with relaxation techniques. This therapist was using a method known as:
    a. aversive therapy
    b. systematic desensitization
    c. stimulus control
    d. token economy

24. Referring back to question 23, the technique described would be most often used by a:
    a. behavior therapist
    b. psychodynamic therapist
    c. Gestalt therapist
    d. client-centered therapist

25. In a nursing home, a female resident who refused to take a shower was rewarded with a plastic card every time she agreed to shower. She knew that when she obtained three cards, she could get her hair permed for free. The technique described is known as:

    a. stimulus control
    b. systematic desensitization
    c. modeling
    d. a token economy

26. Referring back to question 25, the technique described is a form of:

    a. classical conditioning
    b. operant conditioning
    c. aversive conditioning
    d. cognitive therapy

27. As one of the steps of a program designed to help people quit smoking, the participants were instructed to limit their smoking to the outdoors and to eliminate all indoor smoking, including in the house and car. This behavioral technique is known as:

    a. stimulus control
    b. systematic desensitization
    c. a token economy
    d. classical conditioning

28. In cognitive therapy, treatment focuses on:

    a. gaining insight into the causes of dysfunctional patterns
    b. modifying perceptual and thought processes that cause depression
    c. modeling healthy behavior patterns
    d. enhancing the self-concept

29. According to Aaron Beck, a man would be most likely to become depressed if he:

    a. grew up in an abusive household
    b. were unaware of his innate aggressive motives
    c. called himself an idiot every time he made a small mistake
    d. spent most of his time by himself

30. The goal of rational-emotive therapy is to:

    a. promote insight
    b. provide accurate empathy
    c. resolve unconscious conflicts
    d. restructure cognitions

31. A group of third-graders was shown a video of children their age using good table manners at a formal dinner party. The goal was to teach these children through the use of:

    a. stimulus control
    b. modeling
    c. cognitive therapy
    d. classical conditioning

32. Intensive group experiences aimed at increasing self-awareness, improving interpersonal interactions, and realizing the potentials of group members for change are the focus of:

    a. encounter groups
    b. cognitive-behavioral groups
    c. behavioral groups
    d. psychoanalytic groups

33. Virginia Satir is known for:

    a. structured family therapy
    b. conjoint family therapy
    c. systems therapy
    d. self-help groups

34. Salvador Minuchin views the family as a:

    a. behavioral group
    b. nontraditional structure
    c. dysfunctional unit
    d. system

35. Family therapy has been used to treat:

    a. marital problems
    b. anorexic girls
    c. adolescent drug abusers
    d. all of the above

36. The percentage of clients who improve over time even if they receive no therapy at all is between:

   a. 10 and 20 percent
   c. 70 and 90 percent
   b. 30 and 60 percent
   d. 0 and 5 percent

37. Which one of the following statements regarding research on the effectiveness of psychotherapy is the most accurate?

   a. Since most clients experience spontaneous remission, receiving no therapy is just as effective as being in therapy.
   b. Psychoanalytic therapy is more effective than cognitive therapy.
   c. More clients improved with therapy than without therapy.
   d. The Sloane and NIMH studies were too poorly controlled to yield meaningful data on the effectiveness of psychotherapy.

38. Of the following, the approach that dominates the practice of clinical psychology is:

   a. humanistic
   c. behavioral
   b. eclectic
   d. cognitive

39. Which of the following has research shown?

   a. Biomedical therapy is more effective for treating anxiety than is cognitive therapy.
   b. Psychodynamic therapy is more effective for treating sexual problems than is behavior therapy.
   c. All the therapies work equally well for all problems.
   d. There is no overall difference in effectiveness among the therapies.

40. Of the following disorders, psychotherapy is the *least* effective for treating:

   a. schizophrenia
   c. anxiety
   b. depression
   d. anorexia nervosa

41. Of the following, which one is *not* included among the ethical standards for psychologists?

   a. They must recognize the limitations of their competence.
   b. They must always be accountable for the fulfillment of their professional responsibilities.
   c. Positive therapeutic outcome is a professional responsibility.
   d. They must protect their clients.

42. The thank-you proposition is one of the standards used to evaluate:

   a. effectiveness of psychotherapy
   b. mental illness requiring commitment
   c. willingness to commit oneself voluntarily
   d. the right to refuse treatment

43. Which one of the following statements concerning the rights of patients is the most accurate?

   a. Involuntarily committed patients are not required to submit to any routine form of treatment and have the right to refuse psychiatric medications.
   b. The courts have been vague in the requirements of mental institutions to provide a humane environment.
   c. Each patient must receive an individual treatment program.
   d. Controversial treatments can be administered to involuntarily committed patients without family consent.

44. Research has shown that ECT often causes:

   a. permanent memory loss
   c. brain damage
   b. headaches
   d. cardiac complications

45. Electroconvulsive therapy came into widespread use in the treatment of major depression and is also now used very effectively in treating:
   a. schizophrenia
   c. panic disorder
   b. anorexia nervosa
   d. mania

46. Prefrontal lobotomies were first performed in the:
   a. 1900s
   c. 1940s
   b. 1920s
   d. 1970s

47. A cingulotomy is a surgical procedure used in the treatment of:
   a. generalized anxiety disorder
   b. obsessive-compulsive disorder intractable to more routine treatments
   c. schizophrenia
   d. epilepsy when medication fails to control seizures

48. Benzodiazepines are in current use as:
   a. antianxiety agents
   c. antipsychotic drugs
   b. antidepressants
   d. antimanic drugs

49. Rachel, age 35 has spent her life in and out of mental institutions. One of the problems she experiences when left to her own devices is that her hallucinations return when she is noncompliant with taking her medication, which is most likely:
   a. diazepam
   c. a neuroleptic
   b. an MAO inhibitor
   d. Prozac

50. For many years, the antimanic drug of choice has been the mineral salt:
   a. serotonin
   c. phenothiazine
   b. benzodiazepine
   d. lithium

Test Yourself: Fill in the Blanks

Directions: Fill in the blanks with the correct term or name.

1. Increasing dissatisfaction with the exclusive use of large institutional settings for mental health care brought about the _____ movement.

2. _____ refers to the establishment of a helping relationship between a patient and a trained professional, who applies psychological principles to the treatment of emotional or behavioral problems.

3. _____ therapy refers to the use of physiological interventions, such as drugs and surgery, in an effort to treat the symptoms of emotional or behavioral problems.

4. The therapeutic techniques of _____ include free association, dream interpretation, and the analysis of transference.

5. The goal of _____ therapy is to help the patient become more aware of unconscious motives that are producing abnormal behavior and thereby help the patient understand and modify the behavior.

6. _____ psychology deemphasizes the role and power of the irrational id in favor of the rational ego.

7. The _____ approach developed primarily because analysts realized that the problems most often causing patients to seek therapy involved their relationships with other people.

8. _____'s basic principle is that the social values (conditions of worth) imposed on the individual by society underlie self-actualization.

9. _____ emphasizes that we act not on the basis of external reality but rather in accord with our perceptions of that reality.

10. _____ rely on learning principles and processes to change behavior.

11. _____ developed the most influential cognitive theory of depression and a corresponding therapy to treat it.

12. _____, developed by Albert Ellis, attempts to restructure cognitions.

13. _____ psychotherapy involves a systematic, therapeutic interaction among several people with a trained therapist as the group leader.

14. The _____ proposition holds that once a person suffering from mental illness has been successfully treated, he will very likely be thankful that the treatment was forced upon him.

15. More psychologists practice _____ therapy—the use of two or more therapies—than practice within any one school of thought.

16. When all other treatments appear to be unsuccessful, the drastic biological treatment, _____, may be applied.

17. The advent of _____, the use of psychiatric drugs, in the 1950s brought about a revolution in the treatment of the mentally ill.

18. _____ agents act primarily to reduce the effects of stress and make the individual feel more relaxed.

19. _____ agents, or neuroleptics, not only calm the patient but actually reduce the intensity of major schizophrenic symptoms, including hallucinations and delusions.

20. For many years, the _____ drug of choice has been the mineral salt lithium.

Test Yourself: Matching Questions

Directions: For each item in column I, select the item in column II that is most closely associated with it.

I	II
_____1. Phillipe Pinel	a. shock therapy
_____2. Dorothea Dix	b. neuroleptics
_____3. deinstitutionalization	c. eighteenth-century humanitarian
_____4. biomedical therapy	d. innovator in family therapy
_____5. psychoanalysis	e. benzodiazepines
_____6. Carl Rogers	f. reform of treatment in New England
_____7. Fritz Perls	g. improvement with no therapy
_____8. behavior therapy	h. shift to community centers
_____9. cognitive therapy	i. developed Gestalt therapy
_____10. Albert Ellis	j. use of physiological interventions
_____11. Virginia Satir	k. developed RET
_____12. spontaneous remission	l. focuses on thought processes
_____13. ECT	m. developed client-centered therapy
_____14. antianxiety agents	n. abnormal behavior is learned
_____15. antipsychotic agents	o. uses free association

Test Yourself: Answer Key

Multiple Choice

1. d	(598)	11. a	(601)	21. b	(606)	31. b	(609)	41. c	(616)
2. a	(598)	12. b	(601)	22. c	(606)	32. a	(610)	42. b	(616)
3. b	(598)	13. d	(602)	23. b	(606–7)	33. b	(610)	43. c	(616)
4. a	(598)	14. c	(603)	24. a	(606–7)	34. d	(610–11)	44. b	(618)
5. b	(599)	15. b	(602–3)	25. d	(607)	35. d	(611)	45. d	(618)
6. d	(599)	16. a	(604)	26. b	(607)	36. b	(613)	46. b	(619)
7. a	(599–600)	17. c	(605)	27. a	(607)	37. c	(613)	47. b	(619)
8. c	(599–600)	18. d	(605)	28. b	(608)	38. b	(615)	48. a	(620)
9. d	(600)	19. c	(603)	29. c	(608)	39. d	(614)	49. c	(621)
10. b	(600)	20. b	(605)	30. d	(608)	40. a	(615)	50. d	(623)

Fill in the Blanks

1. deinstitutionalization
2. psychotherapy
3. biomedical
4. psychoanalysis
5. insight
6. ego
7. object relations
8. Carl Rogers
9. Gestalt therapy
10. behavior therapy
11. Aaron Beck
12. rational-emotive therapy or RET
13. group
14. thank-you
15. eclectic
16. psychosurgery
17. psychopharmacology
18. antianxiety

19. antipsychotic

20. antimanic

Matching Questions

1. c	6. m	11. d
2. f	7. i	12. g
3. h	8. n	13. a
4. j	9. l	14. e
5. o	10. k	15. b

Do These Mini Projects

1. Obtain a copy of the ethical guidelines developed for psychologists by the American Psychological Association by writing to or calling the APA in Washington, D.C. Read through the ethical standards to get an idea of the types of attitudes and behaviors expected of psychologists and the penalties for violating ethical standards.

2. It is important to distinguish among the types of professionals who are permitted to engage in the practice of mental health. The educational background, specialized training, and practice of mental health differ among social workers, psychologists, and psychiatrists. Make a chart that compares these three types of professionals in terms of type of education and degree required, nature of skills, what they can and cannot do (e.g., who can and who cannot prescribe drugs), and why you would seek out one type over another for a particular problem. If you have the opportunity, it would be of value to interview a social worker, psychologist, or psychiatrist, or all three, to probe more deeply into the similarities and differences in their approaches to the mental health profession.

3. Choose a fear of your own or a fear of a family member or friend to create a hierarchy that at some point could be used for the purpose of systematic desensitization. If you work with another person, be sure that person is a willing participant and that discussion of the fear does not create undue discomfort. Remember that the hierarchy begins with the most feared object or situation and ends with the least feared, with a variety of ordered feared objects and situations in between that in some way resemble the original fear, and are arranged in descending order. Once you have the hierarchy organized and written down, think about how you would use this hierarchy to treat the problem using systematic desensitization.

Pull It All Together

1. Chapter 17 on psychotherapy and biomedical therapies is the culmination of the sequence of preceding chapters, including motivation, emotion, personality, health and stress, and abnormal behavior. The treatment of abnormal behavior is what most introductory students expect to learn about when signing up for an introductory psychology course. Why did you have to wait until chapter 17 to read about psychotherapy? In what significant ways did the information preceding this chapter provide a foundation that is necessary for a full appreciation of the nature of psychotherapy?

2. Psychotherapy and the use of medication to control emotions are topics about which most people have strong opinions. After studying chapter 17, were your original opinions reinforced, or did you change your opinion about any aspect of psychotherapy or biomedical therapy? If you changed an opinion, what opinions did you change and why?

Chapter Outline

Attitudes and Attitude Change

Attitude Formation

Cognitive Consistency

Attitudes and Behavior

Attitude Change

Social Influence

When Others Watch: Social Presence

Conformity

Compliance

Obedience

Group Processes

Theories of Social Affiliation

Sociobiology

Evolutionary Psychology Is *Not* Sociobiology

Group Norms

Group Dynamics

Cooperation and Competition

Environmental Psychology

Personal Space

Crowding

Territoriality

Environmental Stressors

Aggression

The Role of Learning

Triggers for Aggressive Behavior

Biological Factors in Aggression

Chapter Overview

Chapter 18, which discusses the individual in society, is the first of two chapters on social psychology. The topics covered in chapter 18—attitudes and attitude change, social influence, group processes, environmental psychology, and aggression—are all influenced by social cognition (thinking about other people and how you relate to them), the focus of chapter 19. Chapter 18 begins with a definition of social psychology as the study of the behavior of people as they live in, interact with, and are affected by groups. The author of the text also offers Gordon Allport's definition of social psychology as the attempt to understand and explain how the thoughts, feelings, and behaviors of individuals are influenced by the actual, imagined, or implied presence of others.

Chapter 18 contains six major sections: (1) "Attitudes and Attitude Change," (2) "Social Influence," (3) "Group Processes," (4) "Environmental Psychology," (5) "Aggression," and (6) "The Neurophysiology of Social Behavior."

The first section ("Attitudes and Attitude Change") defines an attitude as a relatively enduring predisposition to respond in a reasonably consistent manner toward a person, object, situation, or idea. The author discusses the components of attitudes, sources of attitudes, and how attitudes are acquired, and points out that people tend to maintain consistent attitudes, often in the face of considerable evidence that those attitudes are inappropriate or incorrect. Cognitive dissonance theory and balance theory attempt to explain how we strive to maintain consistency among our attitudes and between attitudes and behavior. This section ends with a discussion of the dynamics of attitude change.

The second section ("Social Influence") defines social influence as the effect of other people on the cognitions and behaviors of any given individual. We are all subject to social influence on a daily basis. Research findings are reported that address the question of why the presence of others sometimes facilitates and sometimes inhibits our behavior. The text discusses research findings on conformity, compliance, and obedience. Conformity is a change in attitudes or behaviors to bring the person in line with group values. Compliance is doing what someone else asks you to do when that person has no specific authority to make the request. Even stronger is obedience, in which a command from an authority figure directly causes an individual to modify his behavior, sometimes against his better judgment.

The third section ("Group Processes") examines our behavior as members of various groups, such as family, ethnic group, professional group, or hobby group. Topics covered in this section include theories of affiliation (social exchange and social comparison), sociobiology and evolutionary psychology (which are not the same thing), group norms, group dynamics, and cooperation and competition. Groups have a powerful impact on the behavior of individuals, and the behavior of the individuals composing and entering a group influence group behavior.

The fourth section ("Environmental Psychology") focuses on the domain of the environmental psychologists—the physical environment in which social interaction takes place. Among the areas addressed are personal space, crowding, territoriality, and environmental stress. Personal space is a definite but invisible psychological boundary that surrounds each of us and into which invaders are not comfortably allowed. Environmental psychologists investigate why people become aroused and threatened when their personal space is invaded, the effects of crowding on our functioning, the nature of territoriality, and the impact of environmental stressors, such as noise.

The fifth section ("Aggression") defines aggression as behavior performed with the intent of physically or psychologically hurting one or more other people. Aggression is distinguished from assertiveness, which means taking a stand and letting one's views be clearly known without any intent to inflict harm. The section discusses the role of learning in the development of aggressive behavior, triggers for aggressive behavior, and biological factors in aggression. The biological factors explored include instincts, evolution, and genetics.

The final section ("The Neurophysiology of Social Behavior") states that there is no doubt that social behavior is mediated by the central nervous system. However, because of the complexity of social behavior, there has been little study of its neuroanatomy and neurochemistry. What has been studied is the neural basis of one form of social behavior—aggression. The text discusses the roles of the hypothalamus, amygdala, serotonin, monoamine oxidase, and testosterone.

How to Master Chapter 18

Refer to These Learning Objectives

You should be able to achieve the following learning objectives after mastering the material in chapter 18:

Attitudes and Attitude Change

1. Define social psychology, and explain what social psychologists do.

2. Define attitude, and describe the process of attitude formation, including sources of attitudes and attitude acquisition.

3. Discuss the nature of cognitive consistency and cognitive dissonance theory.

4. Discuss the relationship between attitudes and behavior.

5. Discuss the nature of attitude change.

Social Influence

6. Define social influence and conformity.

7. Discuss the research on social influenced and conformity.

8. Define and discuss the nature of compliance and obedience.

9. Explain the findings of research on obedience.

10. Define and discuss the nature of social affiliation.

11. Explain the characteristics of social exchange theory.

12. Define and discuss sociobiology, and distinguish it from evolutionary psychology.

Group Processes

13. Define group norms and discuss the research in this area.

14. Define group dynamics, cohesiveness, and group polarization, and describe the research involving these concepts.

15. Explain the prisoner's dilemma.

Environmental Psychology

16. Discuss what is studied by environmental psychologists.

17. Discuss the environmental concepts of personal space, crowding, territoriality, and the nature of environmental stressors, such as noise.

Aggression

18. Define aggression and discuss its nature and origins.

19. Explain the relationship between frustration and aggression.

20. Define deindividuation.

The Neurophysiology of Social Behavior

21. Discuss the biological factors underlying aggression.

22. Discuss what is known about the neurophysiology of social behavior, including the roles of the hypothalamus, amygdala, serotonin, monoamine oxidase, and testosterone.

Debate These Myths

MYTH 1: *The average person would never deliberately harm another person simply because they were told to do so.*

Strategy:

Define obedience:

Discuss Milgram's classic study of obedience and his findings:

Discuss other evidence that average people obey authority against their better judgment:

Other statements or examples for debating MYTH 1:

Change MYTH 1 into a true statement:

MYTH 2: *Aggression is based purely on learning.*

Define aggression:

Discuss the roles of learning and modeling in aggression:

Discuss the roles of frustration, arousal, and deindividuation in aggression:

Discuss biological factors in aggression:

Discuss the neurophysiology of aggression:

Other statements or examples for debating MYTH 2:

Change MYTH 2 into a true statement:

Test Yourself: Multiple-Choice Questions

Directions: Circle the best response for each of the following questions.

1. All of the following are basic components of an attitude *except*:
    a. a belief
    c. a reference group
    b. an emotional response
    d. a pattern of behavior
2. The greatest influence on the developing attitudes of the child is:
    a. TV
    c. peer group
    b. parents
    d. genetics
3. Of the following, attitudes can be best described as:
    a. permanent
    c. fleeting
    b. relatively enduring
    d. easy to change

4.   The statement *If you let your child run wild now, he will be out of control later* is an example of which component of an attitude?

   a.   behavioral   c.   affective
   b.   physical   d.   cognitive

5.   The statement *I set appropriate limits with my 5-year-old so that he can learn self-control* is an example of which component of an attitude?

   a.   behavioral   c.   affective
   b.   physical   d.   cognitive

6.   When Alice observed herself accepting invitations to parties and enjoying herself, she concluded that she must have a positive attitude toward making new friends. Based on this example, Alice formed her attitude through the process of:

   a.   classical conditioning   c.   modeling
   b.   operant conditioning   d.   self-perception

7.   Every time Jim mentioned his upcoming trip to New York City to his parents, they made negative comments. After a few weeks of hearing negative remarks every time he mentioned New York, Jim lost his enthusiasm for the trip. Based on this example, Jim's attitude became negative through the process of:

   a.   self-perception   c.   operant conditioning
   b.   classical conditioning   d.   information-processing

8.   Attitudes are acquired through the process of:

   a.   modeling   c.   mere exposure
   b.   conditioning   d.   all of the above

9.   According to Festinger's cognitive dissonance theory, dissonance would be aroused if you:

   a.   decided to take a break from your diet for one weekend
   b.   knew that your boyfriend treated you badly, but you were nice to him anyway
   c.   voted for the senator whose policies would benefit you the most financially
   d.   baked your best friend a cake on her birthday, not knowing her favorite flavor

10. According to cognitive dissonance theory, dissonance is aroused when you:

   a.   hold simultaneously two cognitions that are psychologically incompatible
   b.   engage in a behavior that is incompatible with your attitude
   c.   either a or b
   d.   neither a nor b

11. According to Heider's balance theory, if you believe in capital punishment and your brother-in-law does not, you would resolve the imbalance by:

   a.   avoiding seeing your brother-in-law
   b.   enlisting your sister's help in changing your brother-in-law's mind
   c.   deciding your brother-in-law is not as well informed as you are
   d.   using relaxation techniques before seeing your brother-in-law

12. That we are most likely to take action based on our stated intent to take that action is the basis of:

   a.   the model of reasoned action
   b.   cognitive dissonance theory
   c.   balance theory
   d.   self-perception theory

13. The model of reasoned action was proposed by:
   a. Heider
   b. Fishbein and Ajzen
   c. Festinger and Carlsmith
   d. Bem

14. According to the model of reasoned action, the man most likely to vote for Councilman Smith is the man who:
   a. belongs to the same political party as Councilman Smith
   b. expressed the intention to vote for Councilman Smith
   c. is the same age as Councilman Smith
   d. shares similar views on the environment as Councilman Smith

15. The most easily persuaded people are those who:
   a. are the least educated
   b. watch a lot of television
   c. have low self-esteem
   d. have high credibility

16. Social judgment theory hypothesizes that attitudes are more likely to be accepted if they are:
   a. expressed by a trustworthy individual
   b. presented before the attitudes of the audience are too ingrained
   c. perceived as beneficial to society
   d. not too different from those already held by the listener

17. When Lisa's mother was present, Lisa felt uncomfortable being spontaneous with her 3-year-old daughter. This is an example of:
   a. social loafing
   b. inoculation theory
   c. social inhibition
   d. dissonance reduction

18. When 14-year-old Jean was with her friends, she was much more likely to use bad language and smoke than when she was under any other circumstances. Jean's behavior supports the concept of:
   a. social facilitation
   b. social inhibition
   c. self-evaluation
   d. self-perception

19. A change in attitudes or behaviors to bring the person in line with group values is known as:
   a. obedience
   b. conformity
   c. compliance
   d. assertiveness

20. Giving up your place in a long line at the bank to a stranger who says she is in a hurry is an example of:
   a. conformity
   b. compliance
   c. obedience
   d. the foot-in-the-door technique

21. Ordering a big dessert because everyone else at the table ordered a big dessert is an example of:
   a. conformity
   b. compliance
   c. obedience
   d. social loafing

22. It can be concluded from Milgram's series of experiments on obedience that:
   a. most people do what they think is right in spite of social pressure
   b. the desire to help others is stronger than the desire to hurt others
   c. most people will obey an order against their better judgment
   d. the desire to maintain existing attitudes is stronger than the desire to obey

23. Milgram's studies present an ethical dilemma because the:

    a. subjects were not debriefed

    b. learners received electric shocks

    c. findings could not be replicated

    d. participants were deceived

24. Social affiliation is the need to:

    a. be with other people   c. please other people

    b. help other people   d. compare ourselves with other people

25. That both human and animal groups form for evolutionary reasons is the basis of:

    a. social comparison theory   c. social exchange theory

    b. sociobiology   d. group dynamics

26. That a major function of groups is to help members assess their own attitudes, abilities, values, and behaviors is the basis of:

    a. sociobiology   c. social comparison theory

    b. evolutionary psychology   d. social exchange theory

27. Unlike sociobiologists, evolutionary psychologists consider the role of:

    a. genetics   c. neuroanatomy

    b. neurochemistry   d. psychological mechanisms

28. All of the following are consistent with the approach of evolutionary psychology *except*:

    a. consideration of environmental demands

    b. a focus on psychological mechanisms in behavior

    c. a belief in a single, domain-general mechanism directing behavior

    d. consideration of adaptive processes

29. Shared expectations about the attitudes and behaviors that should characterize the members of a group are known as:

    a. norms   c. adaptive processes

    b. domain-general mechanisms   d. group dynamics

30. Cohesiveness and polarization are two important aspects of:

    a. competition   c. conformity

    b. group dynamics   d. attitude change

31. Group polarization is most likely to be triggered by:

    a. combining men and women in a self-help group

    b. combining middle school and high school students on a team

    c. selecting individuals at random to form a discussion group

    d. encouraging a group with moderate views on gun control to have a discussion

32. Commitment has been shown to be a powerful force in:

    a. compliance   c. competition

    b. cohesiveness   d. conformity

33. Of the following, which one is the *least* common behavior in our society?

    a. conformity   c. competition

    b. obedience   d. cooperation

34. Social psychologists have tended to ignore:
   a. the physical environment
   b. children's behavior
   c. parental influence
   d. mental processes

35. The most likely explanation for Gloria's feeling uncomfortable when the salesman stood just inches from her as he explained the pros and cons of each computer is that she perceived him as:
   a. taking over her territory
   b. invading her personal space
   c. too assertive
   d. uncooperative

36. Research on the impact of crowding on rats has shown that:
   a. rats and humans respond the same way to crowding
   b. rats adapt well to crowded conditions
   c. female rats adapt more easily to crowding than do male rats
   d. antisocial behavior in rats increased dramatically with crowding

37. Human aggressiveness has been shown to be affected by:
   a. crowding
   b. noise
   c. both a and b
   d. neither a nor b

38. The impact of crowding, noise, and excessive heat are studied by:
   a. sociobiologists
   b. environmental psychologists
   c. evolutionary psychologists
   d. psychotherapists

39. Aggression is to assertiveness as:
   a. learned is to biological
   b. hurtful is to clear
   c. psychological is to physical
   d. male is to female

40. Aggressive behavior can be:
   a. physical
   b. passive
   c. verbal
   d. all of the above

41. Aggressive behavior can be:
   a. instrumental
   b. active
   c. hostile
   d. all of the above

42. A woman who comes home and kicks her dog because she is in a bad mood is engaging in a type of aggression that would be considered:
   a. hostile
   b. instrumental
   c. passive
   d. assertive

43. A man who threatens a burglar with a gun is engaging in:
   a. hostile aggression
   b. passive aggression
   c. instrumental aggression
   d. none of the above

44. A study of over 500 kindergartners showed that those who were more harshly disciplined at home were more likely to:
   a. complain to a teacher about how they are treated at home
   b. be aggressive in school
   c. be compliant in school
   d. demonstrate assertiveness skills in school

45. That children imitate the aggressive behavior they see is the basis of:
   a. social learning theory
   b. social exchange theory
   c. self-perception theory
   d. the frustration-aggression hypothesis

46. Which of the following statements regarding the frustration-aggression hypothesis is the most accurate?
   a. Aggression is always the result of frustration.
   b. Frustration and aggression have been shown to be unrelated.
   c. Aggression is often triggered by situations that are not frustrating.
   d. Men are more easily frustrated than women and, therefore, more aggressive.

47. A group of high school students dressed all in black with their faces painted vandalized a statue in the park. Based on this example, their aggressive act was facilitated by their:
   a. frustration   c. deindividuation
   b. arousal   d. modeling behavior

48. According to psychoanalytic theory, the ôdeath instinctö:
   a. is learned   c. can be modified through aggressive action
   b. is biologically-based   d. is stronger in men than women

49. Research has shown that a cat will become aggressive when stimulated electrically in the:
   a. RAS   c. thalamus
   b. cortex   d. hypothalamus

50. A brain enzyme involved in breaking down a number of neurotransmitters for excretion from the body that has been implicated in aggression is:
   a. serotonin   c. epinephrine
   b. norepinephrine   d. monoamine oxidase

Test Yourself: Fill in the Blanks

Directions: Fill in the blanks with the correct term or name.

1. The groups with which we identify, _____ groups, have a strong influence on our attitudes.

2. Daryl Bem's _____ theory says that attitudes are developed primarily through observation of one's own behavior.

3. Cognitive dissonance theory, proposed by _____, says that dissonance is aroused whenever you simultaneously hold two cognitions that are psychologically incompatible.

4. The balance theory of _____ suggests that we re comfortable only if our attitudes are imbalance.

5. _____ refers to the effect of other people on the cognitions and behaviors of any given individual.

6. Social _____ is evidenced y enhanced performance due to the presence of other people, even if they are not active participants in the task.

7. Social _____ involves putting in less effort when working in a group than when working alone.

8. _____ is a change in attitudes or behaviors to bring the person in line with group values.

9. _____ means doing what someone else asks you to do when that person has no specific authority to make the request.

10. _____ conducted a series of experiments which showed how obedient the average person is.

11. Social _____ is the need to be with other people.

12. According to _____ theory, we associate with groups that provide us with reinforcements or rewards.

13. According to _____ theory, a major function of groups is to help members assess their own attitudes, abilities, values, and behaviors.

14. _____ are shared expectations about the attitudes and behaviors that should characterize the members of a group.

15. _____ is a definite but invisible psychological boundary that surrounds each of us and into which invaders are not comfortably allowed.

16. _____ psychologists study social interaction and the physical environment in which it takes place.

17. _____ means taking a stand and letting one's views be clearly known with no intent to inflict harm.

18. _____ is a breakdown of self-awareness, a reduction in feelings of self-consciousness and distinctiveness.

19. The neurochemical, _____, is strongly implicated in aggressive behavior.

20. _____, a brain enzyme involved in breaking down a number of neurotransmitters for excretion from the body, has been implicated in aggression.

Test Yourself: Matching Questions

Directions: For each item in column I, select the item in column II that is most closely associated with it.

I	II
_____1. attitude	a. social learning and aggression
_____2. reference group	b. enduring, consistent response tendency
_____3. Daryl Bem	c. brain enzyme
_____4. Festinger and Carlsmith	d. strong identification
_____5. Fritz Heider	e. neurotransmitter
_____6. Martin Fishbein	f. extreme positions
_____7. Stanley Milgram	g. self-perception theory
_____8. social affiliation	h. model of reasoned action
_____9. norms	i. frustration-aggression hypothesis
_____10. group polarization	j. obedience studies
_____11. Albert Bandura	k. balance theory
_____12. Neal Miller	l. need to be with others
_____13. Philip Zimbardo	m. cognitive dissonance theory
_____14. serotonin	n. shared expectations
_____15. MAO	o. deindividuation and aggression

Test Yourself: Answer Key

Multiple Choice

1. c	(628)	11. c	(632)	21. a	(636)	31. d	(643–44)	41. d	(648)
2. b	(628)	12. a	(633)	22. c	(639)	32. b	(643)	42. a	(648)
3. b	(628)	13. b	(633)	23. d	(640)	33. d	(646)	43. c	(648)
4. d	(628–29)	14. b	(633)	24. a	(640)	34. a	(646)	44. b	(649)
5. a	(628–29)	15. c	(634)	25. b	(641)	35. b	(646–57)	45. a	(649)
6. d	(629)	16. d	(633)	26. c	(641)	36. d	(647)	46. c	(649)
7. b	(629)	17. c	(635)	27. d	(641)	37. c	(647)	47. c	(650–51)
8. d	(629)	18. a	(635)	28. c	(641–42)	38. b	(646–47)	48. b	(651–52)
9. b	(630–31)	19. b	(636)	29. a	(642)	39. b	(648)	49. d	(653)
10.c	(630–31)	20. b	(637)	30. b	(643)	40. d	(648)	50. d	(653)

Fill in the Blanks

1. reference
2. self-perception
3. Leon Festinger
4. Fritz Heider
5. social influence
6. facilitation
7. loafing
8. conformity
9. compliance
10. Stanley Milgram
11. affiliation
12. social exchange
13. social comparison
14. norms
15. personal space
16. environmental
17. assertiveness
18. deindividuation

19. serotonin

20. monoamine oxidase (MAO)

Matching Questions

1. b	6. h	11. a
2. d	7. j	12. i
3. g	8. l	13. o
4. m	9. n	14. e
5. k	10. f	15. c

Do These Mini Projects

1. The next time you participate in a goal-oriented activity as a member of a group, notice how your attitudes and behaviors are affected by your being part of a group rather than working alone as an individual. Are you a social loafer or an active participant? Does being in the presence of the members of this particular group facilitate or inhibit your behavior and why? Did you find yourself conforming or complying, and to what extent? Were the group members cooperative or competitive, and in what ways? To what extent did your views or the views of others in the group become polarized?

2. Observe parents and their children in natural settings, like the mall, the supermarket, or the bus. Make a mental note of instances in which parents are teaching verbal and physical aggressive behavior by displaying it to their children.

3. When you watch television, make written notes to record verbal and physical aggressive behavior. How frequently is violence displayed on TV and what forms does it take? Do you find differences in the frequency or types of violence displayed when young children are more likely to be watching? What are your views on the relationship between television violence and violence in real life?

Pull It All Together

1. Up until now, the text has focused on individual psychology on many levels, from the biological through the intellectual, cognitively, behaviorally, emotionally, and developmentally. Chapter 18 examines the psychology of the individual within the context of society, including the influence of other individuals, groups, and environmental factors. How is the individual in the context of society influenced by processes described throughout the textbook, including the processes of learning, memory, cognition, and motivation? How would personality factors influence a person's functioning in a group? Give examples of how having any of the various disorders described in chapter 16 could affect how a person would function in a group.

2. What have you noticed in your everyday life experience regarding the tendency of yourself and others to conform, to comply, and to obey? To what extent is your everyday experience with these issues consistent or inconsistent with the research findings presented in chapter 18?

Chapter Outline

Neurochemistry

Industrial/Organizational Psychology

Organizational Psychology

Personnel Psychology

Human Factors Psychology

Chapter Overview

Chapter 19 covers the topic of social cognition—the processes by which you think about other people and your relationship to them. Social cognition takes many forms and is involved in such everyday processes as impression formation, attributing causes of behavior, the perception of ourselves in relation to others, interpersonal attraction, and helping others in need. Our functioning in the workplace also involves social cognition. The author of the text points out that social cognition has adaptive value because it permits interactive processes that enhance the survival of the species.

Chapter 19 contains seven major sections: (1) "Social Perception," (2) "Making Attributions," (3) "Self-Perception and Social Comparison," (4) "Interpersonal Attraction and Romantic Love," (5) "Prosocial Behavior," (6) "The Neurophysiology of Social Cognition," and (7) "Industrial/Organizational Psychology."

The first section ("Social Perception") explains that person perception is the way we organize information about other people in order to arrive at our own internal picture or impression of them. This is a subjective process influenced by past experience and expectations. The process of impression formation, of developing an image and an evaluation of another person, is complex, but even a single behavior on the part of that person can influence our overall impression. First impressions, which are generally lasting impressions, are influenced by our implicit personality theories, reliance on central traits, and expectations. These and other factors in impression formation and impression management are discussed.

The second section ("Making Attributions") discusses the process of attributing causes to behavior. Social psychologists have noted that we tend to arrive at causal attributions—perceptions of why people engage in specific actions—particularly following negative events. Attribution theory, developed by Fritz Heider and others, distinguishes between dispositional and situational attributions. The text also describes other attributional processes, including the fundamental attribution error and the actor-observer hypothesis.

The third section ("Self-Perception and Social Comparison") begins with a definition of self-concept as representing a personal conceptualization, description, and evaluation of one's own characteristics. Components of the self include self-identity, racial identity, self-esteem, and self-image. Our self-concept influences how we respond to people, situations, and events. The self-concept may develop through a process in which we match our own characteristics against those of others—a process of social comparison and the basis of social comparison theory. Self-perception theory is presented in the text as an alternative approach. This section ends with a consideration of the consequences when the self is a distorted, inaccurate structure.

The fourth section ("Interpersonal Attraction and Romantic Love") examines the factors that influence our attraction to and liking and loving of other people. Research has shown that the single most important factor in finding other people appealing or likable is physical attractiveness. The author of the text suggests that we have a strong preference for physically attractive people because of the adaptive value of attractiveness for the continuation of the species. Psychological, situational, and relational factors in interpersonal attraction are also considered. This section ends with a discussion of romantic love, the attraction of opposites, the triangular model of love, and the real difference between liking and loving.

The fifth section ("Prosocial Behavior") defines prosocial behavior, or altruism, as voluntary action that shows concern for and is intended to benefit other human beings. The behavior is performed voluntarily; it is intended to benefit another; it is an end in itself, not a way of benefiting the actor. Evolutionary theory emphasizes the adaptive value of prosocial behavior; equity theory proposes that altruism is a matter of equity or reciprocation; other theories focus on negative affect, empathy, or social norms as causal factors. Characteristics of the helper, the victim, and the situation all contribute to predicting prosocial behavior. The psychological effects on both helper and victim are discussed briefly.

The sixth section ("The Neurophysiology of Social Cognition") explains that work on the complex neural mechanisms underlying social cognition is just beginning. The possibility of a neural module for social cognition is discussed. Researchers are working toward locating specific areas of the brain that are involved in social cognition. The text briefly discusses the role of the frontal cortex in social cognition and the neurochemistry of social cognition.

The final section ("Industrial/Organizational Psychology") defines I/O psychology as the branch of psychology that develops theories and conducts scientific research on the problems of human organizations and the use of human resources by those organizations. Organizational psychology focuses on the structure and functioning of organizations and particularly on the social and emotional adaptations of individuals in organizational settings. The issues of job satisfaction, work motivation, and leadership are discussed within this context. Personnel psychology involves fitting workers to jobs and evaluating that fit. Job analysis, evaluation, employee selection, training, and performance appraisal are discussed within this context. This section ends with a discussion of human factors in psychology.

How to Master Chapter 19

Refer to These Learning Objectives

You should be able to achieve the following learning objectives after mastering the material in chapter 19:

Social Perception

1. Define social cognition, person perception, and impression formation.

2. Explain the factors involved in impression formation and why first impressions are lasting.

3. Explain what is meant by impression management.

Making Attributions

4. Define attribution, and discuss the characteristics of attribution theory.

Self-Perception and Social Comparison

5. Describe the components of self-perception.

6. Describe and give examples of the role of the self in the formation of attitudes, emotional reactions, and ways of thinking.

7. Discuss self-awareness and its effects.

8. Describe the nature of social comparison theory.

9. Discuss self-perception theory and how it differs from social comparison theory.

Interpersonal Attraction and Romantic Love

10. Discuss the nature of interpersonal attraction and romantic love.

11. Explain the role of physical attractiveness in interpersonal attraction.

12. Explain attractiveness in the context of evolution.

13. Discuss the psychological, situational, and relational characteristics of attraction.

14. Discuss the issue of the attraction of opposites, and the triangular model of love.

15. Distinguish between liking and loving.

Prosocial Behavior

16. Define prosocial behavior, and explain why it occurs or does not occur.

17. Discuss theories of prosocial behavior, including evolutionary theory, equity theory, negative affect and altruism, empathy, and prosocial norms.

18. Explain how the characteristics of helpers, victims, and situations can predict prosocial behavior.

The Neurophysiology of Social Cognition

19. Describe a neural module for social cognition.

20. Discuss the role of the frontal cortex and the neurochemistry of social cognition.

Industrial/Organizational Psychology

21. Describe the fields of industrial and organizational psychology.

22. Explain how psychologists study job satisfaction, work motivation, leadership, personnel issues, and human factors.

Debate These Myths

MYTH 1: *Our sense of self is fully formed early in life and remains the same throughout life.*

Strategy:

List and give examples of the components of self-perception:

Explain how we develop self-concept through the process of social comparison:

Explain the role of self-perception in the devlopment of self-concept:

Discuss how we come to view ourselves as others see us:

Give examples of how our views of ourselves can change over time through the processes of social comparison and self-perception:

Other statements or examples for debating MYTH 1:

Change MYTH 1 into a true statement:

MYTH 2: *Physical attractiveness is a superficial and unimportant quality.*

Strategy:

Discuss what research has shown on the importance of physical attractiveness:

Explain the adaptive nature of physical attractiveness:

Other statements or examples for debating MYTH 2:

Change MYTH 2 into a true statement:

Test Yourself: Multiple-Choice Questions

Directions: Circle the best response for each of the following questions.

1. The process of developing an image and an evaluation of another person is known as:

    a. making attributions
    b. social comparison
    c. impression formation
    d. prosocial behavior

2. All of the following concerning first impressions are true *except*:

    a. They can be difficult to change.
    b. They can be based on one characteristic of the person.
    c. They are slow to form because it takes time to know someone.
    d. They can be based on prior events having nothing to do with the person.

3. According to implicit personality theory, which one of the following statements would be the most accurate?

    a. We are attracted to people who remind us of ourselves.
    b. If we view a man as warm, we may also assume he is kind and honest.
    c. Expecting a child to do well in school will lead to that result.
    d. We are most influenced by what we heard most recently about a person.

4. The warm-cold dimension has been shown by research to be:

    a. a central trait
    b. an expectation
    c. an implicit dimension
    d. useful in impression management

5. Jason was told that his new supervisor was arrogant and unfair. As a result, Jason acted defensively when he met him, which brought out the worst in his supervisor. This phenomenon is known as:

    a. impression management
    b. implicit behavior
    c. the recency effect
    d. the self-fulfilling prophecy

6. In a study in which teachers were told that students were expected to improve:

    a. the students improved
    b. the students failed
    c. there was no change
    d. there was no control group

7. In the process known as priming, impression formation can be influenced by prior events:

    a. only when the prior events occur immediately before impression formation
    b. only when the prior event are negative
    c. even when the events have nothing to do with the person you are to meet
    d. if you have low self-esteem

8. When John prepared to meet his girlfriend's parents, he made sure his suit was pressed, he brought a house gift, and he paid them compliments, all as part of his effort at:

    a. attribution
    b. impression management
    c. impression formation
    d. priming

9. Impression formation can be influenced by:

    a. clothing
    b. facial expression
    c. race
    d. all of the above

10. Attributions are primarily:

    a. perceptions
    b. behaviors
    c. emotions
    d. first impressions

11. When Julia saw a man across the street kicking and yelling at a dog, she decided the man was a mean, abusive person. Julia would be making a:

    a. situational attribution   c. false first impression

    b. dispositional attribution   d. divergent perspective

12. Referring back to question 11, what Julia did not know was that the dog had just bitten the man's 2-year-old daughter, who had to be taken to the hospital. If she had known the circumstances surrounding the man's behavior, Julia would have been more likely to:

    a. make a situational attribution

    b. make a fundamental attribution error

    c. engage in impression management

    d. stay with her original impression

13. According to Harold Kelley, when there is considerable distinctiveness, consensus, and consistency, we generally attribute the causes of behavior to:

    a. chance   c. the environment

    b. the person   d. ourselves

14. A correspondent inference is the assumption that a person's intent in performing a behavior:

    a. is unknowable

    b. can be inferred from the behavior itself

    c. generally derives from a positive motive

    d. will be revealed over a period of time

15. The fundamental attribution error involves:

    a. holding on to false first impressions

    b. being overly influenced by priming

    c. taking too much responsibility for how events transpire

    d. overestimating the role of dispositional factors

16. Sharon attributed her failure on her history test to her lack of studying, whereas her father viewed her as lacking intelligence. This difference in attribution between Sharon and her father is an example of:

    a. the actor-observer hyothesis

    b. fundamental attribution error

    c. self-fulfilling prophecy

    d. primacy and recency effects

17. Another term for the actor-observer hypothesis is:

    a. social comparison theory   c. the divergent perspectives hypothesis

    b. the triangular model   d. the expectancy effect

18. Daniel views his toughness as his primary characteristic, and his behavior toward others is consistent with his view of himself. Daniel's picture of himself consititutes his:

    a. self-image   c. self-esteem

    b. schema   d. self-awareness

19. Janet has always struggled to see herself as a good person, perhaps because her parents were overly critical and verbally harsh when she was a child. From this example, Janet's struggle has been primarily with:

    a. the role of self   c. self-esteem

    b. processing information   d. divergent attributions

20. Central themes and cognitive structures that affect social processes are known as:
   a. self-images
   b. schemas
   c. social comparisons
   d. attributions

21. When Kenny's mom and dad found him after he got lost in the mall, his mom cried with relief as she hugged him whereas his dad yelled at him for getting lost. The differences in the reactions of Kenny's parents are most likely attributable to differences in their:
   a. impressions of their son
   b. attractiveness
   c. prosocial behavior
   d. gender schemas

22. Conscious attention directed toward the self as a social object is known as:
   a. self-awareness
   b. self-esteem
   c. social comparison
   d. self-image

23. All of the following statements are true regarding self-awareness *except*:
   a. High self-awareness is associated with greater sensitivity to the needs of others.
   b. The greater your self-awareness, the higher your self-esteem.
   c. Self-awareness can be increased through the process of self-talk.
   d. Low self-awareness makes it difficult to be aware of the perspectives of others.

24. The self as a social mirror in which we learn to see ourselves as others see us is a process of social comparison studied by:
   a. Bandura
   b. Vroom
   c. Bersheid
   d. Cooley

25. When Vicki realized that she had finished her dinner well before everyone else at the table, she judged herself as having eaten too quickly and viewed herself as unfeminine. Her self-evaluation within this social context is in line with:
   a. social learning theory
   b. impression management
   c. social comparison theory
   d. prosocial behavior

26. Self-perception theory and self-theory are alternatives to:
   a. attribution theory
   b. the triangular model
   c. social comparison theory
   d. the actor-observer hypothesis

27. When Joey was first in Little League and hit the ball consistently, he did not know if he was really a good player or was just lucky. Over the years, as he continued to hit well and played under the supervision of several different coaches, Joey came to the conclusion that he was a good baseball player. Joey's ongoing hypothesis testing and conclusion formation based on ongoing behavioral observations are processes most closely associated with:
   a. Festinger's social comparison theory
   b. Epstein's self-theory
   c. Bem's self-perception theory
   d. Heider's attribution theory

28. Referring back to question 27, Joey's positive self-evaluation is likely to affect his:
   a. self-esteem
   b. self-concept
   c. both a and b
   d. neither a nor b

29. Referring back to question 27, Joey's comparing himself to peers who do not play baseball as well as he does would:

    a. be an example of an upward comparison
    b. help raise his self-esteem
    c. both a and b
    d. neither a nor b

30. Distortions in our view of ourselves most likely derive from:

    a. our striving to achieve and maintain a positive self-image
    b. psychological disorders with roots in childhood
    c. an inaccurate perception of others
    d. an innate tendency to view others as more adaptive than ourselves

31. Numerous studies have shown that the single most important factor in finding other people appealing or likable is:

    a. physical attractiveness   c. generosity
    b. monetary wealth   d. sense of humor

32. As compared with less physically attractive people, highly attractive people are judged to be:

    a. happier   c. more socially skilled
    b. better adjusted   d. all of the above

33. Which one of the following statements regarding interpersonal attraction is the most accurate?

    a. Even though physical attractiveness is an important element in attraction, most people set this factor aside and put more weight on personality, particularly when deciding whom to marry.
    b. Thin female figures are rated higher than any other body shape and are perceived as having more desirable personality characteristics.
    c. We are more likely to be attracted to and become friendly with people who are in close proximity and who are familiar to us.
    d. Teachers are unaffected by the attractiveness of students' names and rate students solely on the basis of objective performance and skill level.

34. The types of love studied by Bersheid and Walster are:

    a. committed and intimate   c. passionate and companionate
    b. motivational and emotional   d. fatuous and consummate

35. Alexis and George have been married for 24 years, have mutual respect, feel deep warmth and caring for each other, and consider each other's opinions and desires when making important decisions. According to Bersheid and Walster, this couple is experiencing:

    a. passionate love   c. romantic love
    b. fatuous love   d. companionate love

36. According to Sternberg's triangular model of love, liking involves:

    a. all three components—passion, intimacy, and decision/commitment
    b. at least one component of the triangle
    c. mislabeling true love
    d. nonlove

37. Prosocial behavior is another term for:

    a. altruism   c. attribution
    b. impression formation   d. self-perception

38. With regard to prosocial behavior, which one of the following conclusions is the most accurate?

a. Most psychologists agree that reducing negative affect is the best explanation of prosocial behavior.

b. We are programmed to help others and to expect help from others.

c. Characteristics of the helper, victim, and situation influence prosocial behavior.

d. Most people do not any longer expect to be treated positively by others.

39. The equity theory of prosocial behavior is based on the concept of:

a. adaptation
c. empathy

b. reciprocity
d. norms

40. With regard to prosocial behavior, victims may feel hostile toward a helper when the aid is:

a. spontaneous
c. unexpected

b. volunteered
d. a favor

41. Evolutionary theory hypothesizes that important psychological functions are controlled by neural modules, which are:

a. general brain functions
c. specific to limited areas of behavior

b. in only one area of the brain
d. inconsistent with connectionist theory

42. Research on the neurophysiology has found which of the following parts of the brain to be involved in social cognition?

a. temporal cortex
c. frontal cortex

b. amygdala
d. all of the above

43. Regarding the neurophysiology of social cognition, research has revealed that:

a. oxytocin, a neuropeptide, may be important in the initiation of social cognition

b. frontal lobe damage does not affect the formulation of self-concepts

c. each neural module is located in a specific area of the brain

d. it is not scientifically sound to generalize from monkeys to humans

44. Modern industrial/organizational psychology is divided into three areas:

a. organizational psychology, personnel psychology, and human factors

b. industrial psychology, social psychology, and human factors

c. social psychology, organizational psychology, and human factors

d. personality psychology, social psychology, and human factors

45. Linda, an administrative assistant in a large, impersonal company, made the decision to work at a level consistent with her perception of the rewards for working, not any more or any less. Linda's work motivation can be explained by:

a. leadership ability
c. expectancy theory

b. equity theory
d. contingency theory

46. Job satisfaction, work motivation, and leadership are all subareas of:

a. personnel psychology
c. organizational psychology

b. human factors psychology
d. social psychology

47. The vice president of a financial institution did not allow her subordinates to be involved in decision making, which weakened, rather than strengthened, her ability to lead the group. Which one of the following types of leaders best describes this vice president?

a. task-oriented
c. charismatic

b. authoritarian
d. normative

48. The normative decision theory approach to leadership was developed by:
   a. Fiedler
   c. House
   b. Cattell
   d. Vroom

49. All of the following regarding performance appraisals are true, *except*:
   a. They are used to determine salaries.
   b. Employees don't like to have them done.
   c. Accurate ones are simple to develop.
   d. They are used to determine transfers and layoffs.

50. Human factors psychology was developed in order to:
   a. design equipment and work environments to fit our abilities and limitations
   b. provide better training for the leaders in industry
   c. improve the techniques of employee selection
   d. modernize the process of job analysis and evaluation

Test Yourself: Fill in the Blanks

Directions: Fill in the blanks with the correct term or name.

1. The process of _____ involves developing an image and an evaluation of another person.

2. The primacy effect in impression formation was first demonstrated by the research of _____.

3. The attempt to control the way in which we are perceived and evaluated by others is called _____.

4. _____ are perceptions of why we engage in specific actions.

5. A _____ inference is the assumption that a person's intent in performing a behavior can be inferred from the behavior itself.

6. _____ error is the tendency to overestimate the role of dispositional factors and to under estimate the role of situational factors when making attributions.

7. According to Sandra Bem's _____ theory, we react to a wide range of situations in terms of our perception of ourselves as masculine or feminine.

8. Conscious attention directed toward the self as a social object is called _____.

9. The _____ theory holds that the self-concept grow out of a learned need for self-evaluation.

10. _____ suggested that the self-concept is acually a self-theory.

11. Three basic dimensions of love—passion, intimacy, and decision/commitment—are components of Robert Sternberg's _____.

12. _____ hypothesized that liking and loving differ quantitatively and qualitatively.

13. The _____ theory of prosocial behavior suggests that we help others because we expect help from them.

14. _____ is the ability to sense and deeply understand the feelings and experiences of others.

15. _____ is emotion experienced when observing another person in distress.

16. Evolutionary theory hypothesizes that important psychological functions are controlled not by general brain functions, but by _____ specific to limited areas of behavior.

17. _____, a neuropeptide, may be important in the intiation of social interactions.

18. _____ theory is a cognitive approach which hypothesizes that work performance results from a conscious choice to engage in the behavior that is likely to produce the greatest payoff for the individual.

19. _____ favors a normative decision theory approach, which focuses on the decision-making aspect of leadership.

20. _____ is a technique for ascertaining the exact characteristics of a job by breaking it down into specific components, then determining which are most important.

Test Yourself: Matching Questions

Directions: For each item in column I, select the item in column II that is most closely associated with it.

I	**II**
_____1. Solomon Asch	a. social comparison theory
_____2. Harold Kelley	b. cognitive labeling theory
_____3. Fritz Heider	c. theory of charismatic leadership
_____4. Edward Jones	d. primacy effect
_____5. Daryl Bem	e. contingency theory
_____6. Hazel Markus	f. warm-cold dimension
_____7. Charles Horton Cooley	g. liking vs. loving
_____8. Leon Festinger	h. attribution theory, 1958
_____9. Seymour Epstein	i. information processing and schemas
_____10. Elain Hatfield	j. correspondent inference
_____11. Bersheid and Walster	k. triangular model of love
_____12. Robert Sternberg	l. looking-glass self
_____13. Zick Rubin	m. physical attractiveness
_____14. Robert House	n. self-perception theory
_____15. Fred Fiedler	o. self-theory

Test Yourself: Answer Key

Multiple Choice

1. c	(658)	11. b	(663–64)	21. d	(667)	31. a	(672)	41. c	(683)
2. c	(658–60)	12. a	(663–65)	22. a	(668)	32. d	(672)	42. d	(683–84)
3. b	(659)	13. c	(664)	23. b	(668)	33. c	(674)	43. a	(684)
4. a	(659)	14. b	(664)	24. d	(668)	34. c	(675)	44. a	(685)
5. d	(659)	15. d	(665)	25. c	(669)	35. d	(675)	45. b	(686)
6. a	(659–60)	16. a	(665–66)	26. c	(669)	36. b	(676)	46. c	(685)
7. c	(660)	17. c	(665)	27. b	(669)	37. a	(679)	47. b	(687)
8. b	(663)	18. a	(667)	28. c	(666–67)	38. c	(681)	48. d	(687)
9. d	(662)	19. c	(667)	29. b	(669)	39. b	(679)	49. c	(688)
10. a	(663)	20. b	(667)	30. a	(670)	40. d	(682)	50. a	(689)

Fill in the Blanks

1. impression formation
2. Solomon Asch
3. impression management
4. attributions
5. correspondent
6. fundamental attribution
7. gender schema
8. self-awareness
9. social comparison
10. Seymour Epstein
11. triangular model of love
12. Zick Rubin
13. equity
14. empathy
15. negative affect
16. neural modules
17. oxytocin
18. expectancy theory

19. Victor Vroom

20. job analysis

Matching Questions

1. d	6. i	11. b
2. f	7. l	12. k
3. h	8. a	13. g
4. j	9. o	14. e
5. n	10. m	15. e

Do These Mini Projects

1. The next time you ask yourself about an event, "Why did this happen?" or the next time you ask yourself about someone's actions, "Why did he do that?" you will have an opportunity to observe yourself making attributions. Keep a log for one week in which you record your attributions regarding events and the actions of others. Do you tend to make more dispositional or situational attributions? Under what circumstances do you make dispositional versus situational attributions? Bring your log to class for sharing.

2. In one paragraph, describe a prosocial act in detail. You may use a prosocial act that you were involved in, either as helper or victim; you may use one that you observed; you may use one that you heard about or read about; or you may use your imagination. Make sure you describe the situation, the actions of all the people involved, including the victims and the helper, and how the individuals felt afterward.

Pull It All Together

1. Chapter 19 is the second of two chapters on social psychology. Social cognition involves the processes that underlie our thinking about other people and their actions and our relationships with other people. Most of the chapters in the textbook have focused on the individual and the processes within the individual that account for behavioral, cognitive, and emotional functioning. How is examining the relationships between individuals similar to and yet different from examining the processes within one individual?

2. Most individuals reading chapter 19 will already have preconceptions about impression formation, attribution, interpersonal attraction, and prosocial behavior. To what extent did the information in the text confirm concepts you already had, enhance your understanding, or conflict with your ideas? To what extent will the information on impression formation, attribution, interpersonal attraction, and prosocial behavior have an impact on your future perceptions and behavior?

Appendix

Research Design and Statistical Analysis

Appendix Outline

Appendix Overview

The appendix covers the topics of research design and statistical analysis. The author of the text points out at the start of the appendix that every chapter of this book includes examples of research carried out by psychologists and that statistical analyses are conducted as a basis for drawing conclusions from that research. Therefore, some familiarity with the processes of research design and statistical analysis would enhance one's understanding of the field as a whole.

The appendix contains five major sections: (1) "Why Do Research? Why Use Statistics?" (2) "The Research Process," (3) "Descriptive Statistics," (4) "Inferential Statistics," and (5) "Reporting and Consuming Scientific Results."

The first section ("Why Do Research? Why Use Statistics?") explains that psychologists conduct formal scientific research studies because the knowledge gained through formal research is far more precise, objective, and reliable than the information gathered through casual observation. Statistics is the branch of mathematics that uses numbers, graphs, and calculations to summarize, describe, and draw inferences and generalizations from data.

Psychologists use statistics to quantify information. Doing so allows for a better understanding of the observations, more precise observations, and more effective communication among scientists.

The second section ("The Research Process") describes briefly the five major steps in the research process: (1) get an idea; (2) formulate one or more hypotheses you would like to test; (3) design the study; (4) run the subjects; and (5) analyze the data and reach conclusions.

The third section ("Descriptive Statistics") explains that descriptive statistics are used to condense and summarize data. This section begins with a discussion of the use of graphs and frequency distributions within which data (e.g., scores) are ranked and their frequency indicated. To learn more about the frequency distribution, the psychologist can measure the central tendency, which reveals what scores are typical of the group as a whole. Three measures of central tendency are described: the mode, the median, and the mean. Variability reveals how close together or spread out the scores in a normal distribution are in comparison to the mean. The text demonstrates a calculation of a standard deviation. Remember that the normal distribution is a perfectly symmetrical distribution in which the mean, median, and mode are all identical. This section ends with a discussion and demonstration of correlation, a measure of the degree of relationship between two sets of scores. The text discusses the meaning of positive and negative correlations, how to plot correlational data, the correlation coefficient, and the meaning and importance of correlation.

The fourth section ("Inferential Statistics") explains that inferential statistics are designed to reveal whether it is reasonable to draw inferences from, or generalize to the larger population from, the results of the present experiment. By necessity, experiments are performed on a random sample, and before any generalizations are made based on the data, certain conditions must be met. One of these conditions is statistical significance, which means that the differences found between groups was not due to chance. Tests of statistical significance, in particular the *t*-test, are described. This section ends with a brief discussion of univariate and multivariate statistics.

The fifth and final section ("Reporting and Consuming Scientific Research") describes two processes: (1) publishing the findings of research in a professional journal and (2) locating and reading scientific journal articles.

How to Master the Appendix

Refer to These Learning Objectives

You should be able to achieve the following learning objectives after mastering the material in the appendix:

Why Do Research? Why Use Statistics?

1. Explain the purpose of carrying out formal scientific research in the field of psychology and the purpose of using statistics.

The Research Process

2. List, explain, and give an example of each of the five major steps in the research process.

Descriptive Statistics

3. Define and give an example of descriptive statistics.

4. Define frequency distribution and explain how data is plotted to create a graph.

5. Define and be able to locate the measures of central tendency—the mode, median, and mean—of a normal distribution.

6. Explain what variability reveals about scores, and how a standard deviation is calculated.

7. Describe the nature of a normal distribution.

8. Define correlation and explain its value as a descriptive statistic.

9. Distinguish between positive and negative correlations, define correlation coefficient, and explain the meaning of correlation.

Inferential Statistics

10. Define inferential statistics and distinguish between it and descriptive statistics.

11. Explain what is meant by statistical significance, and describe the t-test.

12. Discuss the use of univariate and multivariate statistics.

Reporting and Consuming Scientific Research

13. Describe the process of publishing research findings.

14. Describe how to locate and analyze a journal article.

Debate These Myths

MYTH 1: *Because the area of statistics is mathematical, everyone would interpret the results of a research study in the same way.*

Strategy:

Discuss the nature of statistics as mathematical and give an example:

Explain what it means to make an inference and give an example:

Explain the purpose of the discussion section of a research article and the meaning of the author interpreting the results (statistics) of the study:

Discuss and give examples of human processes that influence the process of interpretation:

Other statements or examples for debating MYTH 1:

Change MYTH 1 into a true statement:

MYTH 2: *Statistics is too difficult to learn.*

Strategy:

Explain how to graph a frequency distribution:

Describe the features of a normal distribution:

Distinguish among mode, median, and mean:

Explain what knowledge of the standard deviation adds to your findings:

Define and describe the value of correlation:

Explain what is meant by statistical significance:

Now that you have demonstrated that you are capable of learning about statistics, provide other statements or examples for debating MYTH 2:

Change MYTH 2 into a true statement:

Test Yourself: Multiple-Choice Questions

Directions: *Circle the best response for each of the following questions.*

1. A statistic is a:
    a. branch of mathematics
    b. research conclusion
    c. number calculated from data
    d. generalization

2. Psychologists need statistics in order to:
    a. make their observations more precise
    b. understand observations better
    c. communicate findings
    d. all of the above

3. Formulating a hypothesis would take place during which of the following phases of a research project?
    a. toward the end, after running the subjects so that you know what to expect
    b. as the very first step
    c. after getting an idea, but before designing the study
    d. at any point

4. Everything in a research study must be controlled as carefully as possible before the researcher can:
    a. run the subjects
    b. design the study
    c. get an idea
    d. formulate a hypothesis

5. The statement *Reading scores in the group receiving the experimental instruction will be significantly higher than reading scores for the group receiving traditional instruction* is an example of:
    a. a descriptive statistic
    b. a hypothesis
    c. an inference
    d. correlation

6. The purpose of descriptive statistics is to:
    a. interpret data
    b. determine statistical significance
    c. condense and summarize data
    d. report data

7. All of the following are true regarding the nature of frequency distributions, *except:*
    a. They measure central tendency.
    b. You must rank-order scores from lowest to highest.
    c. They can be of any shape.
    d. They can be represented in histograms.

8. Frequency polygon is to histogram as:
    a. normal distribution is to skewed distribution
    b. line graph is to bar graph
    c. descriptive statistics is to inferential statistics
    d. mean is to median

9. The most frequent score in any given set of scores is known as the:
   a. mean
   c. mode
   b. median
   d. standard deviation

10. A spelling test was given to six students and graded from 1 to 10. The scores obtained were 5, 6, 6, 7, 8, and 10. The central tendency, as measured by the mean, would be:
   a. 6
   c. 8
   b. 7
   d. 7.5

11. Based on the example in question 10, the median would be:
   a. 6
   c. 7
   b. 6.5
   d. 7.5

12. Alice, Dana, and Tim all ended the spring semester with an average of 78 in algebra, based on the mean of their test scores. During the semester, Alice's scores ranged from 74 to 82; Dana's from 68 to 91; and Tim's from 76 to 79. Which student has the scores with the greatest variability?
   a. Dana
   c. Tim
   b. Alice
   d. insufficient data to make this determination

13. The standard deviation measures the average difference between the:
   a. mean and the median of a distribution
   b. mean and the mode of a distribution
   c. scores in a distribution and the mean of the distribution
   d. scores in a distribution and the median of the distribution

14. All of the following statements concerning the standard deviation are true, *except*:
   a. It is a measure of variability of a distribution of scores.
   b. Two distributions can have the same mean but a different standard deviation.
   c. The standard deviation is the square root of the variance.
   d. In a normal distribution, 98 percent of scores fall within one standard deviation of the mean.

15. All of the following statements regarding normal distribution are true, *except*:
   a. It is a perfectly symmetrical distribution.
   b. The mean, median, and mode are identical in a normal distribution.
   c. About 68 percent of the scores in any normal distribution fall between one standard deviation above and one below the mean.
   d. The spread of scores in a normal distribution cannot be predicted.

16. In a normal distribution, if the mean is 300, the mode would be:
   a. 300
   c. close to 300
   b. 600
   d. cannot be determined from the information given

17. The degree of relationship between two sets of scores is known as their:
   a. mean
   c. correlation
   b. standard deviation
   d. central tendency

18. If scores on a vocabulary test covary with scores on a test of abstract reasoning ability, then:
   a. skill in vocabulary is positively correlated with abstract reasoning ability
   b. having good verbal skills helps an individual reason abstractly
   c. both a and b
   d. neither a nor b

19. As compared with scatter plots, correlational coefficients are more:

   a. causal
   c. precise
   b. positively correlated
   d. inferred

20. A correlation of -54 between anxiety and performance on mathematical tasks would mean that:

   a. anxiety causes poor performance on mathematical tasks
   b. there is a moderate, negative correlation between anxiety and performance on mathematical tasks
   c. there is a strong negative correlation between anxiety and performance on mathematical tasks.
   d. poor performance on mathematical tasks causes anxiety

21. Inferential statistics are designed to reveal:

   a. measures of central tendency
   b. correlation coefficients
   c. summaries of data
   d. whether results can be generalized

22. In general, results are considered statistically significant if the chances of obtaining the same results by chance are less than:

   a. 1 in 100
   c. 5 in 100
   b. 2 in 100
   d. 10 in 100

23. A multivariate experiment involves more than one:

   a. dependent variable
   c. independent variable
   b. control group
   d. distribution

24. Reporting scientific research in the form of a journal article requires:

   a. data analysis
   c. formulating hypotheses
   b. careful reviews
   d. all of the above

25. The author of a journal article interprets the results of the study in the section known as the:

   a. method
   c. results
   b. discussion
   d. introduction

Test Yourself: Matching Questions

Directions: For each item in column I, select the item in column II that is most closely associated with it.

I	II
_____1. mean	a. *r*
_____2. median	b. arithmetic average
_____3. mode	c. complex determinants studied
_____4. standard deviation	d. based on probability
_____5. normal distribution	e. the middle score
_____6. correlation	f. +.86
_____7. positive correlation	g. the most frequent score
_____8. correlation coefficient	h. degree of relationship
_____9. statistical significance	i. measure of variability
_____10. multivariate research	j. perfectly symmetrical

Test Yourself: Answer Key

Multiple Choice

1. c (692)	11. b (694)	21. d (698)
2. d (692)	12. a (694)	22. c (699)
3. c (692–93)	13. c (695)	23. a (699)
4. a (692)	14. d (696)	24. d (699)
5. b (692)	15. d (696)	25. b (700)
6. c (693)	16. a (696)	
7. a (693)	17. c (696)	
8. b (693)	18. a (697)	
9. c (694)	19. c (698)	
10. b (694)	20. b (698)	

Matching Questions

1. b	6. h
2. e	7. f
3. g	8. a
4. i	9. d
5. j	10. c

Do These Mini Projects

1. Go to page 695 in the textbook and calculate the SD (standard deviation) of section 2 in table 3. Use the steps outlined in table 4 in calculating the SD. What does the standard deviation reveal about the variability in the scores among the students in section 2?

2. Go to your college or university library and find out what types of computer searches are available to search for psychology articles on any particular topic. Then, locate *Psychological Abstracts* and look through it in order to become familiar with the abstracts of journal articles and how to locate journal articles.

3. Select a journal article in an area of psychology of interest to you. Read through the article, noting the six sections described in the appendix: abstract, introduction, method, results, discussion, and references. Summarize the article, using each of these six sections as headings of the sections of your summary.

Pull It All Together

1. Go back to chapter 2, which covers the science of psychology. Review the nature of scientific research, descriptive and correlational methods, and forms of data collection. What does the appendix add to the information provided in chapter 2 about research methods?

2. As stated at the beginning of the appendix, every chapter in the textbook includes examples of research carried out by psychologists. Throughout the book, research findings are not only stated, but also evaluated. Based on your current knowledge of statistics and research design, how would you make a plan to evaluate the findings of a research study? How would you determine whether a researcher was correct or incorrect to generalize from the findings of the study to the general population?